THE MORAL
RHETORIC
OF AMERICAN
PRESIDENTS

SCC Library

D1626990

NUMBER SEVENTEEN

Presidential Rhetoric Series

Martin J. Medhurst, General Editor

E
176.1
.S564
2006

THE

MORAL

Rhetoric

OF

AMERICAN

PRESIDENTS

COLLEEN J. SHOGAN

TEXAS A&M UNIVERSITY PRESS COLLEGE STATION

OCM 62509066

Santiago Canyon College
Library

Copyright © 2006 by Colleen J. Shogan
Manufactured in the United States of America
All rights reserved
Second printing, 2007

The paper used in this book
meets the minimum requirements
of the American National Standard for Permanence
of Paper for Printed Library Materials, Z39.48-1984.
Binding materials have been chosen for durability.

Library of Congress Cataloging-in-Publication Data

Shogan, Colleen J., 1975–
    The moral rhetoric of American presidents / Colleen J. Shogan.—1st ed.
        p. cm.—(Presidential rhetoric series ; no. 17)
    Includes bibliographic references and index.
    ISBN-13: 978-1-58544-522-6 (cloth : alk. paper)
    ISBN-10: 1-58544-522-3 (cloth : alk. paper)
        1. Presidents—United States—History.   2. Presidents—United States—
Language—History.   3. Rhetoric—Political aspects—United States—History.
4. Rhetoric—Moral and ethical aspects—United States—History.   5. Presidents—
United States—Case studies.   6. Rhetoric—Political aspects—United States—Case
studies.   7. English language—United States—Rhetoric.   8. Political leadership—
United States—History.   9. Political oratory—United States—History.   10. Political
ethics—United States—History.   I. Title.   II. Series.
    E176.1S564   2006
    352.23'8014—dc22   2005034159

ISBN-13: 978-1-58544-639-1 (pbk.)
ISBN-10: 1-58544-639-4 (pbk.)

FOR MY PARENTS,
WHO TAUGHT ME ABOUT
THE IMPORTANCE
OF MORALITY
AND RELIGION

CONTENTS

ACKNOWLEDGMENTS

I began research on this study before George W. Bush assumed office in 2001. Even prior to September 11, I believed that the topic of presidential moral rhetoric was potentially important for understanding executive power and authority. Throughout several years of writing first a dissertation and then this book, I remained enthusiastic about the topic. That optimistic confidence was buoyed by generous individuals who never wavered in their support of my work.

Leading this list are the political science faculty members who influenced me over the years. Stephen Skowronek was a dedicated and cooperative advisor who spent countless hours providing insight and helpful comments. He always believed that the topic was significant and spared no expense in efforts to improve my understanding of the presidency. David Mayhew read versions of the manuscript even after I left graduate school, always providing constructive recommendations that helped me develop this book. Likewise, Hugh Heclo gave the historical case studies a thorough reading and provided timely and much-needed advice from a fresh perspective. Outside the realm of American politics, Steven Smith served as a careful reader and reminded me not to forget my education in political philosophy. Norma Thompson's seminar provided me with the framework to understand rhetoric in a classical sense, which was essential in completing the book. At conferences, I also received helpful commentary from Jeffrey Tulis, Michael Nelson, Peri Arnold, Sid Milkis, and Mary Stuckey. I am indebted to the mentoring of Marc Landy, Kay Schlozman, Robert Faulkner, and Robert Scigliano during my time as an undergraduate at Boston College. They are responsible for initiating and fostering my interest in the presidency, American politics, and the history of political thought.

In graduate school, I was fortunate to have several friends who also supported the project. Dan Galvin and I indulged our taste for coffee and executive power in many fruitful discussions. Matt Glassman, Matt Green, and Chris Mann listened patiently to my research presentation on presidential moral rhetoric several times. David McKenzie, Nancy

Epling, Barry McMillion, Rachel Seher, Jason Marino, and Eileen Hunt Botting provided the type of companionship that makes graduate school enjoyable. I am also indebted to Jonathan Berkon, an undergraduate at Yale who worked as my research assistant to replicate the content analysis contained in chapter 2.

I also received generous institutional support to complete my research. The National Science Foundation Graduate Fellowship kept me in graduate school and was indispensable in the completion of my degree. The Institute for Human Studies also provided me with several grants, including funding to present my research at conferences as a graduate student. The Robert Leyland Dissertation Fellowship and Enders Research Grant at Yale offered financial assistance as I finished the final stages of research and writing. The Capitol Hill Campus program of the Mercatus Center at George Mason University has provided me, as a faculty member, with numerous opportunities to present my research to an engaged audience of congressional staffers.

I would like to express appreciation to the Public and International Affairs faculty at George Mason University. They made my transition from graduate school to professional life an easy one. I am extremely fortunate to have smart, collegial, and supportive colleagues at my home institution.

The staff at Texas A&M University Press was a pleasure to work with on the production of this book. I am grateful for the comments provided by Martin Medhurst and an anonymous reviewer. Their helpful criticisms greatly improved the finished product. All remaining errors are mine alone. I am also thankful to Jim Pfiffner for introducing me to Texas A&M University Press.

Portions of chapter 2 appeared previously in "Rhetorical Moralism in the Plebiscitary Presidency: New Speech Forms and Their Ideological Entailments," *Studies in American Political Development* 17 (2003): 149–67. These excerpts were reprinted with permission from Cambridge University Press.

I would like to thank my family: parents Joy and Dick Shogan, brother Greg Shogan, sister-in-law Susan Shogan, and niece Alyssa Shogan, who urged me to persist throughout graduate school and the completion of this book. I especially thank my mother, one of a few individuals who willingly read my dissertation. I also enjoyed support from my extended family—numerous aunts, uncles, and cousins—who always offered kind words of encouragement.

Finally, I thank my husband, Rob Raffety. A word to the wise: no one should try to finish a book and plan a wedding at the same time. More than anyone, he listened patiently to all of my complaints and frustrations. I am blessed to have such an understanding person in my life.

THE MORAL
RHETORIC
OF AMERICAN
PRESIDENTS

CHAPTER 1

PRESIDENTIAL MORAL

LEADERSHIP AND RHETORIC

Four months after the September 11 terrorist attacks, Pres. George W. Bush stood before Congress to give the annual State of the Union Address. With an 85 percent approval rating from the American public and firm support from legislators on both sides of the aisle, Bush seized this rhetorical opportunity to showcase his role as the nation's moral spokesman. In his speech, Bush called the war in Afghanistan a "just cause" and announced that times of tragedy have made Americans realize that "God is near." Not content with that, Bush pushed the moral dimensions of his presidential rhetoric further: he described North Korea, Iran, and Iraq as an "axis of evil" that threatens "the peace of the world." The President ended his speech with the observation that "evil is real, and it must be opposed."[1]

Bush's moral posturing would be remarkable and noteworthy, even if the "axis of evil" remark had not started an international controversy. A president who lost the popular vote in the 2000 election asserted the moral authority to speak for the nation only a year after taking office. During his first presidential campaign, the media often depicted Bush as a lightweight ingénue of less-than-admirable mettle. In little over a year, Bush had become not just a beacon of patriotic inspiration but a leader confident enough in his political authority to judge which of the world's countries should be damned as evil.

Bush might have described North Korea, Iran, and Iraq as dangerous "rogue nations" that posed a security risk to the United States. But the term "axis of evil" brought a purposeful moral dimension to his leadership posture.[2] Bush used his rhetoric to redefine the war against terrorism; his words implied that terrorism was not a foreign policy problem but a moral struggle. The categorical language in his speech ("America will lead by defending liberty and justice because they are right and true and unchanging for all people everywhere") assaulted the realist belief that morality is indeterminate in world affairs. Through his rhetoric, Bush elevated his authority by depicting the president as the defender of eternal moral values shared by not just Americans, but the entire human race.

The impact of Bush's address was significant. A Gallup poll administered after the speech reported that 91 percent of Americans believed Bush's policies were "taking the nation in the right direction."[3] Beyond the influence of his speech on public opinion, the forcefulness of his rhetoric generated discussion that a "Bush Doctrine" of foreign policy had been born. Alternatively, some members of the foreign policy community categorized Bush's use of the term "axis of evil" as a blank check for aggression.[4]

While the diplomatic merits of Bush's "axis of evil" terminology can be debated, it is unquestionable that his rhetoric strengthened his governing authority. With strong political support from both the American public and the Washington community, Bush reached beyond the specific constitutional powers of the office to tap into the moral dimensions of presidential leadership. In a time of threatening uncertainty, Bush found strength by appealing to fundamental moral beliefs and values. The power of Bush's speech came not only from his moralistic words but also from his strong constitutional position as commander-in-chief. Bush's 2002 State of the Union Address exemplifies how presidents can use moral and religious rhetoric to enhance their political leadership and strengthen existing authority. In this light, moral and religious argumentation can be viewed as a strategic political tool used by presidents to augment their formal, constitutional powers.

In the past several decades, presidents have highlighted the moral and religious dimensions of their leadership through expanded media outlets. For example, in an obvious attempt to advertise his religiosity, Jimmy Carter took the oath of office in 1977 with not one but two Bibles. All presidents now participate in the annual White House prayer breakfast. In his first act as president, Ronald Reagan stated that future inaugurations should be declared a "day of prayer." When Richard Nixon resigned from office, his last words were a prayer: "May God's grace be with you in all the days ahead." Despite his reputation for immoral behavior and less-than-admirable character, Bill Clinton used moral and religious appeals frequently in his presidential rhetoric, until his impeachment made moralistic references extraordinarily imprudent.

With an emphasis on piety surrounding us, it is hard to imagine that a presidential candidate could prevail without revealing his religious and moral beliefs to the American public. During the 2004 Democratic primary, even the intensely private Howard Dean felt the need to explain publicly why he switched churches to become a Congregationalist. In contemporary politics, we expect presidents to make moral affirmations as much as we expect them to engage in rhetoric touting their partisan affiliation. Although the moral and religious persona of presidents has become commonplace, we know little about the historical evolution of this role.[5] Is rhetorical moralizing an embedded executive behavior or a product of modern plebiscitary politics?

Another reason to study how presidents use moral and religious rhetoric is that people are interested in ideas and, in particular, the ideas espoused by presidents. Recent bestsellers such as David McCullough's *John Adams,* Richard Ellis's *His Excellency George Washington,* and Edmund Morris's *Theodore Rex* are obvious examples. We consider a president's rhetoric as an articulation of his ideas, making an examination of presidential moral and religious rhetoric intellectually relevant. In particular, political scientists are eager to discover new ways in which they can study ideas systematically. Many are convinced that ideas, values, and moral beliefs affect institutional development but do not know how to study these phenomena scientifically.[6] From a methodological perspective, ideals and principles are hard to classify and categorize. But presidential rhetoric is suited to overcome these problems. An investigation that utilizes scientific analysis to study the moral and religious language contained in presidential rhetoric can facilitate historical comparisons and test commonly held perceptions. Has George W. Bush used moral and religious appeals more frequently than his predecessors? Have presidents of one party emphasized moral and religious argumentation to a greater degree? By reducing selection bias and the likelihood of incorrect inferences, quantitative analysis enables social science to answer these questions.

Scholars concerned with how rhetoric influences the presidency as an institution are uniquely positioned to offer important insights that are broadly applicable to studying the political uses of moral and religious speech. Political scientists who study presidential speeches from a historical perspective have analyzed rhetoric's impact on the polity, with a particular interest in the institutional development of the presidency within the constitutional framework, the cultivation of a public philosophy or national symbols, and dilemmas of executive governance.[7] These scholarly contributions view rhetoric as a reflection of wide systematic development rather than as a strategic tool presidents have used to enhance their leadership and authority. Concerned with rhetoric's historical evolution, its instrumental purpose is often minimized. On the other hand, communication scholars routinely consider rhetoric from a strategic perspective. Several have paid considerable attention to the moral and religious dimensions of presidential rhetoric, although none with the distinct combination of quantitative methodology and broad historical analysis utilized in this effort.[8] In this book, I merge the strengths of both disciplines, paying particular attention to the political circumstances that influence rhetorical choices and also monitoring how rhetoric affects the institutional development of the presidency.

The importance of moral leadership has not gone unnoticed in presidential studies. Scholars who emphasize the moral dimension of presidential leadership typically adopt a biographical approach that either analyzes the individual characters and religious backgrounds of presidents or builds upon the president's role as the symbolic prophet of a national civil religion.[9] These efforts treat moral leadership as either a character issue or as an articulation of American political culture, but neither approach directly relates the contingent moral dimensions of leadership to the president's exercise of political power. An exception is Erwin Hargrove's *The President as Leader*, which offers a philosophically based model designed to explicate the fundamental tensions between the political and moral demands of presidential leadership.[10] I follow in Hargrove's footsteps and provide more precise observations about the political contingencies of moral leadership and its connection to political authority in the presidency, using rhetoric as the lens for monitoring the relationship. Previous research has demonstrated that presidents act as purveyors of civil religion, serving as national leaders who articulate the beliefs, values, and morals that constitute the American civic tradition. However, the analysis needs to probe deeper into the political context of these actions. The simple fact is that no one knows whether this behavior has compromised or enhanced the exercise of executive power, and what specific political circumstances encourage or constrain presidential moral leadership.

Two recent books are closely related to an investigation of presidential moral and religious rhetoric. Vanessa Beasley's *You, the People* and Mary Stuckey's *Defining Americans* examine how presidents throughout history have used rhetoric to articulate definitions of American national identity. It is important to explain how this book grounds itself in comparison to these efforts. Stuckey examines the choices presidents make regarding rhetorical constructions of the nation's identity and determines how these decisions impact the shared understanding of America's diversity. Stuckey pays attention to moral and religious arguments in presidential speeches as a tactic for expanding or contracting the definition of American civic identity. For example, the concept of "virtue" as a requirement for citizenship has changed throughout American history as the demand for political inclusion increased.[11] Stuckey's focus on the rhetorical choices presidents make is similar to my own approach, but her broader concentration on national identity diverges from the specific subject matter of this book, which concentrates on moral and religious appeals.

Beasley argues that presidents have used the language of civil religion to promote shared civic beliefs. Although Beasley and I are both interested in the moral and religious arguments contained in presidential rhetoric, Beasley's motivation is distinct from my own in that she analyzes such language as a self-described "rhetorical critic" who is primarily interested in the constitutive, rather than instrumental, aspects of presidential rhetoric.[12] Beasley explores how presidents throughout history have used the language of civil religion ideationally. In contrast, I rely heavily upon analyses of particular rhetorical situations, focusing on how political context either restrains or promotes opportunities for presidential moral leadership.[13] In this respect, I rely upon both quantitative and qualitative methodologies to analyze the relationship between political and moral leadership in the presidency.

INVESTIGATING THE USUAL SUSPECTS: QUANTITATIVE CONTENT ANALYSIS

To understand why presidents have spoken moralistically, it makes sense to search for empirical patterns.[14] After all, it might be the case that party affiliation or economic prosperity determines the level of moral and religious appeals, or that wartime presidents speak much more moralistically than non-wartime chief executives. It is necessary to determine if the variables often used to examine fluctuations in presidential behavior can reliably predict the frequency of presidential moral and religious rhetoric.[15] To examine the ebb and flow of presidential moral and religious rhetoric throughout American history, I develop a historical dataset consisting of the Annual Addresses (or State of the Union Addresses) and Inaugural Addresses. The purpose of collecting empirical data is to determine if one or more political variables can explain varying levels of presidential moral and religious rhetoric and also to measure how moralistic rhetoric has changed over time. The content analysis, which consisted of coding over five thousand pages of text, was guided by firm rules and definitions that are outlined in the appendix. Although the Annual and Inaugural Addresses are distinct genres of presidential rhetoric, there was considerable variation of moral and religious rhetoric within both categories, enabling sound empirical analysis. Furthermore, in the qualitative case studies, I analyze many genres of presidential rhetoric, thus expanding the scope of my investigation.

Coming up with a comprehensive definition of moral and religious argumentation was one of the more difficult tasks of this project. As stated earlier, the tough decisions that arise from attempting to operationalize abstract ideas, principles, and ideals usually deter social science from undertaking such ventures. For the purposes of the quantitative content analysis, I defined moral and religious rhetoric strictly, using the specific moral and religious phrases outlined in the appendix. The coding rules were developed as I interacted with primary source material, although the complete coding rules were used uniformly on all the speeches and addresses analyzed.

Throughout the course of my research, I found that presidents have utilized moral and religious language in making a variety of rhetorical arguments. Presidents use moral or religious language to describe segments of the American citizenry or the nation as a whole. They also use moral or religious language to defend their proposed policies or the actions they have already undertaken. On certain occasions, presidents employ moral or religious language to condemn domestic or international actions. Finally, presidents make general appeals or pronouncements about the importance of morality, virtue, or religion that are unrelated to any specific domestic or international policy concern. In my content analysis, I have attempted to construct a broad, yet explicit, definition of moral and religious rhetoric that can be used by other social scientists interested in this subject.

One final note on definitions should be made clear. Throughout the book, I often use the term "moral rhetoric." However, this term is not limited to moralistic language, such as references to virtue, values, and justice. Instead, I use the abbreviated term "moral rhetoric" to signify both moral and religious appeals. I do this to showcase the fact that the president often fulfills the moral leadership role through rhetoric. Throughout the book, I do not divide moral and religious rhetoric into separate categories. Future research might consider the distinct ways in which presidents use moral versus religious arguments in their rhetoric. However, the purpose of this book is to determine how moral and religious arguments *collectively* contribute to presidents attempting to fulfill the moral leadership role.

With my original dataset, I am able to provide a comprehensive descriptive picture of how the frequency of moral and religious rhetoric has fluctuated over time. I also use multivariate regression to test the influence of several political variables on varying levels of presidential moral rhetoric throughout American history. Surprisingly enough, the regression models demonstrate that most measurable political characteristics (party affiliation, historical period, times of war or economic strife, eras of divided government) do not predict fluctuating levels of presidential moral rhetoric. In other words, when it comes to their rhetorical choices, presidents can be unpredictable. If empirical patterns are indeterminate, then what can we learn about the political effects of moral and religious rhetoric? The inability of the quantitative measures to explain rhetorical patterns paves the way for the remainder of the book, which investigates the political benefits and costs of moralistic rhetoric. The question worth answering concerns itself with political capacities and the contingencies of moral leadership. More specifically, when does engaging in moralistic rhetoric enhance the president's political position, and when does it hurt him?

Strategic Choices and Presidential Moral Rhetoric

As stated earlier, this study of presidential moral and religious rhetoric elucidates the more general relationship between political leadership and moral leadership. Instead of viewing moral leadership as separate from political demands, I illuminate the powerful historical interplay between them by relating rhetoric to the strategic exercise of power and demonstrating that some presidents have used moralistic rhetoric instrumentally as a tool to enhance their constitutional position. William Riker identifies rhetorical strategy, or *heresthetic,* as "structuring the world so you can win."[16] The arguments a president chooses to emphasize in his rhetoric are important ingredients in the construction of his own political reality. Quite simply, a president's decision whether to moralize or not has political consequences that can affect prospects for effective governance.

Why focus on the strategic capacities of presidential moral and religious rhetoric? The emphasis stems from a theoretical conception of executive power that views American presidents as perennially plagued with the problem of authority. The ambiguous structure of the presidency motivates the consistent desire for building political support.[17] Because good government depends upon an energetic executive, the Founders included institutional incentives for the chief executive. According to the *Federalist Papers,* unity, duration, adequate support, and competent powers gave the president the tools to govern independently. But as much as the Founders insulated the president from the whimsy of democracy, the strength of the office itself still relies upon the people's conferral of democratic legitimacy. To sustain authority, presidents must build political support. Throughout American history, presidents have used their rhetoric as a means to establish their credibility and to nurture existing authority. Moral and religious appeals are especially useful because they have the power to connect the pragmatism of policy to the passion of emotions and elevate political discourse to a discussion concerning first principles. Moral legitimacy can easily translate into the perception of political control, and presidents find this potential source of power enticing, and sometimes irresistible. The moral dimensions of rhetoric and the cultivation of political support are inextricably linked; a consideration of one must include an analysis of the other.

Presidents in a variety of political and historical situations might find it expedient to justify their actions and proposed policies using moral argumentation. Because ethical principles signify both constancy and change, moral appeals are not always transformative. Moral ideals such as "justice" and "virtue" are typically thought of as ethical standards that transcend time or political situation. First-order principles are often "order-affirming."[18] Besides providing affirmation to an existing political regime, moral argumentation can also be used to usher in a new one; new realizations and formulations of principled ideals can serve as justifications for a changed polity. Thus, presidents can adapt moral language as both agents of affirmation and change; such language can either confirm the status quo or create new standards.

Given the political attractiveness of moral rhetoric, why doesn't every president utilize this type of rhetoric? If moralistic rhetoric has the power to augment already existing political authority and can be employed in a variety of situations, we might expect high levels of moral and religious references in every presidential speech. It turns out that the political reality of rhetoric's potential is more complicated. It is better to think of presidential moral rhetoric as a *contingent* source of authority.

In keeping with the theoretical contributions of the "new institutionalism" in presidential studies, I depict moral rhetoric as an instrumental tool resulting from political judgments about the costs and benefits of specific institutional environments.[19] When rhetoric is a product of a strategic choice, it can enhance executive authority. From a political standpoint, presidents should not consider giving moralistic speeches a destiny that they must fulfill. Rather, the political utility of moral rhetoric depends upon the presence of supporting circumstances that recommend its use. In this light, the analysis contained in this book places greater emphasis on the institutional belief that structure and circumstance, more than personality or leadership style, determine the political effects that result from presidential choices and decisions. Individuals certainly make a difference, particularly when morality and values are being discussed. Nonetheless, a stable political structure exists that either rewards or penalizes presidents based upon the rhetorical choices they make. The political environment conditions the rhetorical effectiveness of a president's moral ethos, rather than the reverse.

Even though moral rhetoric often stems from an articulation of abstract principles, I argue that presidents should view it from a prudential lens. The concept of prudence, or *phronesis,* plays an important role in the rhetorical tradition. An extended discussion of *phronesis* appears in Book VI of Aristotle's *Nicomachean Ethics,* but the practical application of prudence becomes evident in his *Rhetoric.* For example, it is often difficult for a political leader to know what level of emotion is appropriate for a given rhetorical engagement, and the possession of prudence enables the rhetor to choose wisely. In the words of Robert Hariman, prudence "is the mode of reasoning about contingent matters in order to select the best course of action."[20] With regard to rhetoric, prudence involves choosing the appropriate means to persuade and inform listeners about the best possible choice. Prudent speakers realize that rhetorical limits exist and that one type of argument will not work in all situations. In the spirit of Aristotelian political science, presidents who have viewed rhetoric from a prudential lens have benefited politically from this orientation.

Although *phronesis* serves the conceptual purpose of bridging the gap between the study of moral ethics, rhetoric, and politics, there has been little research focused on the contingent nature of presidential moral rhetoric. With a few notable exceptions, previous attempts to analyze the political circumstances that influence the use of moral and religious speech have focused on individual presidents and their rhetoric.[21] These accounts are illuminating but do not provide theoretical observations about the broader institutional relationship between presidential moralizing and political authority. By examining a number of presidents across time, we can move toward building a general theory about the complex relationships between moral and political leadership, as well as presidential rhetoric and political authority. Indeed, a variety of case studies that seek to illuminate broader conclusions may show us rhetoric's political limits and its potential strengths.

Assigning motivation to presidential decision-making is always a difficult enterprise. The historical case studies included offer a range of evidence to substantiate the strategic hypothesis. In some instances, actual documents offer evidence that strategic considerations affected rhetorical choice. In other examinations, secondary historical literature helps tell the story at hand. Oftentimes, the personal moral dispositions of presidents do not match their rhetorical choices. Because a president's rhetoric does not always mimic his privately held beliefs, strategy's influence is advanced. Also, I carefully monitor when presidents change their rhetoric within their administration, either increasing their moral and religious references or decreasing them. Abrupt alterations provide corroborative evidence for the strategy hypothesis and further substantiate the inference of political motivations.

With this book, I hope to facilitate a discussion about the strategic timing of moral posturing. As scholars, we know that presidents have served as the "prophet" of civil religion, using moralistic and religious rhetoric as a political symbol to impact the formation of American political culture. Furthermore, certain genres of presidential rhetoric (Inaugurals, Farewell Addresses, Annual Addresses) routinely include moral and religious appeals or references.[22] But when is the inclusion of moral and religious rhetoric politically desirable for presidents? Are there specific political circumstances, apart from the historically pervasive characteristics of rhetorical genres, which make moral and religious rhetoric an effective tool for enhancing a president's authority? There has been no comprehensive historical analysis of the specific political conditions that encourage or discourage presidential moralizing; we don't know *when* presidents *should* engage in moral leadership through speech to enhance their political authority. Adopting the terminology of Clinton Rossiter, scholars have approached the president's moral spokesman role as a "hat" that can be worn at will, paying little attention to the political context of moralizing.[23] On the contrary, moral leadership does not exist within a political vacuum. The political context of moral and religious rhetoric is vitally important to studying its impact upon the broader concept of presidential political authority.

POLITICAL CIRCUMSTANCES AND RHETORICAL CHOICE

A perennial conundrum of Aristotelian *phronesis* is that it is difficult to extrapolate any specific instructions towards practical applications. After all, it is politically naïve to think that a president studies his copy of Aristotle's *Rhetoric* the night before an important speech. Rather, presidents and their advisors are interested in concrete applications of theory. In particular, when will moral and religious rhetoric enhance the political authority of the president? In the context of this book, the term "authority" is defined as the president's capacity for accomplishing political goals within the confines of a particular historical situation. Stephen Skowronek defines authority as "the warrants that can be drawn from the moment at hand to justify action and secure the legitimacy of the changes effected."[24] A president's authority is a reflection of his political standing, the ability to move his agenda forward and solidify the political goals he has accomplished. Rhetoric is a presidential resource, and how a president decides to use his rhetoric impacts his broader exercise of authority.

Throughout the case studies contained in this book, the impact of seven recurring political conditions on rhetorical choice is considered. Four circumstances encourage presidents to engage in moral rhetoric, and three conditions recommend moral restraint. In contrast to the quantitative portion of my research, in which I used a deductive approach akin to hypotheses testing, I arrived upon these specific conditions through inductive reasoning, moving from specific observations when conducting the historical research to the broader generalizations that are described here. This "bottom up" approach enabled me to detect recurring patterns and regularities in the case studies. Since previous historical research has not analyzed the political circumstances that make the use of moral and religious rhetoric politically advantageous to the president, a more open-ended or exploratory research direction was appropriate. The seven circumstances outlined below were limited in an attempt to value the simplicity and parsimony of the model.[25]

In the case studies, four recurring political conditions suggest that moral argumentation is the preferred rhetorical choice for presidents. First, when faced with the imminent task of rallying the nation around a particular cause, in which public support is uncertain or marginal, moral and religious rhetoric can enhance the authority of the president and substantiate the seriousness of his claims. Second, when justifying complicated legislation that is otherwise difficult to explain to a national audience, moral rhetoric can prove beneficial. Defining a complex policy in moral terms simplifies rhetorical explanations and also enables the president to avoid becoming mired in details that could potentially endanger a proposal. Third, when presidents are elected on the premise of providing moral leadership for the nation, moralistic rhetoric bolsters a president's authority by reinforcing and fulfilling expectations. If a president elected on a "moral leadership platform" refuses to speak moralistically, he risks diminishing an important source of his authority. The final political circumstance that encourages presidents to engage in moral rhetoric is when Congress threatens to assume leadership on a national issue. In this light, the institutional context of presidential rhetoric can be seen as influential. Moral rhetoric can prove helpful in this situation because strong moral arguments enable presidents to reassert their relevance and defend their political position. Under these conditions, presidents are forced to either take a principled stand or risk ceding authority. Moral and religious rhetoric facilitates principled position-taking and gives the president a strong voice in which to "shout down" those who try to steal his thunder.

At least three conditions recommend that presidents refrain from moralistic rhetoric. The most prevalent condition recommending restraint is divisiveness within a president's own party. When an explosive issue with potentially explicit moral overtones sharply divides the president's party, moral restraint is the more advisable option. Morally principled arguments are frequently too blunt for the skillful maneuvering required for intra-partisan battles. It is particularly difficult for presidents to back away from bold moral pronouncements and seek political compromises. If they do strike a deal, they run the risk of alienating all concerned factions. Moral restraint can prove powerful in these situations if the president can use careful rhetoric to maintain party unity, whereas moral appeals that take sides on conflict-ridden issues threaten to exacerbate existing tensions.

Second, when presidents suffer a public condemnation or scandal, moralistic pronouncements are misplaced, and rhetorical restraint is the more advantageous option. In particular, if a scandal calls the moral authority of a president or his administration into question, more secular rhetoric should be adopted. A "slippage between character and role" can precipitate a strategic mistake.[26] Presidents do not need to be paragons of virtue to speak the language of morality forcefully, but if the Washington community or the public seriously doubts their ethics, moral stances will be seen as fulsome.

Finally, if a president is in a position of weak political authority, moral and religious appeals lead to a further denigration of his leadership position. Out of a desire to create political authority where little exists, presidents often resort to desperate measures, but moralistic rhetoric in these situations will prove counterproductive and project an image of feebleness instead of strength. Lacking *political* legitimacy, presidents sometimes seek *moral* legitimacy. Moralistic rhetoric cannot create political authority from nothing; it can only strengthen or build upon already existing authority. Rhetoric is a powerful political tool, but there are limitations to its effectiveness and influence. In the presidency, these limits are determined, in large part, by structure.[27] The constitutional framework imposes such limitations; the president must compete for political authority to secure his position vis-à-vis other institutional actors. Moral leadership is not an adequate substitute for exercising fundamental institutional powers. Instead, moral leadership through speech is a unique opportunity available to presidents that can improve their credibility and capacity. Even the most morally inspirational president cannot escape the structural confines that surround him.

These circumstances constitute the strategic framework of presidential moral rhetoric. Of course, political scenarios are often complicated. At times, presidents will encounter situations in which circumstances encourage both moral argumentation and moral restraint. For example, Lincoln became president during a national crisis in which support for action was tenuous, but he also dealt with the morally divisive issue of slavery that threatened to tear apart the Union coalition and his own Republican Party. The evidence presented in subsequent chapters suggests that when political conditions move in opposite directions, moral restraint is the more advantageous strategy. Moral posturing is often a risky endeavor for presidents that can incur political costs as well as benefits. For a president to enhance his political authority through moral rhetoric, the situation at hand must be free of restraining circumstances that encumber the moral force of his claims. Furthermore, political conditions may shift within a term of office. The nuances explored in the case studies of chapters 3 through 5 allow for such possibilities and monitor how presidents who respond strategically are rewarded politically.

Finally, it is important to keep in mind that the conditions outlined above are not predictions of how presidents will speak or act. Presidents are not calculating robots who always abide by the political constraints of a given situation. However, this examination demonstrates that when presidents throw caution to the wind and neglect the strictures that bind them, their political authority suffers. From a political perspective, rhetorical choice matters.

THINKING ABOUT MORAL LEADERSHIP STRATEGICALLY

Thinking about moral and religious rhetoric as a strategic response to political circumstances allows us to make additional observations about the relationship between political and moral leadership. First, presidential moralizing often runs counter to expectations drawn from the persona of the incumbent. Leaders with strong moral beliefs do not always advertise these sentiments through their presidential rhetoric, while those who did not demonstrate strong moral convictions before sometimes find themselves engaging in moral argumentation as president. James Madison's moralizing in office is surprising, as is Abraham Lincoln's moral restraint. The political reasons why presidents often go against their prior dispositions provide the analytic framework for the historical case studies.

Second, by focusing on rhetoric's strategic nature, we learn that sometimes presidents make bad choices.[28] Despite the presence of political circumstances that either encourage or discourage moralistic rhetoric, not all presidents heed this calculus. Some employ moral arguments when political factors suggest they should not. Others refuse to change their restrained leadership style to adopt a morally inspirational stance when that might be to their advantage. When presidents do not adjust their rhetoric to suit their circumstances, they suffer political consequences, finding their authority diminished because their rhetoric is out of sync with the political contingencies of the moment. Throughout history, presidents have paid a price for not heeding the political constraints of their rhetorical leadership.

Third, looking at presidential rhetoric with a strategic eye suggests that presidents can exercise moral leadership in a variety of different ways. Obviously, presidents serve as moral leaders by frequently invoking the ethical and religious ideals in their public rhetoric. However, an examination of Lincoln's rhetoric indicates that another possibility exists: presidents can exercise moral leadership by restraining their rhetoric and deliberately avoiding high platitudes in their public statements if they believe that public arguments about moral and religious principles will ultimately harm the common good instead of promoting it.

Determining why certain presidents engage in heightened levels of moral and religious rhetoric is a complicated enterprise. When presidents assume office, they inherit a strategic position based upon electoral results and the strength of the political ideology with which they are affiliated.[29] Furthermore, presidents constantly face new challenges that often arise due to circumstances largely outside of their control. Despite these constraints, presidents have the ability to construct their own response to the situational context they operate within. Presidents exist in an opportunity structure, and their political authority rests upon the choices they make and the leadership rationales they adopt. Although this examination specifically focuses on rhetoric and moral leadership, in a broader sense, it also analyzes the ability of presidents to enhance and justify their independent political authority and influence. How presidents exercise executive power and the choices they make in pursuit of their political goals is the primary concern of the book.

OVERVIEW OF THE BOOK

Chapter 2 presents a quantitative overview of presidential moral and religious rhetoric. To determine if any persistent circumstantial trends across time reliably predict the rhetorical choices presidents make, I provide content analyses of the Annual and Inaugural Addresses that compare rates of presidential moralizing throughout American history and also measure the predictive value of independent variables.

The nine case studies of chapters 3 through 5 illustrate the situational constraints of presidential rhetoric and are divided into three scenarios: moral reinforcement (chapter 3), rhetorical restraint (chapter 4), and strategic moralizing (chapter 5). These three categories were based on two variables: the moral dispositions of presidents and their rhetorical practices. The case studies were organized in this way to show that the effectiveness of a president's rhetorical choices is determined not by moral ethos or disposition but by the president's willingness to adapt his rhetoric to the political situation at hand. Consequently, there are rhetorical "successes" and "failures" within each chapter. A rhetorical success enhances the president's political authority, and a failure diminishes it. For example, chapter 4 demonstrates that moral restraint is advantageous when it is a purposeful strategic response but not when it emanates from a rigid philosophical belief that moralistic rhetoric is inappropriate.

All three "moral reinforcement" presidents of chapter 3—George Washington, Theodore Roosevelt, and Jimmy Carter—highlighted their known moral personas through moral and religious rhetoric. The strong moral dispositions of these presidents lead us to anticipate that they would moralize frequently, and they fulfill these expectations. However, because rhetoric's political utility varies as circumstances change, their rhetoric met with different degrees of political success. Chapters 4 and 5 describe presidents who purposefully engaged in moral argumentation or restraint, often going against their dispositions or inclinations. Chapter 4 analyzes Thomas Jefferson, Abraham Lincoln, and John Kennedy, three presidents who refrained from using moral and religious appeals, again with variable effects tied to circumstances. Chapter 5 considers James Madison, James Buchanan, and Lyndon Johnson, three presidents who employed moral and religious language in their rhetoric. Within each chapter, I draw conclusions about when rhetorical practices work effectively and when they do not. These observations substantiate the contention that moral rhetoric is best viewed as a strategic tool to enhance political authority.

There are three layers of analysis in each case study. First, to examine how personal inclinations influence rhetoric, I briefly discuss each president's moral ethos and then determine if a relationship existed between who he was and what he said. For example, such a relationship did not exist in the case of Lyndon Johnson, whose moralistic rhetoric in the 1965 Voting Rights Address did not match his reputation as a secular politico. On the other hand, Jimmy Carter's moralistic presidential rhetoric certainly reinforced his self-description as a born-again Christian. The fact that a president's persona does not always determine his rhetorical choices substantiates the supposition that moralistic rhetoric is often a strategic, institutional tool used by presidents to enhance their authority.

This paves the way for the second level of analysis in the case studies, which considers how political circumstances influence rhetorical decisions. Each case study evaluates whether or not a president's rhetoric matched the political circumstances he faced and also examines the political consequences of his rhetorical choices. Some matches may be fortuitous, a coincidence of persona and situation. Others will be intentional, a departure from what personality alone leads us to expect. Several presidents discussed in the case studies enhanced their political authority by using moral arguments in a strategic and supple manner, whereas those who failed to adjust their speech paid a price for their inappropriate rhetoric.

The third and final level of analysis in each case study focuses on the political benefits and costs of a president's chosen rhetoric. By showing that presidents who speak strategically increase their authority and those who speak haphazardly are penalized, I demonstrate the political importance of rhetorical decisions and moral leadership. It may be the case that presidents feel it is their duty to speak moralistically regardless of the political constraints that warn them against such behavior. Without discounting the altruism that can motivate presidents, I consider the political ramifications of their rhetorical decisions. As far as success or failure is concerned, my primary concern in this book is instrumental rather than ethical or constitutive.[30]

Finally, in chapter 6, I conclude with an assessment of modern developments in presidential rhetoric. The nine case studies analyze when moralistic speech enhances a president's political authority. Chapter 6 discusses how twentieth-century trends in moral rhetoric affect its political and strategic utility, which is based upon the premise that political conditions must be ripe for presidents to moralize without suffering a loss of authority. As contemporary expectations for moral posturing increase, it is likely that even more presidents will fall victim to the deleterious consequences of imprudently crafted rhetoric. Instead of being used as a sharp political tool to assert independence, presidential moral rhetoric runs the risk of becoming a political liability. Presidents need to acknowledge and understand these modern challenges if they wish to preserve the powerful independent authority that moral and religious argumentation can afford.

CHAPTER 2

RHETORICAL PATTERNS

OF THE ANNUAL AND INAUGURAL

ADDRESSES, 1790–2003

From time to time, all presidents use moral and religious appeals in their rhetoric. But the only way to determine if historical fluctuations or empirical patterns exist is by creating a research design that incorporates quantitative content analysis. The data presented in this chapter are drawn from the Annual and Inaugural Addresses of George Washington through George W. Bush and are used to analyze how moral and religious rhetoric varied in two different respects.[1] The first line of inquiry is concerned with historical development. Have levels of moral and religious rhetoric changed over time? Were particular time periods in presidential history infused with moral and religious rhetoric? The second line of inquiry examines whether or not specific political variables affect the frequency of presidential moral rhetoric.

The Annual Addresses were analyzed to keep the specific rhetorical task—providing information on the state of the union—constant throughout my analysis. Since all presidents have given Annual Addresses, this form of presidential communication offers a consistent method to monitor fluctuations in moral and religious rhetoric. Furthermore, Karlyn Campbell and Kathleen Jamieson explain that the Annual Addresses are quite varied as a genre. Some are "eloquent" and others are "dull." The speech is typically used to explain policy proposals, but many Annual Addresses also include an assessment of values; the Annual Address can be considered a "rhetorical hybrid" that invites scholars to investigate its recurrent and variable characteristics. In particular, presidents include policy recommendations and meditations on values to "varying degrees."[2] The bottom line is that not all presidents approach the Annual Address in the same way. For the purpose of measuring presidential usage of moral and religious rhetoric across time, the Annual Address is the most appropriate genre of presidential discourse to analyze, because fluctuation in the dependent variable is high.

While the official audience of the Annual Address is Congress, most presidents have used the Annual Address to reach a national audience. Writing in 1898, Mary Parker Follett, an early student of Congress, observed that the Annual Address serves as an "address to the country" rather than a speech intended for Congress.[3] During the nineteenth century, when the president issued the Annual Address in writing, newspapers throughout the country routinely reprinted the message.

While the Annual Addresses serve as the primary data source for evaluating rhetorical trends, my research is not limited to this particular genre. I also analyze the Inaugural Addresses to investigate divergent types of moral and religious argumentation. To further supplement the quantitative analysis of the Annual and Inaugural Addresses, in chapters 3 through 5 I discuss a wide variety of presidential rhetoric, including proclamations, replies to addresses, "swings around the circle," radio addresses, and televised speeches.

Coding

Using content analysis, I sought to determine how frequently presidents used moral or religious argumentation in their Annual Addresses. In my coding, I looked for sentences that contained one of five types of moral and religious rhetoric. These five definitions were developed prior to the content analysis and were based upon my preliminary examination of presidential addresses throughout American history. The definitions employed in the coding were intended to be as exhaustive as possible and are listed in the appendix.

Measuring presidential moral and religious argumentation throughout American history is a difficult enterprise. It is important to note that the content analysis was designed to measure *explicit* moral and religious argumentation in presidential rhetoric. Phrasing that might contain *implied* or *tacit* moral or religious allusions are not included. There are several reasons for this decision. First, an explicit definition of moral and religious argumentation enables replication of the content analysis. Including implicit references would diminish the likelihood that the analysis could be repeated soundly by someone else. Second, the general standard for inclusion is that all listeners and readers of the address would agree (regardless of their religious or educational background) that the phrase was explicitly moral or religious in nature. For example, allusions to biblical passages that were not explicitly attributed to the Bible, Christian principles, or religion were not counted as moral and religious rhetoric. Also, broad visionary or inspirational statements that did not employ explicitly overt moral or religious language were not counted.[4]

The rationale for firmly following explicit coding rules is twofold. First, measuring moral and religious argumentation in speeches throughout presidential history is an abstract task from the outset, and if a rigid standard is not set for inclusion, the empirical results will depend upon the whims and impressions of the coder. The purpose of the study is not to code for *inspirational* rhetoric but explicit moral and religious argumentation. Second, although some presidents have used implied allusions to religion and the Bible in their speeches (such as Clinton's "forcing the spring" theme in his First Inaugural Address) these references may not be recognized uniformly as possessing moral and religious significance.

The unit examined was the sentence. I counted the number of sentences that contained moral or religious rhetoric in each Annual Address. Other quantitative analyses of presidential rhetoric have employed similar methodologies in their coding.[5] I also kept track of how presidents used moral and religious appeals in their rhetoric, classifying each coded instance of moral and religious rhetoric as referring to domestic policy, foreign policy, or no policy. The purpose was to monitor fluctuations in the contextual purpose of moral and religious rhetoric throughout American history. Upon completion of the coding, I used a word processing program to determine how many sentences each address contained.[6] By dividing the total number of moral and religious references of each president by the total number of sentences contained in his Annual Addresses, I was able to compare, across history, the *rate* of presidential moral and religious rhetoric.

Additionally, the content analysis also enables an alternative time series that compares the average *overall amount* of presidential moral and religious rhetoric. In this secondary measurement, a president's total number of moral and religious references is divided by the number of Annual Addresses he issued. This analysis allows us to observe the fluctuations in *aggregate* presidential moralizing throughout American history. An aggregate measure may help to assess the overall political impact of moralizing and also detect the possible presence of a "layering effect" due to varying lengths of speeches over time. The longest Annual Addresses occurred during the period of 1890–1912, in which addresses averaged 576 sentences in length, or roughly twenty-one-thousand words. It could be the case that the amount of presidential moral rhetoric has remained constant over time, but the overall length of addresses has changed. Used in tandem, these two measures provide a fuller empirical picture of the phenomenon at hand.

MORAL RHETORIC AND HISTORICAL DEVELOPMENT

Political scientists, particularly presidency scholars, are inclined to think about institutional change and development using periodization. The concept of the "modern presidency" is an anchoring paradigm in presidential studies today. The predominant understanding is that the presidency has undergone a fundamental transformation, which pits "premodern" and "modern" presidents on opposite sides of a historical divide. One important developmental change has been the tendency of most twentieth-century, or modern, presidents to govern by rhetorical appeal.[7] Although political development is often more complicated than any blunt periodization scheme can describe, it is an appropriate place to start the investigation. From what we already know about the historical development of the presidency as an institution, it is reasonable to expect patterned variation in moral and religious rhetoric. In particular, previous scholarship suggests that higher levels of moral rhetoric should be anticipated in the early years of the presidency and the post-Wilsonian era.

Republican cultural norms elevated eminent virtue and the common good in late-eighteenth-century politics. Ralph Ketcham argued that the first six presidents uniquely reflected this understanding of politics, aspiring to disinterested statesmanship and integrity.[8] In these administrations, the president's most reliable resource for power and authority was his individual character and reputation. After the patrician era, starting with Andrew Jackson and Martin Van Buren, presidential politics shifted ground, with incumbents tied to organizations of interest and a party apparatus demanding distribution of political patronage. The importance of emanating a virtuous personal reputation lessened as party organization and patronage became a more prominent resource for power in the 1830s.[9] If patrician leadership affected rhetorical choices, moral and religious rhetoric should be very high during the administrations of the first six presidents and then lessen considerably when personal reputation and virtue no longer served as the main resource of presidential authority.

On the other end of American history, Jeffrey Tulis has argued that Woodrow Wilson permanently altered the accepted norms of presidential rhetoric in an attempt to reinvigorate the executive office and its leadership potential. According to Tulis, presidents before Wilson based their policy recommendations on a legalistic interpretation of Constitutional principles. After Wilson, presidential rhetoric became more symbolic, visionary, and inspirational. Instead of drawing upon their Constitutional authority, post-Wilsonian modern presidents have come to rely on a figurative moral authority, speaking like a "moral trumpet." In Tulis's depiction, Woodrow Wilson is a pivotal figure in the metamorphosis of presidential rhetoric because his rhetorical innovations pave the way for the remainder of the twentieth century. Given the influential nature of *The Rhetorical Presidency,* it makes sense to test Tulis's bifurcated account, although others have already challenged several of his claims.[10]

To investigate historical changes in presidential rhetoric, the data have been organized into two line graphs, figures 1 and 2. Figure 1 displays the percentage of moral and religious sentences in the Annual Addresses from George Washington through George W. Bush. Figure 2 displays the average aggregate number of moral and religious sentences per Annual Address.[11]

First, a few general observations can be made about the data. For the most part, the graphs present similar results. Jackson, Buchanan, Andrew Johnson, Reagan, and George W. Bush are "high" points on both graphs, and Lincoln, Taft, Kennedy, and Clinton are "low" marks on both measures. A "layering effect" does not exist; there are significant fluctuations in the aggregate measure displayed in figure 2. The graphs display noteworthy discrepancies in only two instances. First, the early patrician presidents rank highly on figure 1 but not in figure 2. This disparity is due to the fact that the Annual Addresses of the first six presidents were short, averaging just 74 sentences or roughly 2,700 words. Their rate of moralizing was high, but due to the abbreviated length of their addresses, their aggregate score is comparatively low. The second discrepancy is Theodore Roosevelt, who does not stand out in figure 1 but appears quite high in figure 2. Of all the presidents, Roosevelt's Annual Addresses were the longest (averaging 628 sentences or about 23,000 words). Although he moralized quite frequently, the lengthiness of his addresses minimized his overall rate. The full impact of Roosevelt's

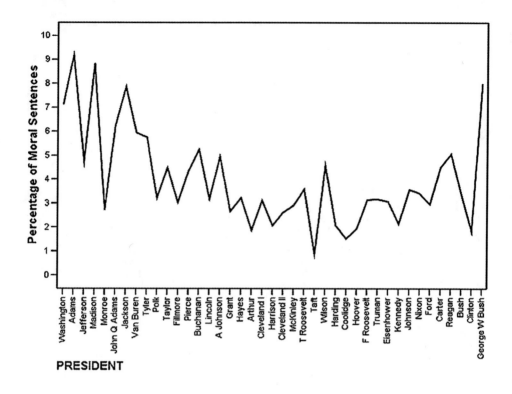

Figure 1. Percentage of Moral and Religious Rhetoric: Annual Addresses

moralistic rhetoric is displayed in the auxiliary measure, which shows that he averaged about twenty moral or religious appeals per Annual Address. As much as possible, both measures of presidential moral rhetoric will be used throughout the empirical analysis.

Figure 2 also enables a comparison of presidents in similar eras. For example, the Annual Addresses issued by presidents from Jackson through Cleveland's first term were similar in length (approximately 250–300 sentences per address). During this time period, there was a large fluctuation in presidential moralizing, with Jackson, Van Buren, and Buchanan leading the way and, surprisingly enough, Abraham Lincoln trailing behind. The contrast of Buchanan (17.75 moral/religious appeals per address) and Lincoln (7.50 moral/religious appeals per address) is quite interesting and will be explored in chapter 4.

Figure 1 shows that the patrician presidents engaged in moral and religious rhetoric at higher *rates* than presidents of any other time period.[12] However, moral and religious rhetoric in the Annual Addresses did

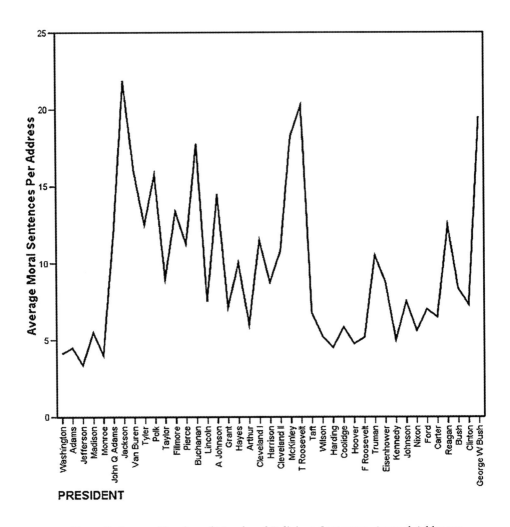

Figure 2. Average Number of Moral and Religious Sentences: Annual Addresses

not disappear after the patrician era. If patrician norms or the political primacy of a virtuous reputation explained rhetorical choices, we would expect a sharper decline after this time period. In particular, as the first "party" president, Andrew Jackson's rhetoric should contain lower levels of moral and religious rhetoric than his predecessors. Figures 1 and 2 do not indicate that Jackson engaged in less moral rhetoric than his "patrician" predecessors and suggests that the advent of the party era did not depress presidential moralizing.

The influence of modernity is more complicated, but both graphs indicate that moralistic rhetoric did not begin with Woodrow Wilson.

Instead, presidents have invoked principles, ideals, and morals in their Annual Addresses since the days of George Washington. Wilson was a standout but not because he changed rhetorical leadership without historical precedent, as previously suggested. Wilson did not drastically change the substance or content of presidential rhetoric. Instead, Wilson changed *how* presidents used moral and religious rhetoric. This phenomenon can be observed by looking at a second set of data, displayed in figure 3. This line graph shows the percentage of moral and religious rhetoric of each president that does not refer to a policy issue.[13]

As described earlier, I classified each moral and religious reference as referring to foreign policy, domestic policy, or no policy. Figure 3 shows

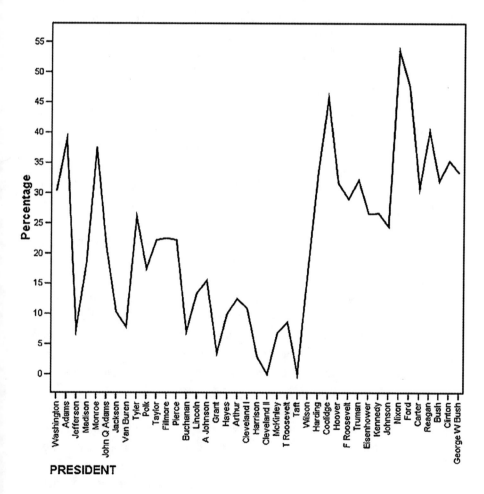

Figure 3. Non-Policy Moralizing: Annual Addresses

that Wilson, along with Coolidge (who followed Wilson's lead), began a trend of presidential moralizing without a particular policy goal in mind. After Wilson, moral and religious rhetoric in the Annual Addresses became much more detached from policy recommendations. Notice that this detachment originated before technological innovations such as radio and television became "modern" tools of presidential persuasion.[14]

Presidents now use moral and religious argumentation to pontificate about the "spiritual health of the nation" or the importance of "values" in American society. These moralistic statements are separate from arguments about policy decisions, proposals, or executive actions. Presidents engage in pronouncements such as Reagan's in 1984, "There is a hunger in the land for a spiritual revival" or Nixon in 1970, "Today, let it not be recorded that we lack the moral and spiritual idealism which made us the hope of the world at the time of our birth." Such moralistic observations aim to inspire or convey ideology rather than provide an argument about a specific policy proposal or issue.

While the data presented in figure 3 clearly indicates that Woodrow Wilson changed how presidents use moral rhetoric, it is possible that such a transformation resulted from Wilson's return to the oral mode of delivering the Annual Address. From Jefferson to Taft, presidents issued their Annual Addresses to Congress in writing. Wilson broke this precedent in 1913 when he appeared in the House of Representatives chamber and gave his address in person. However, due to his illness, Wilson did not deliver his final two Annual Addresses orally. Similar to his previous six speeches, these two written addresses continued to use non-policy moralizing. Calvin Coolidge's rhetoric also raises questions about the validity of attributing the proliferation of non-policy moralizing to the change in delivery. Of the six Annual Addresses he issued, Coolidge gave only one speech in person. Coolidge's five written addresses employed non-policy moral and religious rhetoric at high rates, similar to his 1923 Annual Address, which was broadcast over the radio. If the oral mode of address explained the post-Wilsonian phenomenon of non-policy moralizing, then we would expect that Coolidge's position on figure 3 would be very low, since he submitted five of his six addresses in writing. However, figure 3 demonstrates that Coolidge used non-policy moral and religious rhetoric at very high rates. While choosing not to imitate Wilson's method of delivery, Coolidge did mimic his rhetorical practices.

Wilson is clearly responsible for detaching policy concerns from moral argumentation. But did he also permanently change the *substance* of moral argumentation itself, moving it towards a more "visionary" or "inspirational" approach and away from disciplined, traditionalist, backward-looking speech? According to Tulis in *The Rhetorical Presidency*, Wilsonian visionary speech articulates a "picture of the future" and "impels a populace towards it" rather than focusing on retrospective "established principles."[15] Glen E. Thurow concurs, arguing that Wilson's Inaugural Addresses paved the way for a "new standard" of virtue in American life that created "a new point of view in the nation as a whole." Wilson's virtue is more democratic and compassionate; it is not the traditional virtue of "outstanding persons" that had been emphasized previously by presidents.[16] To figure out if Wilson is a transformational president in this regard, I examine another dataset, collected from the Inaugural Addresses, to determine if visionary rhetoric began with Woodrow Wilson and continued with his modern successors.

The Inaugural, as an example of epideictic or ceremonial rhetoric, is particularly well suited to answer this question. From a message-centered perspective, the defining characteristic of epideictic rhetoric is "praise or blame." The Inaugural Address emphasizes the former. Typically a celebration of American ideals, the Inaugural Addresses contain many references to principles and morals that can be classified as either retrospective or visionary. Campbell and Jamieson argue that as epideictic rhetoric, inaugurals "link past and future in present contemplation" and provide presidents with their greatest opportunity to engage freely in visionary and retrospective appeals. Celeste Condit explains that defining shared importance in an inaugural is possible when the speaker links the audience to its past and indicates the boundaries of hopes and expectations for the future.[17]

In the content analysis of the Inaugural Addresses, "visionary" rhetoric refers to the changing, evolving nature of morality and values and emphasizes the collective nature of a shared cultural ethos. In distinction, "retrospective" rhetoric includes references to traditional morals that do not change over time.[18] Retrospective rhetoric is often categorical and talks about the individual as the primary source of moral activity and decision. The complete coding definitions of "visionary" and "retrospective" rhetoric are included in the appendix.

Before Andrew Jackson's presidency, Inaugural Addresses contained very few examples of both visionary and retrospective moral argumentation. Instead, the first six presidents often spoke about their own venerable character or sense of duty that served as a qualification for public office. For this reason, they have been omitted from this analysis.[19] The coding results support the claim that visionary rhetoric began with Woodrow Wilson. A comparison of the premodern and modern Inaugural addresses in table 1 shows that prior to Wilson, visionary appeals were rare. Wilson's two Inaugural Addresses alone contained more visionary appeals than the preceding ninety years of presidential history.

Table 1 substantiates Tulis's observation that as president, Wilson was a rhetorical innovator.[20] However, the results also demonstrate that post-Wilsonian presidents did not employ visionary rhetoric at the expense of retrospective appeals. The modern Inaugural Address is a mixture of visionary and retrospective moral argumentation. As often as presidents articulated the changing nature of ideals or the creation of new ideals, they also lauded the constancy of older, time-honored principles. Visions of the future were tempered by rhetorical retrospection and traditionalism. Table 1 does not support the claim that Woodrow Wilson altered twentieth-century presidential rhetoric by *replacing* appeals to established principles, morals, and ideals with visionary speech. Rather, Wilson introduced a new rhetorical tradition that now exists alongside earlier practices.

In summary, presidents did employ moral and religious arguments in their rhetoric prior to Woodrow Wilson. Wilson's presidential rhetoric was transformative in that he permanently changed moral rhetoric in the Annual Address by detaching it from policy concerns. Within this genre, all subsequent presidents have imitated Wilson's example and engaged

TABLE 1. VISIONARY AND CATEGORICAL MORAL APPEALS: INAUGURALS, 1829–2001

Presidential Era	Number of Visionary Appeals	Number of Retrospective Appeals
Jackson through Taft	11	64
Woodrow Wilson	12	5
Harding through George W. Bush	114	128

in non-policy moralizing. By introducing a new visionary component, Wilson also changed presidential moral rhetoric in the Inaugurals. Unlike non-policy moralizing, Wilson's successors have not uniformly adopted his visionary example, and retrospective appeals to time-honored values still exist in modern presidential rhetoric. While agreeing with Tulis and other scholars who recognize Woodrow Wilson as a rhetorical innovator, my analysis questions the portrayal of the modern "rhetorical presidency" as unidimensional and structurally determined. As far as moral and religious rhetoric is concerned, modern presidents do not uniformly labor under the expectation of "visionary" leadership. Wilson successfully introduced a new rhetorical tradition, but did not displace the old.

MORAL RHETORIC AND POLITICAL INFLUENCES

A comprehensive historical dataset enables further empirical investigation beyond descriptive analyses. Figures 1 and 2 demonstrate that levels of presidential moral and religious rhetoric vary, but why? Perhaps Republican or wartime presidents engaged in higher levels of moralizing. Or perhaps a strong electoral mandate encourages more frequent moral appeals. Some political contexts may make it more likely for presidents to employ moral rhetoric in their speeches. To answer these questions, we need a systematic evaluation of the political variables that may influence rhetorical choice.

Party Affiliation

Historical research concerning the composition and cohesiveness of American political parties reveal a pervasive, ideological division concerning the role of morality and religion in political life. John Gerring showed that the Whig and Republican Parties, which shared a cohesive political ideology despite an organizational transformation, exhibited a moralistic, evangelical ethos that was distinct from the more secular Democratic Party. A Yankee Protestant piety persisted throughout the nineteenth and twentieth century within the Whig-Republicans. In particular, Whig-Republicans believed strongly in human perfectibility and moral reform. Robert Kelley also described sharp ideological differences between the two parties. According to Kelley, the Whigs became the party of decency, piety, sober living, proper manners, thrift, and steady habits, while the Democrats, who welcomed deists and agnostics, became the staunch enemy of the moralists.[21] If party ideology affects rhetorical choice, Whig and Republican presidents should use moralistic and religious appeals more frequently than their Democratic counterparts.

Wars

Because wars are often times of sacrifice, presidents might use moral and religious argumentation to establish legitimacy for American intervention in foreign conflicts. Several communication scholars have noted the tendency of presidents to use moral and religious argumentation during times of war. Denise Bostdorff observed that presidents often draw on traditional American values to provide legitimation for foreign policy decisions. According to Rachel Holloway, a presidential expression of faith serves as a rhetorical strategy to inspire trust and conviction. During times of foreign crisis, presidents engage in "prophetic dualism" rhetoric, which includes appeals to religious faith, moral insight, and God's laws. Finally, Campbell and Jamieson conclude that presidents frequently describe foreign conflicts as credible threats to the nation's shared values and beliefs.[22] Based upon these observations, it is reasonable to hypothesize that during times of war, presidents engage in higher levels of religious and moral rhetoric.

Divided Government

For much of the past century, divided government was the norm rather than the exception to the rule. Scholarship has focused on determining if divided government affects legislative behavior. For example, David Mayhew shows that divided control has not made a significant difference in the production of important legislation and the frequency of high-publicity investigations. Less research has focused on how divided government affects executive behavior. The research that does exist examines how divided government alters a president's legislative or policy leadership.[23]

It seems reasonable to postulate that divided government might also affect a president's rhetorical decisions. During times of divided government, presidents might find political appeals less efficacious. In an attempt to "shout down" their partisan opponents in Congress, presidents might resort to moral and religious appeals, which may foster the illusion of transcending political divisiveness and ideological conflict. In this scenario, moral rhetoric might be a sharp tool utilized by the president when competing institutions threaten his political authority.

Electoral Mandates

A president's political strength might affect his willingness to engage in moralizing rhetoric. Presidents with strong electoral victories might believe that they possess a mandate to speak moralistically. Presidents since Andrew Jackson have used their significant electoral margins to claim that they represent the interests and desires of the American people. Mandate claims occur when elections signal strong public support for the president's proposed policy agenda.[24] Presidents with a larger percentage of electoral support may take their mandate claims a step further and interpret their victories as a confirmation of moral authority as well as political legitimacy.

Economic Conditions

The nation's economic prosperity may influence whether presidents employ higher levels of moral and religious argumentation in their rhetoric. Over time, the public has come to expect the president's involvement in economic management, and the president is held responsible for the nation's economic prosperity. Scholars have demonstrated that economic events influence presidential behavior and action. Furthermore, extensive research has shown that economic conditions affect the outcomes of elections.[25] Economic crises encourage resolute action on the part of the chief executive, and justifications for such leadership are likely to be found in the president's rhetoric. Therefore, in times of economic depression, presidents may use moral appeals to rally the nation and boost confidence.

Political Authority

Stephen Skowronek describes recurrent structures of presidential political authority. First, a president is either affiliated or opposed to the ideological commitments of the established institutional regime. Second, the governing capabilities of a regime are either resilient or vulnerable. These two variables produce a typology of four leadership structures: reconstruction, disjunction, articulation, and preemption.[26] The nature of a president's authority may influence his rhetorical choices. In particular, it seems reasonable to hypothesize that reconstructive presidents moralize more than their counterparts, given that they repudiate the basic principles and fundamental values of their predecessors and replace them with their own governing ideologies.

In two regression models, I test the independent influence of the political variables discussed above on levels of moral and religious rhetoric. In table 2, the shaded portion of each independent variable reports the results when the dependent variable was the *percentage* of moral and religious sentences in the address. The non-shaded portion reports the results when the dependent variable was the total *number* of moral and religious sentences in each address. Instead of collapsing all of a president's addresses into one observation, the unit of analysis was the individual Annual Address, with 198 yearly data points to examine.[27] The patrician and modernity variables were included in the model as controls to prevent bias.

The regression results do not substantiate the hypothesis that a president's party affiliation affects levels of moral rhetoric in the Annual Address. There is no evidence to suggest that the strong moralistic ethos of the Whig and Republican parties heightened moral and religious appeals within this genre. Table 2 shows a small, yet statistically significant, difference between Democrats and Whig-Republican presidents, with Democrats registering slightly higher levels of moral and religious rhetoric across time. This finding runs against the grain of anticipated results.

Consequently, I took the analysis one step further to examine the interaction between party affiliation and historical time period. Table 3 separates the effect of party into two distinct time periods (before and after Woodrow Wilson's presidency). Although the Democrats used moral and religious rhetoric more in the premodern era, differences between the parties were small during the twentieth century, with the Republicans engaging in slightly higher numbers of aggregate moral and religious appeals than the Democrats (8.5 versus 6.7).

Aggregate measures of moral and religious rhetoric might not tell the whole story of party affiliation's effect. I return to the Inaugural Addresses dataset and find that differences between Democrats and Republicans do appear when different types of moral argumentation are analyzed. Although party affiliation does not influence overall quantities of moral rhetoric, modern Democratic and Republican presidents adopted divergent (the "visionary" versus the "retrospective") rhetorical practices.

Tables 4 and 5 investigate partisan differences. Table 1 shows that pre-Wilsonian presidents engaged in retrospective appeals much more often than visionary rhetoric in the Inaugurals. Table 4 demonstrates that

TABLE 2. REGRESSION ANALYSIS: ANNUAL ADDRESSES, 1801–2003

Independent Variable	Unstandardized Coefficients		T	Sig.
	B	Std. Error		
War				
1=War-time	.142	.569	.250	.803
0=Non war-time	−.271	1.279	−.212	.833
Party				
1=Republican/Whig	−.679	.408	−1.666	.097
0=Democrat/Dem. Republicans	−1.400	.917	−.112	.129
Modern				
1=Modern (1913–2003)	−.370	.415	−.893	.373
0=Pre-Wilson	−5.191	.933	−5.560	.000
Patrician				
1=Patrician (1801–29)	1.588	.595	2.671	.008
0=Post-Jackson	−8.615	1.338	−6.439	.000
Divided Government				
1=Divided	.079	.418	.190	.850
0=Unified	.369	.940	.393	.695
Mandate	−.031	.013	−2.418	.017
% Electoral College vote	−.029	.029	−.999	.319
Economic Conditions	.010	.034	.304	.761
% Growth rate in real GDP	.046	.077	.590	.556
Orthodox Innovator				
1=Orthodox Innovator	−.646	.471	−1.371	.172
0=All others	.170	1.061	.160	.873
Disjunctive				
1=Disjunctive	−.189	.666	−.283	.777
0=All Others	2.157	1.499	1.439	.152
Reconstructive				
1=Reconstructive	1.149	.583	1.972	.050
0=All Others	1.816	1.311	1.385	.168

N=198, shaded dependent variable = percent of moral/religious sentences per address; non-shaded dependent variable = number of moral/religious sentences

TABLE 3. PARTY AFFILIATION AND THE ANNUAL ADDRESSES

Party	Era	% Moral Sentences (σ)	N	Average number of moral/religious sentences per address (σ)
Democrats/ Democratic Republicans	1801–1912	5.4% (3.1%)	60	10.9 (7.7)
	1913–2003	3.4% (2.4%)	47	6.7 (1.9)
	Total	4.5% (2.9%)	107	9.3 (6.6)
Whigs/ Republicans	1801–1912	3.0% (1.7%)	52	11.1 (6.2)
	1913–2003	3.5% (2.0%)	41	8.5 (4.8)
	Total	3.2% (1.9%)	93	9.9 (5.9)

both Democratic and Whig-Republican presidents of the nineteenth and early twentieth century employed retrospective appeals. Table 5 shows that Democrats continued to employ appeals to traditional morals in the modern era. In fact, their rate of such appeals remained unchanged from one century to the next, remaining constant at approximately four retrospective references per Inaugural Address. The real change occurred with Whig-Republicans, whose retrospective references jumped from 2.1 mentions per speech in the pre-Wilsonian era to 7.5 in the twentieth century. Even more than their nineteenth-century predecessors, modern Republican presidents made it a priority to emphasize traditional, backward-looking moral principles. Furthermore, table 5 shows that modern Republican and Democratic presidents emphasized different types of moral argumentation in their rhetoric. In twentieth-century Inaugural Addresses, Republicans were more likely to employ retrospective appeals than visionary claims while Democrats emphasized the opposite.

This partisan divergence was not overwhelming; Democrats and Republicans utilized both visionary and traditionalist moral arguments. In an Inaugural Address, we can expect a post-Wilsonian Republican president to include three more traditional appeals than a typical Democrat (7.5 versus 4.3). Such a difference is not enormous, but considering that

TABLE 4. PARTY DIFFERENCES: INAUGURAL ADDRESSES, 1829–1909

	Total Visionary Appeals	Total Retrospective Appeals	Number of Inaugural Addresses	Average Visionary Appeal per Address	Average Retrospective Appeal per Address
Democrats	4	33	8	.5	4.1
Whig/ Republicans	7	31	15	.5	2.1
Total	11	64	23	.5	2.8

modern Inaugural Addresses are usually quite brief, this partisan divergence can be noticeable. This empirical evidence suggests that moral and religious arguments contained in modern Inaugural Addresses can be used to promote and reinforce partisan ideological beliefs.[28]

To test effect of war on rhetorical choice, I classified each Annual Address as either "war-time" or "non-war-time" rhetoric. "War-time" rhetoric was initially defined as addresses issued during times of officially declared wars—the Mexican War, Spanish American War, World War I, and World War II. Upon analyzing the data, the influence of war on levels of moral and religious rhetoric was insignificant. I repeated both regression analyses a second time, this time operationalizing the war variable as the five declared wars plus five major undeclared conflicts—the Civil War, the Korean War, Vietnam, Operation Desert Storm, and the War on Terror.[29] The results of the more inclusive "war" variable are reported in table 2 and are statistically insignificant. This finding questions scholarly

TABLE 5. PARTY DIFFERENCES: INAUGURAL ADDRESSES, 1913–2001

Total	Total Visionary Appeals	Number of Traditionalist Appeals	Number of Inaugural Addresses	Average Visionary Appeal per Address	Average Traditionalist Appeal per Address
Democrats	77	51	12	6.4	4.3
Republicans	49	82	11	4.5	7.5
Total	126	133	23	5.5	5.8

characterizations of wartime or crisis rhetoric. Presidents may use moral and religious language in wartime, but Annual Addresses during these episodes are no more moralistic than during times of peace.

To test the divided government hypothesis, I classified each Annual Address as either given during "divided government" or "unified government." Divided government was defined as years in which the president's party was not the majority in either one house of Congress or both houses. As the results demonstrate, divided government is a poor predictor of moral and religious rhetoric. Although coefficients were positive as hypothesized, in both models the standard error overwhelms the estimate. Economic conditions also do not predict fluctuating levels of moral and religious rhetoric in the Annual Addresses. The economic variable is the annual percentage increase or decrease in real gross domestic product.[30] According to table 2, no statistical relationship exists between economic conditions and presidential moralizing.

To test the mandate hypothesis, I calculated the percentage of Electoral College votes obtained by the president in his most recent election. Electoral College vote percentage was used instead of popular vote percentage.[31] In the model using the percentage of moral and religious rhetoric as the dependent variable, the mandate variable is statistically significant, but surprisingly demonstrates that presidents with smaller Electoral College vote shares engage in higher levels of moral and religious rhetoric. This finding indicates that presidents elected with slimmer margins may use their rhetoric to establish moral legitimacy when their political legitimacy is tenuous. In subsequent chapters, several case studies examine why presidents with weak political authority often resort to moral and religious appeals in their rhetoric.

The final series of variables included in the regression models were dummy variables testing the influence of Skowronek's typology on rhetorical practices. Both models demonstrate that reconstructive presidents, who enter office with strong mandates for change, engage in higher levels of moral and religious rhetoric in their Annual Addresses. One model also suggests that disjunctive presidents, who are politically disadvantaged due to their affiliation with a dying regime, also engage in higher levels of moral and religious rhetoric. The possible relevance of the disjunctive variable substantiates the negative relationship between the strength of a president's electoral mandate and his level of moral and religious rhetoric.

To further assess the relationship between Skowronek's typology and rhetorical choices, the percentage of moral and religious sentences contained in the Annual Addresses was compared for all presidents (except George Washington) using an analysis of variance test.[32] The results show that reconstructive and disjunctive presidents moralize at higher rates than orthodox innovators and preemptive presidents, and that the differences are statistically significant. Once again, it is not surprising that reconstructive presidents employ religious and moral arguments at elevated levels. Reconstructive presidents possess the disruptive political authority to condemn the governing ideologies of the previous regime and replace them with their own. In reconstructive scenarios, the distinction between moral and political leadership becomes blurred. Reconstructive presidents dedicate themselves to recapturing the nation's fundamental values and conceiving a new political order. These ambitious endeavors almost require the president to employ moral and religious language in his rhetorical justifications.

A more unexpected result hinted at in the regression models and substantiated by the analysis of variance model is that disjunctive presidents moralize most frequently. Disjunctive presidents find themselves in an "impossible leadership situation" in that they are associated with a regime whose governing commitments and ideologies have been deemed as failures.[33] Unlike reconstructive presidents, disjunctive presidents cannot impose their ideals and principles upon newly created political institutions. It seems that moralizing would be a stretch for disjunctive presidents. However, it is possible that presidents in divergent leadership situations have different motivations for moralizing. Whereas reconstructive presidents may moralize because their political authority encourages such behavior, disjunctive presidents might moralize in an attempt to boost their credibility. Disjunctive presidents are left with few strategic options. Saddled with a defunct governing ideology, they must try to paint themselves out of a corner and justify their leadership. Because their political authority is damaged, table 6 indicates that disjunctive presidents fall back upon their moral authority, which they attempt to cultivate through their rhetoric.

LIMITATIONS

The content analysis brings to light a general weakness of using quantitative methods to study presidential rhetoric. Content analysis reveals the frequency of presidential moralizing and even the important ways in which this behavior has changed over time. Quantitative methods also

TABLE 6. POLITICAL AUTHORITY AND MORAL RHETORIC

Reconstruction (N=38)	Disjunction (N=24)
Jefferson, Jackson, Lincoln, Franklin Roosevelt, Reagan	John Adams, John Quincy Adams, Pierce, Buchanan, Hoover, Carter
Mean=5.09% (2.85%)	Mean=5.53% (3.75%)
Articulation (N=90)	Preemption (N=52)
Madison, Monroe, Van Buren, Polk, Grant, Hayes, Garfield, Arthur, Harrison, McKinley, Theodore Roosevelt, Taft, Harding, Coolidge, Truman, Kennedy, Lyndon Johnson, George H W Bush, George W Bush	Tyler, Taylor, Fillmore, Andrew Johnson, Cleveland, Wilson, Eisenhower, Nixon, Ford, Clinton
Mean=3.50% (2.73%)	Mean=3.61% (2.35%)

(ANOVA: SS=131.00, df=3, Mean Sqr=43.667, F=5.569, p<.01)

can show which variables influence a president's rhetorical choices. But it is necessary to turn to a qualitative, historical methodology to figure out how a president's convictions and character interact with the political circumstances he faces. In each of the nine case studies included in chapters 3 through 5, attention is paid to the president's moral and religious ethos and his views about moral leadership.

A cursory examination of the coding results indicates that moral and religious beliefs do not reliably predict a president's rhetorical choices. In fact, the empirical evidence implies that presidents with secular dispositions sometimes engage in moral and religious argumentation while presidents with professed moral and religious convictions often exercise moral restraint. For example, Andrew Jackson and James Buchanan engaged in moral and religious argumentation at higher levels than anticipated. Although Andrew Jackson became more religious as he grew older, he believed in a strict separation between church and state. One of James Buchanan's governing beliefs was that political institutions could not settle moral disputes, yet he chose to utilize moral and religious rhetoric at a surprisingly high rate.

On the other hand, if a president's moral and religious persona determines his rhetorical practices, we would anticipate high levels of moral and religious argumentation from presidents such as Abraham Lincoln and Dwight Eisenhower. However, the data do not support this supposition. In early speeches, Lincoln used moral and religious appeals to make his arguments, but his presidential Annual Addresses avoided such language. Although not a member of any particular religious sect until he joined the Presbyterian Church as president, in 1948 Eisenhower announced publicly, "I am the most intensely religious man I know."[34] Given this pronouncement, we would expect Eisenhower's rhetoric to reach the heights of George W. Bush, Carter, and Reagan, but the content analysis results fail to corroborate this intuition.

Some presidents do fulfill our expectations of heightened moral and religious rhetoric. The moralistic rhetoric of George W. Bush, Ronald Reagan, Woodrow Wilson, Jimmy Carter, Theodore Roosevelt, John Adams, and George Washington matched their personas. Given that there are several exceptions to this hypothesis, we must conclude tentatively that personal moral and religious beliefs do not reliably predict rhetorical choices. A critical evaluation of this hypothesis will continue in the historical case studies, in which the professed moral and religious personas of several presidents will be analyzed more closely in connection with their rhetorical practices.

CONCLUSION

The topic of presidential moral leadership is interesting in itself, but political scientists strive to determine how specific behaviors and decisions affect outcomes. The remainder of the book will use case studies to explore the complex relationship between a president's moral leadership and his political constraints. The way in which presidents approach this relationship affects their ability to use rhetoric as an effective tool to supplant their political legitimacy. This approach also enables a more nuanced evaluation of how rhetorical choices are either constrained or strengthened by a president's authority and the political circumstances that surround him.

The next three chapters will examine how and why nine presidents, situated in various eras of American history, decided to engage or refrain from rhetorical moralizing. The sketches are attempts to explore presidential decision-making processes with regards to moral leadership and rhetoric and were constructed with the intent to illuminate the strategies and choices behind rhetorical leadership and its political consequences. With this goal in mind, the subsequent case studies demonstrate that certain political circumstances either encourage or discourage presidents from engaging in moral argumentation. In other words, depending on a given political context, it makes strategic sense that a president will engage in or refrain from moralistic rhetoric.

I consider a rhetorical choice as strategic if a purposeful desire to craft particular rhetorical arguments to the political circumstances of the situation motivated the decision. The presidency is embedded in a separated powers constitutional structure riddled with conflict and competition. Constantly trying to assert a sphere of independent leadership, a president's strategic rhetoric can strengthen his encumbered constitutional position. Sometimes framing arguments in moralistic language helps; sometimes moral restraint is advisable. The contribution of these nine rhetorical sketches is to describe the circumstances that facilitate moral argumentation and moral restraint and to highlight how successful assertions of independence are influenced by whether or not presidents adapt their rhetoric to match circumstantial demands. The analyses explore rhetoric's power to augment or diminish a president's constitutional position and authority. Political leaders constantly make moral choices. However, the precise question of this investigation is *when* should presidents use rhetoric to emphasize the moral dimensions of their decisions and *when* should presidents refrain from moral justifications?

The case studies are meant to be indicative but not exhaustive; other presidents in American history may be arranged in these categories. For example, Andrew Jackson and John Tyler engaged in "strategic moralizing," William Howard Taft and James Monroe in "rhetorical restraint," and John Adams and Ronald Reagan in "moral reinforcement." The presidents chosen for chapters 4 and 5 were selected because of their historical proximity to one another. Jefferson versus Madison, Buchanan versus Lincoln, and Kennedy versus Johnson show how political contexts can change from one president to the next and demand different rhetorical practices. Therefore, the rhetorical sketches in chapters 4 and 5 can be read sequentially or as pairs. Regardless of the order in which they are read, the case studies emphasize the politically contingent nature of presidential rhetoric and the tenuous relationship between moral leadership and executive authority.

CHAPTER 3

THE POLITICS OF REINFORCING

MORAL RHETORIC

A political cartoon from the 1990s illustrates how presidential leadership has changed in the past two centuries by comparing Bill Clinton to George Washington. In the depiction, Washington uttered famously, "I cannot tell a lie." In response to the first president, Clinton's contorted visage boomed, "Amateur." The cartoon is humorous but points to a larger question about public expectations of presidential moral leadership. Upon occasion, Americans select presidents who emphasize their capacity for moral leadership as a powerful political advantage. Once in office, these presidents often resort to moral claims in their speech regardless of mitigating factors. Since "moralists" revert to predictable justifications for their actions, they provide a good source of information about when moral rhetoric enhances political authority and when it does not.

This chapter investigates three presidents who used their strong moral dispositions as a primary source of political authority. They are classified as "reinforcing moral leaders" because their moral beliefs buttressed their rhetoric. While we expect George Washington, Theodore Roosevelt, and Jimmy Carter to engage in heightened levels of moral speech, this discussion explores the different political contexts in which they moralized and compares the varying levels of success their rhetoric achieved. Washington successfully capitalized on the authority of moral leadership, establishing the president's role as the nation's moral spokesman. Roosevelt's moralizing was a mixed bag that both helped and encumbered his leadership. As a president with weak political support, Carter's moral stances proved the most problematic and damaging.

George Washington: The Patriot King Realized in Speech

Political scientists and historians characterize Washington's presidential and military leadership as a fulfillment of Bolingbroke's patriot king ideal.[1] Many scholarly works celebrate Washington's personal character, public virtue, disinterestedness, moderation, and religious piety. Although historical and rhetorical analyses of Washington's Farewell Address are plentiful, his other presidential orations have received less scholarly attention.[2] Prior to the Farewell Address, Washington often used his public addresses to discuss the importance of moral virtue and religion in political life.

Presidential scholars have recognized Washington's precedent-setting activities. Washington created the cabinet, instituted a two-term limit, established the "advise and consent" procedure with the Senate regarding treaties, and fortified the constitutional authority of the national government vis-à-vis state governments. Less noted amongst scholars is Washington's establishment of the president as the nation's moral spokesman.[3] Washington embraced the symbolic possibilities of the office and used his distinguished reputation to increase his own political authority and, even more broadly, the power of the presidency as an institution.

This section investigates Washington's precedent-setting rhetorical leadership. In this pursuit, three pieces of Washington's presidential rhetoric are analyzed: the First Inaugural Address, his rhetoric concerning the Whiskey Rebellion, and the Farewell Address. In these presidential addresses, Washington emphasized the importance of strong moral and religious beliefs in a republican democracy. Washington utilized such frequent appeals not only to enlighten citizen listeners but also to forestall the growth of factions and political parties. His moralistic rhetoric served a political as well as a pedagogical purpose. Using his eminent reputation as leverage, Washington urged his compatriots to rise above ideological divisiveness and reject the formation of political parties. Historical descriptions of Washington's presidency typically mark the controversial Neutrality Proclamation as the origin of his crusade against factional strife, but a careful reading of the First Inaugural Address clearly demonstrates that the battle against faction began much earlier. Moral argumentation was particularly appropriate for Washington's rhetoric since eighteenth-century political culture viewed faction as dangerous and opposed to republican virtue.[4]

Washington's abhorrence of factional divisions and political parties is well documented.[5] As a general during the Revolutionary War, Washington grew dubious of localism and state government, which he believed threatened national unity. During the Articles of Confederation era, Washington became critical of Virginia's highly personalized and divisive politics that often frustrated the administration of government. In Washington's view, faction threatened the existence of national harmony. As a product of classical republicanism rather than liberal pluralism, Washington stood firmly against the proliferation of sectional conflict and diverse interests.

It is no surprise that Washington used his presidential rhetoric to denounce the growth of political parties. The more interesting observation is *how* he chose to frame his rhetorical arguments concerning faction. Washington showcased his own reputation as a patriot king to demonstrate the political benefits of non-partisanship. By arguing that personal morality serves as the soundest foundation of representative democracy, Washington hoped to dampen self-interested and localized political beliefs in favor of his more holistic, republican theory of government.

The First Inaugural Address

In writing his first presidential address, Washington turned to the rhetorical model he employed when he accepted the generalship of the Continental Army in 1775. The First Inaugural exemplified patrician leadership by highlighting Washington's personal character and virtue, emphasizing his gratitude and humility.[6] In the speech, Washington presented his own controlled ambition as an imitable example. In the first paragraph of the speech, Washington discussed his reluctant accession to the presidency. Unlike the first draft of the address, Washington did not directly attack his enemies. Instead, Washington offered his own difficult decision as an example of republican disinterestedness, virtue, and duty: "On the one hand, I was summoned by my country, whose voice I can never hear but with veneration and love. . . . On the other hand, the magnitude and difficulty of the trust to which the voice of my country called me . . . could not but overwhelm one with despondence. . . . In this conflict of emotions, all I dare aver, is, that it has been my faithful study to collect my duty from a just appreciation of every circumstance by which it might be affected."[7] Washington depicted the presidency as a stewardship above self-interested concerns and, in the process, set a high bar for the presidency. While even Washington could not avoid political intrigue in his own administration, his Inaugural Address created a rhetorical expectation that presidents embody the qualities of a patrician statesman who stands above the fray.

Washington actually established a broad institutional precedent in the speech: the importance of the president's "head of state" role. On the surface, the First Inaugural did not concern itself with the pressing political issues facing the United States in 1789. Washington's rhetoric suggested that the president's constitutional authority gave him a broader vantage point that allowed him to discuss the moral health of the nation. Washington's noted reputation as a moral leader allowed him to speak in such a manner. Over two hundred years later, we take the president's role as the nation's moral spokesman as given, but without Washington's rhetorical example, such a role might not have developed at all.

However, Washington's emphasis on developing a unified moral vision did have an underlying political purpose. As Washington took the oath of office, Rhode Island and North Carolina had not adopted the Constitution, and Anti-Federalists still opposed the new centralized government of the United States. Washington's reliance upon moral and religious rhetoric was a strategic reaction to the political doubt that still permeated the national mindset. Stephen Lucas commented, "Cloaking the government with the mantle of divine consecration was one way to allay those fears and to create trust in the new government."[8]

The most notable feature of the First Inaugural was its religious tone. At the end of his oath, Washington added the phrase, "I swear, so help me God," which was typically included in English coronation services.[9] In previous circulars addressed either to the states or the Continental Army, Washington always recognized the power of "Divine Providence" or the "blessed Religion," but one-third of the sentences in his Inaugural Address contained religious references. Washington explicitly emphasized that his first action as president involved religious devotion: "Such being the impressions under which I have, in obedience to the public summons, repaired to the present station, it would be peculiarly improper to omit, in this first official act, my fervent supplications to that Almighty Being who rules over the universe; who presides in the councils of nations; and whose providential aid can supply every human defect. . . ." James Flexner argued that Washington included so many religious appeals because he felt the need for more celestial guidance as president.[10]

While Flexner's biographical conclusion might be correct, Washington's use of religious imagery also articulated his overarching argument concerning the problems of political factions. The first segment of the speech presented Washington's moral qualifications for the office, and the remainder of the address attempted to remind citizens why moral virtues are important in a democratic republic. According to Washington, democracy depended upon private morality, which in turn can only be developed through religious piety and devotion. A rhetorical appeal to morality served as the consensual alternative to the dividing force of faction. The connection between Washington's use of religious rhetoric and his condemnation of political faction rings true in the following concluding excerpt from his Inaugural Address: "I shall take my present leave; but not without resorting once more to the benign Parent of the human race, in humble supplication, that, since he has been pleased to favor the American People with opportunities for deliberating in perfect tranquility, and dispositions for deciding with unparalleled unanimity on a form of government for the security of their union, and the advancement of their happiness, so his divine blessing may be equally conspicuous in the enlarged views, the temperate consultations, and the wise measures, on which the success of this Government must depend."[11] To conquer the debilitating threat of faction, citizens must find themselves enlightened with "enlarged views" that are made possible by a "divine blessing." A devotion to moral and religious ideals produces the "temperate consultations" required in a democracy.

Washington tried to drive home one encapsulating political point in his First Inaugural: elected representatives should base their decisions on immutable standards of morality and religion rather than self-interest. In this sense, Washington spoke from a position of power and circumstance, using moral argumentation to substantiate his independent position and transcend political divisiveness. In the following excerpt, Washington explicitly highlighted his reliance on moral standards as a solution to the immediate threat of divisive factions: "I behold the surest pledges that, as on one side no local prejudices or attachments—no separate views, nor party animosities, will misdirect the comprehensive and equal eye which ought to watch over this great assemblage of communities and interests; so on another, that the foundations of our national policy will be laid in the pure and immutable principles of private morality. . . ."[12] In this passage, it becomes evident that Washington's distaste for factions did not stem from a personal hatred of political parties. Rather, Washington's concern was much more subtle. As the first president of a new democratic republic, Washington sought to establish binding ties between the citizenry and the nascent government. Through his rhetoric, Washington purposefully chose to ground the federal government in the firm principles of morality and religious piety. In this light, appeals to moral and religious standards enhanced the political legitimacy of the newly formed national institutions.

With no constitutional precedent to rely upon, Washington rested his claims on moral grounds. Considering that Washington's eminent and virtuous reputation probably was the most durable and reliable aspect of the new government, his moral and religious tone in the First Inaugural constituted a sound political strategy that also allowed him to discredit the formation of political parties and alienate Anti-Federalist criticisms of the new government. Furthermore, whether unintentional or purposeful, Washington also institutionally established the president's role as the nation's moral spokesman. In his very first executive action, Washington created a legitimate rhetorical precedent that enhanced the scope of presidential authority. From 1789 thereafter, the president not only executed the political duties explicitly outlined in the Constitution but also functioned periodically as the nation's moral and spiritual leader.

The Rhetoric of the Whiskey Rebellion

Washington's presidential rhetoric concerning the Whiskey Rebellion used moral and religious language to denounce the Pennsylvania insurgents and, more broadly, the dangerous spirit of faction that permeated the country. The political circumstances of 1794 recommended moral argumentation as an appropriate rhetorical response. Faced with a domestic insurrection, Washington needed to defend the use of force to quell the disturbance. Support for military intervention was divided along ideological lines: the Jeffersonians criticized military intervention while the Federalists endorsed it. Washington relied heavily upon favorable public opinion to justify his executive decision to call up the militia. In particular, his rhetorical explanations served as a means in which to drum up wider support for his actions.[13] Furthermore, a sizable component of Washington's political authority rested on his eminent reputation and demonstrated moral leadership. As Washington sought to assert his leadership, the political situation suggested that heightened levels of moral and religious rhetoric would be strategically beneficial while no circumstances cautioning moral restraint existed.

Persuaded by Alexander Hamilton, the federal government began levying a tax on whiskey in 1791 in an effort to decrease the nation's war debt. Farmers in western Pennsylvania, who distilled their grain crop into whiskey for easier transportation, found themselves unable to evade this new excise. Despite Congress's ameliorating attempt to remove the strictest provisions of the tax, tension mounted steadily in the region. In the summer of 1794, four counties grew openly hostile towards the federal government and its whiskey tax.

The region's two Democratic Societies, particularly the Society of Mingo Creek, were rumored as the source of the escalated discontent. In the winter of 1794, Democratic Societies began to appear across the United States. Inspired by the democratic fervor in France, these "societies" discussed politics, spread political information, and celebrated patriotism. The members of these political clubs were self-professed Republican followers of Jefferson and Madison, although the leaders of the societies were not the most prominent Republicans of the area. Whether or not Mingo Creek instigated the insurrection is a matter of historical interpretation, but Alexander Hamilton's lengthy analysis of the trouble in western Pennsylvania, written in a letter to President Washington, certainly emphasized the baneful role of the region's Democratic Societies.[14]

The Whiskey Rebellion culminated in a raid on exciseman John Neville's mansion in which two men were killed. The following weeks were filled with "impassioned meetings, radical oratory, and threats to take Pittsburgh by force and oust all federal authority." Undoubtedly influenced by Hamilton, Washington placed much of the blame on the Mingo Creek society. He wrote to Henry Lee on August 26, 1794, that the Democratic Societies constituted "the most diabolical attempt to destroy the best fabric of human government and happiness that has ever been presented for the acceptance of mankind."[15] From the tone of his letter, we can anticipate that Washington's rhetoric about the rebellion not only addressed the immediate insurrection at hand but also the broader political issue of faction's dangers.

In his public condemnations of the Whiskey Rebellion, Washington used moral and religious appeals to justify his actions. Prior to the federal government's actual use of military force, Washington employed moral and religious language to rouse law-abiding members of the Pennsylvania state militia to march against their fellow citizens. Washington needed to convince Pennsylvanians to take up arms against Pennsylvanians. To add fuel to the fire, Pennsylvania's Governor Mifflin was a strident Jeffersonian who publicly professed his dislike of Washington.[16] The likelihood for cooperation and unified action appeared dim. To sway public opinion, Washington appealed to the moral sense of Pennsylvanians in his September 27, 1794, proclamation entitled "Concerning the Western Insurrection." In an attempt to induce militia members to march, Washington equated the domestic insurrection to a religious transgression: "And I do moreover exhort all individuals . . . to call to mind, that as the people of the United States have been permitted under the Divine favor, in perfect freedom, after solemn deliberation, in an enlightened age, to elect their own Government, so will their gratitude for this inestimable blessing be best distinguished by firm exertion to maintain the Constitution and the laws."[17] In this passage, Washington used a religiously based argument to chastise those citizens who failed to fulfill the dictates of republican virtue. The people of the United States, reasoned Washington, enjoyed "perfect freedom" only because God permitted it. It is the duty of citizens to follow the laws in a democratic republic, especially, Washington stressed, if such a government existed under "Divine favor."

Earlier in the proclamation, Washington declared that force "is already in motion to the scene of disaffection." As president, he could declare the use of force "in obedience to that high and irresistible duty consigned to me by the constitution" and also because of his "reliance on that gracious Providence, which so signally displays its goodness towards this country."[18] Besides invoking his constitutional duty to execute the laws, Washington verbalized his reliance on a religious deity. The Constitution gave Washington the legal power to quell the disturbance while "Providence" provided him with the resolve to preserve the nation's "goodness."

Before troops even arrived in Pittsburgh, the insurrection had diminished significantly. Several men were arrested for their leadership roles in the rebellion and stood trial in Philadelphia. All were acquitted except two, whom Washington eventually pardoned.[19] Although the crisis was over quickly, Washington seized upon a rhetorical opportunity to articulate publicly the moral lessons to be learned from the incident. In his Sixth Annual Address given on November 19, 1794, Washington used the insurrection in western Pennsylvania to emphasize the importance of virtuous moderation in a democracy and the dangers of faction. The moral disappointment in his fellow countrymen was apparent in Washington's opening statement: "When we call to mind the gracious indulgence of Heaven by which the American people became a nation; when we survey the general prosperity of our country . . . with the deepest regret do I announce to you that during your recess some of the citizens of the United States have been found capable of an insurrection."[20] Much like his earlier proclamation, Washington used a religious appeal to condemn the insurrection. Despite the "gracious indulgence of Heaven" that enabled democracy to flourish in the United States, some citizens still decided to participate in the uprising.

The body of the speech included a history of the rebellion and justifications for the administration's use of military force. In his detailed description of events, Washington mentioned "certain self-created societies" that assumed a "tone of condemnation" that threatened the effect of "moderation on the discontented."[21] As much as possible, Washington insinuated in the speech that the Democratic Societies intensified the passions of citizens, pushing them into an active insurrection. According to Washington's arguments, factions frustrated the exercise of controlled moderation and republican virtue.

At the conclusion of the address, Washington severely condemned the insurgents, ending with a biting conclusion of moral and religious censure: "Let us unite, therefore, in imploring the Supreme Ruler of nations to spread his holy protection over these United States; to turn the machinations of the wicked to the confirming of our Constitution; to enable us at all times to root out internal sedition and put invasion to flight."[22] The embodiment of moral certitude above the fray, Washington as the patriot king never stood so eminently as president. To sustain a moral community in which the public good transcended the private, Washington labeled the insurgents of western Pennsylvania as "wicked." As portrayed in Washington's rhetoric, the Whiskey Rebellion posed a serious challenge to democratic governance guided by the "pure and immutable principles of private morality" emphasized in his First Inaugural Address. The "internal sedition" of faction threatened to undermine the moderation needed in a large democratic republic to identify the common good. Faction degraded political motives from virtuous intentions to narrow self-interest. Notice the distinct difference between Washington's rhetoric and his actions. While Washington bestowed considerable forgiveness and mercy on the Pennsylvanian "rebels," he was not lenient in his speech. Washington wanted to hold these insurgents up as a rhetorical example and equate their wrongdoing with political factions. The "machinations of the wicked" served as a moral example for the public at large.

Washington's Whiskey Rebellion rhetoric strongly argued against the continued prevalence of the Democratic Societies. Washington's moral eminence failed to convince some political insiders that a serious transgression had been committed; an unmoved Thomas Jefferson stated, "An insurrection was announced and proclaimed and armed against, but could never be found." James Madison also expressed his dislike of Washington's rhetoric surrounding the Whiskey Rebellion, particularly the Sixth Annual Address. However, Washington's authority extended beyond the Philadelphia insider community. While he failed to make Jefferson a believer, his words found their power within a broader public venue through the newspaper coverage of his speeches. By 1795, most Democratic Societies disbanded in the United States. Washington's strong rhetoric was one of several political factors which contributed to their demise.[23]

Using the tools of popular leadership, Washington employed powerful moral and religious language to achieve his political goal of destroying factions and passionate self-interest. Of course, in the long run, Washington's moral posturing was not enough to prevent the formation of political parties in the United States. However, the response to the Whiskey Rebellion was a short-term rhetorical success. Through his intense and passionate public messages, Washington encouraged the downfall of the Democratic Societies he detested.

The Farewell Address

In writing his Farewell Address, Washington received substantial help from Alexander Hamilton. Before Hamilton, James Madison wrote an earlier version of the address for Washington. Despite the help Washington received, the ideas contained in the address belonged to Washington. Washington knew which important political and moral beliefs he wanted to emphasize while Hamilton possessed the ability to translate these complex principles into words. With regards to the composition of the Farewell Address, Samuel Bemis described Washington as the "trunk of the tree" and Hamilton as the "shimmering foliage."[24]

Washington hoped that all citizens of the United States would read his address and pay heed to his pedagogical efforts. In a letter to Hamilton, Washington instructed him to compose the Farewell Address in language that was "plain and intelligible" so that the yeomanry could easily understand his arguments. On September 19, 1796, the Farewell Address appeared in the *American Daily Advertiser,* a Philadelphia newspaper. Shortly after the first printing, hundreds of other newspapers published the address across the country. Washington intended his observations to be enduring rather than ephemeral, characterizing them as "all important to the permanency of your felicity as a People."[25] The Farewell Address solidified the president's role as the nation's moral spokesman. In the address, Washington firmly established the president's unique ability to stand above the fray and make powerful moral judgments about politics and policy. This pedagogical function supports the contention that moral rhetoric can bolster the president's constitutional powers. Speaking with one voice, no other institutional actor can issue moral pronouncements or teachings that carry the same degree of legitimacy as the president. In his Farewell Address, Washington seized upon this rhetorical opportunity.

Well known for its commentary on American foreign policy, the Farewell Address remains Washington's most lasting rhetorical contribution. It has achieved a heralded spot in American political culture, demonstrated by the fact that every year, one senator is chosen to read the Farewell Address aloud on Washington's birthday. Even though a revived intellectual interest in Washington's life and presidency has occurred in recent years, the scholarly discourse about the Farewell Address largely concerns itself with Washington's opinions regarding American isolationism, thus narrowly focusing on the foreign policy themes of the message. Washington's reasoned defense of foreign neutrality certainly comprised a significant part of the Farewell Address, but his discussion of virtue, morality, and religion was equally prominent. Despite Campbell and Jamieson's observation that Farewell Addresses rely upon moral suasion and the fulfillment of the president's priestly function, Washington's arguments about the importance of morality and religion are often overlooked in textual analyses of the speech.[26] The failure to consider Washington's emphasis on virtue is especially problematic because many of the policy arguments advanced in the address relied upon his observations regarding morality and organized religion. Washington framed his discussion of political parties and foreign affairs, two of the main subjects of the address, as battles between self-interest and republican virtue.

Washington organized the Farewell Address with the goal of encouraging citizens to deliberate about the complex ideas he offered. To ensure that readers would engage his ideas in a meaningful manner,

Washington made two important rhetorical decisions. First, he coupled the announcement of his retirement with his exposition of governing ideals and principles. Washington knew that his retirement from public life would generate a considerable buzz and wanted to capitalize on this interest to entice citizens to also read his more pedantic thoughts. Second, Washington's sentences in the Farewell Address were "lengthy and complex."[27] Although the message was written so that everyone could understand his meaning, his ornate rhetoric was purposeful. It forced all interested citizens to read the sentences more than once, encouraging reflection and deliberation about the ideas he advocated.

In the Farewell Address, Washington repeatedly emphasized the importance of unity in government. The greatest danger the United States faced was the dissolution of a unified purpose. Geographic differences, sectional strife precipitated by faction, and foreign entanglements represented possible threats to the "Unity of Government." If allowed to intensify, Washington warned, self-interest could "enfeeble the sacred ties which now link together the various parts" of American political society.[28]

A steadfast devotion to morality and religion served as self-interest's antidote. Immediately after discussing the dangers of faction, Washington emphasized the importance of religion and morality. This juxtaposition was not accidental. The unifying aspects of virtue and morality offered an alternative to the divisiveness of political faction. According to Washington, faction "agitates the Community with ill founded jealousies and false alarms, kindles the animosity of one part against another, foments occasionally riot and insurrection." To avoid such entanglements, citizens must turn from self-interested concerns to a morally unified perspective: "Of all the dispositions and habits which lead to political prosperity, Religion and morality are indispensable supports. In vain would that man claim the tribute of Patriotism, who should labour to subvert these great Pillars of human happiness, these firmest props of the duties of Men and citizens. The mere Politician, equally with the pious man ought to respect and to cherish them." In this passage, Washington described a symbiotic relationship between private morality and republican government. On one hand, a moderate government encourages the cultivation of virtue in the citizenry. On the other, individual morals pave the way for sound government. Because the lines of causality run in both directions, a strong interdependence exists between government and morality. If allowed to grow, faction threatened to undermine the interdependence and self-sufficiency perpetuated by a strong national character. The effects of faction posed the most serious threat to the American republic. The cornerstone of the Farewell Address is its attempt to inform citizens about the common moral and religious political principles that strengthened the conception of "union" in the young United States.[29] By providing it with a shared moral element, Washington's parting words sharpened the unique definition of the American political community.

Washington's commentary on foreign policy also relied upon the continued existence of strong morals. Washington began his discussion of foreign affairs by emphasizing the role of moral sentiments in policy decisions: "Observe good faith and justice towds. all Nations. Cultivate peace and harmony with all. Religion and morality enjoin this conduct: and can it be that good policy does not equally enjoin it? Can it be, that Providence has not connected the permanent felicity of a Nation with its virtue?"[30] As this excerpt demonstrates, the arguments used in the section on political factions resembled his foreign affairs commentary. With regards to both political factions and foreign policy decisions, the passions must be subordinated (or "excluded") to the cooler response of moderation and virtue. The connection between a nation's happiness and well-being depends upon the proper cultivation of its morals. The United States must steer clear of foreign alliances because such relationships potentially undermine the dictates of morality and religion, thus damaging the maintenance of the national character Washington so valued.

In a constitutional system in which co-equal branches share power, politicians often search for independent sources of leadership to enhance their authority and influence. The two policies Washington staunchly advocated—the demise of political parties and an avoidance of foreign alliances—were not adopted as permanent governing principles. Rather, the value of Washington's moral rhetoric was its precedent-setting ability to enhance the independent authority of the office. His pedagogical use of moral and religious rhetoric strengthened the formal, constitutional powers of the presidency. Washington's own laudable reputation validated his rhetoric, lending credibility to the president's moral spokesman role. Washington cultivated this rhetorical role to situate the executive office above the fray, thus giving subsequent presidents the possible authority to make moral judgments that would influence policy.

THEODORE ROOSEVELT: MORAL REFORM
AND THE BULLY PULPIT

Theodore Roosevelt brought to the presidency strong opinions on the importance of a vigorous national character, the need for honest and efficient administration, and the reincarnation of morally principled business practices. Prior to his presidency, TR built his political career on a crusade to square government service and the formation of public policy with the higher dictates of ethical principles and morality. For example, when Roosevelt accepted the Republican nomination to run for mayor of New York City in 1886, he campaigned against Tammany Hall with a call to institute moral reform in urban government. Roosevelt lost but established his reputation as a moral crusader through his efforts.[31]

Roosevelt argued that the development of intellectual abilities was less important than the development of a strong moral character. According to Roosevelt, American progress would perpetuate itself only if citizens continued to lead morally upright and courageous lives. Roosevelt's political ideology contained a Darwinian component that combined a "survival of the fittest" mentality with a strong emphasis on moral character. He advertised his morally charged views in a speech entitled "The Strenuous Life" given before Chicago's Hamilton Club on April 10, 1899. Far from hiding his moral beliefs, Roosevelt explicitly described the speech as an act of "preaching" that recommended his characterization of the "strenuous" life:

> I preach to you, then, my countrymen, that our country calls not
> for the life of ease but for the life of strenuous endeavor. . . .
> Let us therefore boldly face the life of strife, resolute to do our
> duty well and manfully; resolute to uphold righteousness by
> deed and by word; resolute to be both honest and brave, to serve
> high ideals, yet to use practical methods. Above all, let us shrink
> from no strife, moral or physical, within or without the nation,
> provided we are certain that the strife is justified, for it is only
> through strife, through hard and dangerous endeavor, that we
> shall ultimately win the goal of true national greatness.[32]

Roosevelt's depiction of a strong virtuous character never wavered during his public career. Material and moral prosperity were inextricably intertwined for Roosevelt, with each condition influencing the other symbiotically. For TR, political power was a means towards achieving order and morality in a democracy.[33]

Roosevelt's moral posturing encompassed an important part of his political persona and governing ideology. This examination analyzes Roosevelt's rhetoric concerning railroad regulation and the Hepburn Act and explores the costs and benefits of Roosevelt's moralizing. Anxious to convince the nation of the justice of railroad regulation, Roosevelt engaged in an extended public campaign in 1905. Focusing on his railroad legislation rhetoric enables a consideration of Roosevelt's famous "swings around the circle" speeches, as well as his more formal Annual Addresses. It also highlights the negative political effects felt by presidents when they engage in moralistic rhetoric haphazardly. While TR's rhetoric achieved its immediate political purpose, his strong statements and promises diminished his authority when conservative Republicans forced him to accept a compromise version of the Hepburn Act in 1906.

The Political Strategy of TR's 1905 Rhetoric
As president, Roosevelt used moral and religious appeals to sell many of his political programs. Most notably, TR engaged in moral argumentation when speaking about the build-up of the navy, conservation policies, Panama Canal construction, and the regulation of corporations.[34] I concentrate on Roosevelt's use of moral argumentation to justify his pro-regulatory stance towards big business, focusing on the passage of the Hepburn Act. Railroad regulation required Roosevelt to engage in intricate political strategizing, which involved choosing appropriate and effective rhetoric. Other scholars such as Leroy Dorsey, John Morton Blum, and Robert Friedenberg have noted that Roosevelt's rhetoric concerning railroad regulation adopted a strongly moralistic tone but have not analyzed how the political circumstances of 1905 and 1906 presented difficulties to this rhetorical approach.[35]

From 1901 until the 1904 election, Teddy Roosevelt was an "accidental" president who had been branded as a "wild man" by McKinley's Old Guard disciples. During this time period, TR battled Republican boss Sen. Mark Hanna for control of the party. Aware of the divisions within the party on the tariff and corporate regulation, Roosevelt kept the two issues distinct. In particular, Roosevelt evaded the tariff as much as possible and accommodated the protectionists within the GOP, reaffirming the existing tariff policy in the 1904 Republican Party platform.[36]

After his landslide victory in the 1904 election, Roosevelt turned immediately towards formulating a legislative program that stressed railroad regulation. Many railroads charged large industrial companies such as Standard Oil a discounted rate. Forced to pay higher costs for shipping, smaller companies suffered. Roosevelt considered correcting this inequality a moral duty, and his legislative proposal gave the Interstate Commerce Commission (ICC) the power to set maximum railway shipping rates. To insure that his party would stand behind his regulatory legislation, Roosevelt offered a deal to conservative Republicans. In return for railway regulation, the president would sideline his efforts to amend the tariff. For Roosevelt, the tariff was a means to achieving what he really wanted: administrative control of railway rates through the ICC.[37]

Through his bargain, Roosevelt sought to unite the Republican Party behind a policy that had caused deep divisions within it. The progressive wing of the party wanted both railway regulation and a revision of the tariff while conservative standpatters supported a continuation of *laissez-faire* nineteenth-century economic policy.[38] A considerable contingent of the Republican Party opposed TR's railroad legislation. Yet, Roosevelt strategized that the bargain alleviated these partisan divisions, giving the progressives railroad regulation while the conservatives retained the protective tariff.

Roosevelt went on a public speaking tour throughout 1905 to sell his party's railroad policy to the American people. During the spring of 1905, the railroad industry conducted an extensive propaganda campaign to warn the public about the potential negative consequences of railroad regulation. The press eagerly reported the claims of the railroads, and it appeared that Roosevelt's opponents were making considerable headway with public opinion.[39] Roosevelt's speaking tour was designed to combat the publicity campaign waged by the railroads and to advertise the Republican Party's policy on railroad regulation.

Two political conditions recommended moral argumentation on the tour. First, Roosevelt used moral argumentation as a rhetorical tool to explain complicated economic policy. As the Senate debated the minute intricacies of railway legislation in the spring of 1905, eventually producing an impenetrable five-thousand-page document that even government agencies did not want to publish, the president took his arguments to the people by explaining why administrative control of shipping rates was morally necessary. Instead of becoming mired in economic details,

Roosevelt characterized his support for regulatory policy in moral terms, painting regulation as a safeguard against those few trusts that refused to act ethically without legal restraint.

Second, TR engaged in moral argumentation as a fulfillment of electoral expectations. In the election of 1904, Roosevelt based his candidacy on his personal qualities, such as his strong character and his belief in honest government. In a letter to William Allen White in 1904, Roosevelt characterized his supporters as Americans who "sympathize with my appeal for common sense, courage, and common honesty." TR's electoral landslide over Alton Brooks Parker represented a mandate only insofar as voters clearly wanted another four years of Theodore Roosevelt's style of leadership. The 1904 campaign amounted to a referendum on Roosevelt's character and its impact on his aggressive view of the executive. Although he handled intraparty disputes skillfully, Roosevelt's greatest political asset in 1904 was his masterful public exploitation of his forceful personality. The electorate clearly expected and anticipated moral leadership from Roosevelt, who believed deeply in the importance of strong individual and national character in a democracy.[40]

Because of the deal struck with the conservative members of the GOP, Roosevelt believed that his party was not deeply divided on railroad regulation. Roosevelt claimed responsibility for breaking up the connection between the Republican Party and the "so-called Wall Street men" of wealth and prestige. Roosevelt's rationale had some merit. William Harbaugh argued that by 1905, the Old Guard of the Republican Party had been shaken significantly by mounting pressures for reform. According to Harbaugh and Gabriel Kolko, conservative Republican senators agreed with Roosevelt on the basic regulatory purpose of the Hepburn Act.[41] However, Roosevelt's belief that he had ameliorated all of the tensions within his party was misguided.

Under the impression that he had bargained successfully for ICC control of railway rates, Roosevelt engaged in moralistic rhetoric during his 1905 speaking tour. Because support for railway regulations divided along nonpartisan lines, Roosevelt viewed it as a moral issue that deserved a principled defense.[42] The tour's immediate political goal was to combat the railroad industry's propaganda and sell regulatory policy to the American public. But TR also wanted to use moral rhetoric for two broader purposes. First, Roosevelt hoped his strong moral rhetoric would mitigate the behavior of the trusts. By stressing the importance of honesty and virtue in business practices, TR aimed to achieve a moral redemption of corporate leaders. No matter how much regulatory legislation eventually became law, TR believed that just business practices could only be achieved if the so-called industrial robber barons based their business decisions on firm moral principles.[43] By exhorting businessmen to act morally, TR anticipated that his rhetorical pedagogy might reach where regulatory legislation could not. No matter how tightly Congress constructed a law, the possibility for circumvention always existed. The only way to guarantee just business practices was to change the culture of corporate America by appealing to the moral consciences of its leaders.

Second, Roosevelt engaged in moral rhetoric in an attempt to fulfill a broader moral purpose. In his speeches, TR brought a vision of a morally fortified country to the fore. The "bully pulpit" provided an opportunity for Roosevelt to reconstitute the moral purpose of American life.[44] TR saw a changing world in which the United States must hold onto its traditional values while adapting to new economic realities. Without losing the "manly" virtues embodied by nineteenth-century citizens, Americans needed to embrace the industrial age. A balance between new materialist demands and traditional virtues could be achieved, according to President Roosevelt: "Each man must be able to pull his own weight, to carry his own weight; and therefore, each man must show the capacity to earn for himself and his family enough to secure a certain amount of material well-being. That must be the foundation. But on that foundation he must build as a superstructure the spiritual life."[45]

Through his rhetoric, Roosevelt encouraged Americans to build a "superstructure" of the "spiritual life." Just as TR sought to build an administrative state that would serve as the superstructure of American government and the executive branch, his rhetorical pedagogy directed itself towards building a moral superstructure that would insulate the materialistic world from unhealthy selfishness and greed. TR strongly believed that a "reconstitution" of the civic spirit was vitally important to the future of American life. Without a moral awareness, Roosevelt feared that the United States's power would decline gradually within an international system that valued a vigorous and martial class of men. TR's rhetoric attempted to forestall this threatened deterioration.

Roosevelt clearly viewed regulatory policy and class politics in moral terms. With his 1905 rhetoric, Roosevelt wanted to create a new dimension of authority. Standing above divisions of economic class, Roosevelt contended that the positions advocated by labor or the trusts were not the answers to the nation's economic woes. Instead, the moral position he crafted through his bargaining with the Republican Party provided a just solution to the problem of rate inequality.

Even in early 1905, TR spoke from a supreme confidence that he possessed the power "to translate his conscience into politics."[46] Roosevelt believed his political bargain enabled him to carve out a larger realm for government involvement in corporate regulation. In a January 30, 1905, speech in Philadelphia, TR outlined the state's moral duty regarding oversight: "In some body such as the Interstate Commerce Commission there must be lodged in effective shape the power to see that every shipper who uses the railroads and every man who owns or manages a railroad shall on the one hand be given justice and on the other hand be required to do justice. Justice—so far as it is humanly possible to give and get justice—is the foundation of our Government." This excerpt can be contrasted to Roosevelt's 1902 comments in Fitchburg, Massachusetts, in which he described the government's circumscribed role in regulation as "determining what are the real evils and what of the alleged evils are imaginary."[47] By 1905, the purpose of the state was much broader and extensive: to "give and get justice." Furthermore, Roosevelt clearly stated that the ICC would possess the power to dispense the "justice" he referenced.

On the 1905 speaking tour, TR used moral argumentation as a unifying tactic to negate class warfare. Reminiscent of George Washington's pedagogical rhetoric, Roosevelt used moral language to denounce the formation of economic classes or factions. As the independent policy leader on railroad regulation, TR sought to stand above the fray by denouncing class distinctions. According to TR, the issue wasn't about capital versus labor; it was about justice defeating injustice and good opposed to evil. By standing above class and party barriers, TR claimed a new vantage point that allowed him to lead the fight on regulatory policy. Moral arguments gave Roosevelt's position a fresh dimension that did not fall neatly on the labor-capital continuum: "This is an age of organization, the organization of capital, the organization of labor. Each type of organization should be welcomed when it does good, and fearlessly opposed when it does evil. Our aim should be to strive to keep the reign of justice alive in this country so that we shall above all things avoid the chance of ever dividing on the lines that separate one class from another, one occupation from another."[48] Roosevelt's rhetoric positioned him to hover above the two extremes of the political fray. The president could orchestrate the "reign of justice" that would negate the divisiveness of economic strife and faction.

After uniting his party on the issue of railroad regulation through his tariff deal, Roosevelt used his rhetoric to project his authority above economic divisiveness. This type of rhetoric—which painted Roosevelt as a Washingtonian "patriot king" above the fray—seemed out of place in 1906 when the Old Guard of the Republican Party forced TR to the extreme left and then back to the right of his original position as part of the political maneuvering surrounding the passage of the Hepburn Act.

In his 1905 rhetoric, Roosevelt spoke from moral principle, basing his efforts on the "eternal and immutable principles of justice." TR's rhetoric set a high standard for regulatory legislation, demanding an "administrative body with the power to secure fair and just treatment among all shippers who use the railroads."[49] When using "good versus evil" rhetoric, presidents must be certain that the political climate can support such strong claims. As Republican Party cleavages reasserted themselves in the Senate negotiations of 1906, it became clear that Roosevelt's 1905 rhetoric had overstated its promises. Once firm moral standards are set in place, it is difficult to retract such assurances. The political value of moral arguments is their ability to persuade listeners from different backgrounds and perspectives towards a common goal. The political liability is that moral promises constitute a rhetorical contract that is costly to break or amend.

1906 and the Hepburn Act: The Aftermath

Roosevelt's rhetoric did achieve its immediate political purpose. The 1905 tour made the mass movement for railroad regulation "politically irresistible."[50] While the railroads enjoyed early success with their propaganda campaign, they were no match for Roosevelt's mastery of the bully pulpit. By the end of Roosevelt's speaking tour, it was evident that Congress would pass some form of railroad regulation in 1906.

However, in the long run, Roosevelt's moralizing damaged his political authority. Because he believed the tariff deal had ameliorated the differences within his party, Roosevelt infused his rhetoric with strong moral pronouncements and promises. TR did not anticipate that the Old Guard of the GOP might challenge him on the details of his proposal. In 1906, the House of Representatives accepted Roosevelt's provisions, but conservative Republicans in the Senate challenged his version of railway regulation. While Roosevelt's legislation gave the ICC the power to amend railway rates, Sen. Nelson Aldrich sought to change TR's proposal by giving the courts final authority over the amendments. An alteration of this magnitude to Roosevelt's version of the Hepburn Act would have been devastating to his authority as a progressive reformer. Throughout the 1905 speaking tour, Roosevelt had spoken strongly on the issue of railroad regulation and the ICC's administrative capacity to secure "fair and just treatment" to all shippers. The ICC's control over rates was the linchpin of Roosevelt's program, creating a lofty "moral superstructure" that would eradicate unjust business practices in the United States. While Aldrich could not stop railroad regulation altogether, his opposition to ICC control of rates made it likely that Roosevelt would be unable to fulfill all of the strong rhetorical promises he had made on his 1905 tour.

To save his legislation and his reputation as a moral reformer, Roosevelt was forced into an unholy alliance with Democrat Ben Tillman and La Follette Republicans to create a new, liberal coalition. Because the coalition placed him in a position to the left of his original proposal, Roosevelt attempted to appease the influential centrists within his party by giving a rousing speech on April 14, 1906, denouncing investigative journalists as "muck-rakers": "If the whole picture is painted black there remains no hue whereby to single out the rascals for distinction from their fellows. Such painting finally induces a kind of moral color-blindness; and people affected by it come to the conclusion that no man is really black, and no man really white, but they are all gray. . . . Hysterical sensationalism is the very poorest weapon wherewith to fight for lasting righteousness."[51] Forced to enter a political alliance with his opponents, TR attempted to moderate his position through a moral condemnation of reform-minded journalism. Roosevelt's speech failed to influence undecided GOP senators and intensified divisions within the Republican Party.[52] In addition, the speech also angered journalists, whom Roosevelt had previously supported. The "Muck-rake" speech demonstrated that the political circumstances for moral argumentation are not appropriate when partisan divisions are growing. In a desperate attempt to placate conservatives, Roosevelt used moral rhetoric to condemn reporters, but his plan backfired, implying that moral stances are too blunt for intricate political maneuvering.

When the Senate conservatives defeated the new liberal partnership, Roosevelt lurched rightward and accepted a version of the bill that gave the courts the power to annul any ICC order. Subject to the whims of his party, Roosevelt accepted a watered-down version of railway regulation. The rocky passage of the Hepburn Act intensified the political feud between Roosevelt and the Old Guard and also instigated tension between the president and the progressives led by La Follette. Because the judiciary's power to control rates remained vague in the final version of the bill, the pro-railroad senators claimed victory.[53] The weaknesses of the Hepburn Act angered the progressives from the Midwest. Consequently, La Follette and his followers believed they could not trust Roosevelt with their progressive agenda. In his autobiography, La Follette chastised Roosevelt's decision to accept the weaker version of the Hepburn Act:

> I state the facts here just as they transpired, because they illustrate the difference in methods which sometimes rendered it impossible for President Roosevelt and myself to cooperate on important legislation. He acted upon the maxim that half a loaf is better than no bread. I believe that half a loaf is fatal whenever it is accepted at the sacrifice of the basic principle sought to be attained. Half a loaf, as a rule, dulls the appetite, and destroys the keenness of interest in attaining the full loaf. A halfway measure never fairly tests the principle and may utterly discredit it. It is certain to weaken, disappoint, and dissipate the public interest.[54]

Even though TR signed railroad regulation into law, his progressive reputation was tarnished. The problem was that TR had advertised the "full loaf" in his swings around the circle and subsequently failed to deliver all of his promises. Rather than alleviating the divisions within his party, Roosevelt intensified them.

Roosevelt's miscalculation about the fictive unity of his party influenced his rhetorical choices and political authority. While Roosevelt's moralizing did generate public support for railroad regulation, it also boxed him into a corner. Moral pronouncements are bold but not flexible. Roosevelt's strong rhetoric required him to support regulatory policy that matched his promises. The rhetorical license Roosevelt thought he earned through the tariff deal was more tenuous than he surmised. Roosevelt demonstrated that using bold moral language to justify the "party line" is a dangerous rhetorical practice, particularly when intra-partisan divisions persist. Through his strong rhetoric in 1905, Roosevelt sought to create an independent policy position, but staking out such a position is risky for a president subject to the turbulence of his party. Roosevelt moralized to push the Republican Party in a direction he wanted it to go, an effort to make his old party "progressive again," as he recounted in his autobiography.[55] But when the conservative members of the GOP refused, Roosevelt found his authority vulnerable to attacks from both the right and the left.

The political effectiveness of Roosevelt's rhetoric can be compared to the moral and religious rhetoric Washington issued after the Whiskey Rebellion. Because political circumstances recommended moral argumentation, Washington's strong rhetoric enhanced his authority and encouraged the Democratic Societies to disband. Washington emerged from the Whiskey Rebellion with a stronger leadership position. In comparison, Roosevelt's rhetoric was subject to the whims of his party, thereby placing his moral posturing on an unstable foundation. Rather than emerging as a stronger leader like Washington, Roosevelt faced even more scrutiny and criticism after the passage of the Hepburn Act. Roosevelt's rhetoric fueled progressive insurgency and Old Guard resistance.

Rather than moralizing in 1905, moral restraint might have enhanced Roosevelt's leadership by allowing him to respond to changing circumstances within the Republican Party. Instead of making railroad regulation a moral crusade, Roosevelt should have spoken about the issue with more caution and suppleness. Roosevelt's tough rhetoric in 1905 created the expectation, especially amongst progressives, that the president could deliver his version of railway legislation. Because of the rift within his party, TR could not fulfill these expectations.

Lastly, Roosevelt's 1905 rhetoric did not succeed in its broader objectives. John Milton Cooper observed that TR's greatest presidential failure "lay in his attempt to get the people to avoid class politics and rise above material concerns."[56] Economic divisions had become too strong by the turn of the century; even TR's best rhetorical efforts could not undermine the growing factional force of materialism in American political culture. Roosevelt's rhetoric also failed to convince industrial captains to adopt a moral code of business ethics. No evidence suggests that TR's rhetorical campaign to infuse the business community with a sense of moral responsibility had any effect on corporate practices. In fact, during his last year in office, Roosevelt frequently complained of big business' reluctance to adopt high moral standards. The president's growing frustration with the trusts and the Old Guard led him to engage in radical rhetoric at the end of his term. As the next section illustrates, political conditions in 1908 recommended moral restraint, but Roosevelt refused to heed all warnings and consequently endured the damaging consequences of his strident moralizing.

1908 Rhetoric: No Holds Barred

After winning the election in 1904, Roosevelt announced that he would not seek another term. By the end of 1907, TR's relationship with congressional Republicans, continually encumbered by differences over the protective tariff, had worsened. Roosevelt feared that many of the legislative proposals he sent to Congress in his 1907 Annual Message would be ignored. To awaken the "Do-Nothing Congress," Roosevelt decided to issue a Special Message on January 31, 1908. At this point, Roosevelt still maintained his reputation for strong moral leadership. However, the split within the Republican Party between the Old Guard and progressives had grown stronger than ever.

Clearly aware of the costs of issuing divisive rhetoric at this time, it is possible that Roosevelt's goal was not persuasion but exhortation.[57] His January 31, 1908, Special Message contained such radical language, it is almost impossible to conclude that Roosevelt thought his address would improve his relationship with Congress. In the message, Roosevelt unleashed all of the frustration he felt towards the Old Guard, whom he believed were nothing more than minions of wealthy business interests: "The Federal Government does scourge sin; it does bid sinners fear, for it has put behind bars with impartial severity the powerful financier, the powerful politician, the rich land thief, the rich contractor—all, no matter how high their station, against whom criminal misdeeds can be proved. All their wealth and power can not protect them."[58] Notice that the federal government's role regarding business regulation had changed from an impartial moral arbiter between capital and labor to an active state agent who imposed "fear" upon the financially privileged "sinners." With this type of rhetorical appeal, Roosevelt abandoned the independent "above the fray" position that had temporarily strengthened his position during the Hepburn campaign.

Roosevelt also vented his frustration with business leaders, who had not heeded his rhetoric and changed their immoral ways: "The keynote of all these attacks upon the effort to secure honesty in business and in politics is well expressed in brazen protests against any effort for the moral regeneration of the business world, on the ground that it is unnatural, unwarranted, and injurious, and that business panic is the necessary penalty for such effort to secure business honesty. The morality of such a plea is precisely as great as if made on behalf of the men caught in a gambling establishment when that gambling establishment is raided by the police." Roosevelt's analogy—comparing the immorality of the business world to gamblers that cower from the law—showed that he had lost all confidence that capital would comply voluntarily to establish ethical standards of practice. TR ended the message with a vehement statement that resembled the rhetoric he adopted in the 1912 Bull Moose campaign: "We strive to bring nearer the day when greed and trickery and cunning shall be trampled under foot by those who fight for righteousness that exalteth a nation."[59] This statement was perhaps a precursor to Roosevelt's famous concluding statement at the 1912 Progressive Party nominating convention, in which he trumpeted, "We stand at Armageddon, and we battle for the Lord." The moral dividing line had been drawn, and TR threatened to "trample under foot" those who challenged "righteousness."

It is unlikely that Roosevelt thought his January 1908 Special Message would influence or persuade Congress to adopt his legislative program. It is more likely that TR believed that his crusading rhetoric might generate strong public opinion that would force Congress into action. In his *Autobiography*, Roosevelt recalled that near the end of his presidency, he abandoned persuasive efforts with Congress and instead decided to appeal "over the heads of the Senate and the House leaders to the people, who were the masters of both of us." Roosevelt's Special Message earned him wide acclaim from the country at large. Newspaper editorials across the nation urged Congress to pay heed to Roosevelt's message and enact his legislative program. However, the morally righteous tone of the address enraged Old Guard Republicans and made them even more disposed towards inaction.[60] Roosevelt's rhetoric irritated conservative GOP members so much, they chose to withstand public condemnation rather than give in to the president's demands.

For the remainder of his term in office, Roosevelt paid a heavy price for his moralizing. First, Congress stymied TR's legislative program with a "vengeance" reminiscent of Andrew Johnson's presidency. In most cases, Roosevelt's proposed bills were destroyed in committee. In particular, this antipathy haunted Roosevelt in the spring of 1908 when he tried to form a coalition to pass new legislation that would give the president strong discretionary powers to regulate interstate commerce and labor. Unable to hold his delicate coalition together, the bill never made it out of committee in the Senate until after the 1908 election, and then it faltered. TR's righteous position engendered "hostile fire" amongst coalition members, and the alliance fell apart quickly.[61] This legislative loss was hard for Roosevelt. By highlighting his morally righteous beliefs in his rhetoric, Roosevelt effectively eliminated any possibility of winning legislation that would have enlarged the president's independent regulatory power. Roosevelt moralized to demonstrate power and control, but rhetorical restraint might have increased his executive authority to a greater degree by facilitating passage of the bill he desired.

Most of Roosevelt's other legislative proposals met a similar fate in 1908—the inheritance tax, child labor protection, increased powers for the ICC, and regulation of stock ownership in railroad companies never made it out of committee for consideration. Of the many requests the president made to Congress in his 1907 Annual Address, only currency legislation survived intact.[62]

Besides the legislative realm, the Old Guard also struck back at Roosevelt in early 1909. In his last Annual Address, issued on December 8, 1908, Roosevelt stated that Congress opposed an expansion of the Secret Service because they feared investigation themselves. The only benefactors of such a policy were the "criminal classes." Roosevelt had finally crossed a line with his bold rhetoric. Conservative members of the Republican Party had not forgotten the moralistic ire of the 1908 Special Message issued a year earlier, and the 1908 Annual Address pushed the Old Guard over the edge. Led by Republican Speaker Joseph Cannon, the House voted on January 8, 1909, to censure Roosevelt for his actions. The *New York Times* observed that "not since the time of Andrew Johnson had a quarrel between Congress and President reached such dimensions."[63]

The final consequence of Roosevelt's inopportune rhetoric did not directly diminish his authority as president but the strength of the regime he bequeathed to his successor. Roosevelt never considered a progressive Republican successor; he preferred Elihu Root and William Howard Taft, two well-known GOP conservatives. After his year of militant and moralistic rhetoric directed at the Old Guard, Roosevelt urged Taft to make amends with the conservative wing of the party and continue a moderate program of progressive reform. Roosevelt's instructions were doomed to failure. As this analysis has shown, Roosevelt paid a considerable price for his rhetorical agitations. Roosevelt pushed the divisions of his party to the fore, and by 1908, those tensions came to a head. John Milton Cooper concluded that while Roosevelt's presidential rhetoric elevated the tone of discourse, his exhortations "were as foredoomed as any evangelist's call for permanent renunciation of self-interest."[64] TR bequeathed a party riddled with schisms to Taft and urged him to preserve the regime, despite intensifying the divide within his party during his last year in office. Consequently, Roosevelt handed Taft a difficult leadership situation.

Theodore Roosevelt is testimony to the perils of reinforcing moral leadership. Roosevelt's popular appeal stemmed from his vigorous belief that the party organization could be used to pursue moral causes.[65] TR's moralistic rhetoric resonated well with the American public, particularly in comparison to his colorless opponent in the 1904 presidential campaign. Nonetheless, a popular expectation of moral leadership can prove problematic if the political climate recommends restraint. In Roosevelt's situation, tough moral stances increased tensions within his own party. As a moralist who refused to practice moral restraint, Roosevelt suffered the consequences of weakened authority, legislative defeat, and a tarnished progressive legacy.

JIMMY CARTER: MALAISE, MORALITY, AND M.E.O.W.

This analysis of Jimmy Carter's rhetoric demonstrates that moralizing cannot build political support on its own. Moral and religious rhetoric can strengthen existing political support but cannot create political legitimacy. Presidents with little political support, such as James Buchanan and Carter, often resort to moral appeals because such assertions can help executives establish an independent policy position. Both Washington and Roosevelt used strong moral argumentation to condemn potential divisions in the polity that threatened to undermine their executive independence. But any success enjoyed by Washington and Roosevelt rested upon a political contingency; their moralistic arguments matched the circumstances at hand. This was not the case with Jimmy Carter. Instead, Carter demonstrates that when presidents moralize with scant political support, their claims diminish their authority even further.

Jimmy Carter found himself in an unfortunate political situation as a reinforcing moral leader. His strong moral stances played well during the presidential campaign of 1976 but failed as a governing strategy. During his 1976 campaign, Carter emphasized his ability to lead a White House administration that embodied high ethical standards. In his campaign rhetoric, Carter often promised that he would never lie as president. During a 1976 campaign speech in Sacramento, Carter stated: "Our people

have been through too much. . . . They are crying out not for government that is liberal or conservative or ideologically pure, but just honest
and efficient and compassionate. If I had to sum up one word what this
campaign is all about, the word would be 'faith.'"[66] After Watergate and
Nixon's impeachment, the country yearned for a candidate who could
promise, with some credibility, that he would restore moral character to
Washington. Carter's decision to emphasize his moral leadership in the
campaign was partially a strategic decision. In 1972, aide Hamilton Jordan
prepared a blueprint for the 1976 election that argued the nation needed
a moral leader who could demonstrate administrative competence. It
is no coincidence that Carter's campaign autobiography, entitled *Why
Not the Best?*, emphasized two themes: the importance of honest, decent
government and administrative competence. In addition to the strategic
advantages of moral posturing in 1976, Carter genuinely viewed politics
as a moral activity and considered his religious faith a central part of his
life. Carter's outlook led him to believe that America's greatness rested
primarily on its morals and ideals rather than national policies. Former
speechwriter James Fallows believed that Carter possessed moral and
religious beliefs but lacked a strong political ideology.[67]

Carter's July 15, 1976, acceptance speech at the Democratic National
Convention in New York once again stressed the importance of restoring
ethics to the federal government. However, one excerpt in the speech
foreshadowed future problems regarding Carter's moralism: "The test
of any government is not how popular it is with the powerful but how
honestly and fairly it deals with those who must depend on it."[68]

In this sentence, Carter outlined both his successful electoral stance
and his governing failure. As part of his campaign rhetoric in 1976,
Carter utilized moralistic appeals that labeled the Washington crowd as
dishonest and indecent. This moral repudiation resonated soundly with
voters who admired Carter's personal character but eventually hindered
Carter's ability to govern as president. In a post-presidential interview,
Carter admitted that he didn't "have any obligations to the people in
Washington" for his election.[69] Journalists, lobbyists, and members of
Congress were skeptical of Carter before he even began his term, and
Democrats had been out of power in the White House for eight years
prior to his 1976 win. Moralistic condemnations of political insiders exacerbated an already tenuous situation and contributed to a governing
style that put Carter at a distance from Beltway power brokers, paving
the way for his own political isolation. The next section examines the

political circumstances that made Carter's moralism politically costly and theorizes when Carter should have shelved his prophetic rhetoric for a more restrained tone. To narrow the scope of the analysis, I concentrate on Carter's rhetoric concerning his energy policies.

Political Constraints of Carter's Rhetoric

Political circumstances suggested that Carter should have practiced moral restraint throughout most of his presidency. While conditions for moral argumentation existed in the early months, by the fall of 1977, Carter's opportunity to speak moralistically had ended. First, a series of scandals involving members of the White House staff plagued Carter in the first year of his term. Besieged with accusations of financial improprieties, budget director Bert Lance resigned less than a year after Carter took office, and Chief of Staff Hamilton Jordan suffered accusations of drug use. Both scandals seriously damaged his moral authority, but Carter did not adjust his rhetorical choices to reflect the problems at hand. Reflecting upon his presidency, Carter confessed that he "felt a particular need to reassure people" that his administration was "honest and benevolent and moral."[70] Second, as his presidency progressed, Carter found himself in a position of weak political authority. In 1979, Carter's public support ratings fell below Nixon's Watergate approval numbers. His extremely weak political position signaled that moral stances had become inopportune.

Political circumstances recommended moral restraint for most of Carter's term in office. Before Carter faced any public scandals and did not suffer from weakened liberal coalitions, Carter did enjoy a brief opportunity for moral leadership. Carter could have engaged successfully in high levels of moral rhetoric during the spring and summer months of 1977. However, after the Bert Lance incident began to garner attention in September of 1977, Carter's ability to speak moralistically began to wane. Certainly, by 1979, Carter's rhetorical circumstances had changed. Despite his extremely weak political support from both the public and Congress, Carter still issued his most morally charged speech on July 15, 1979, popularly known as the "malaise" speech.[71]

Carter could have used moral argumentation as an early rhetorical strategy to sell his energy policies. As his term progressed, Carter needed to retreat from such posturing and replace his moralistic lectures with more straightforward rhetoric. Instead, when backed into a corner in the summer of 1979, Carter reverted to his version of "Old Faithful," the political sermon that addressed the problems of the national spirit. Carter's rhetorical miscalculation illustrates a main point: moral stances do not exist in a political vacuum. Without some degree of political support, whether from public opinion or Washington insiders, moral leadership based solely on rhetoric is futile. Political authority is a prerequisite for presidential moral leadership.

The Moral Equivalent of War

Carter's decision to make energy the first initiative of his administration was a surprise. While Carter had spoken occasionally about the nation's energy problems during his campaign, he seemed to classify tax and welfare reform as issues with a higher priority. After winning the presidency, Carter catapulted energy to the top of the list for two reasons. First, his mentor from the navy, Adm. Hyman G. Rickover, strongly encouraged Carter to tackle the nation's energy problems immediately. Secondly, Carter became convinced that solving the energy crisis was his "moral responsibility" as president. Carter's decision to elevate energy policy to the top of his agenda did not result from an electoral mandate, an immediate crisis, or calls to action from Congress or the public. Instead, Carter believed that as president, he shouldered the moral responsibility to deal with complicated, national problems and set his sights on solving the energy crisis as his first presidential task.[72]

Despite Carter's moral dedication, energy legislation would not be an easy sell. An energy plan based on conservation and increased regulation had the potential of alienating many constituencies and members of Congress. Specifically, Carter's energy proposals increased taxes on domestically produced oil and gasoline, created tax penalties for less-efficient cars, instituted price increases for natural gas, and placed more reliance on renewable sources of energy. Three groups in Congress immediately opposed the president's plan. First, on ideological grounds, conservative Democrats and Republicans disagreed with creating additional government regulations. Second, members from oil- and gas-producing states opposed regulation due to economic concerns. Third, liberal Democrats from consuming regions feared higher energy prices for constituents.

To sell his plan, Carter needed to work closely with Washington insiders to overcome these problems and also mobilize public support for his plan. Carter realized that it would difficult to arouse public support for a "complicated program" like his energy plan.[73] To overcome this difficulty, Carter proceeded in 1977 and 1978 on the premise that his energy package was morally right. Because of this strident belief, Carter's political handling of energy legislation suffered, including the public appeals he chose to employ. His less-than-stellar rhetoric comprised only one part of his political troubles. Publicly introducing a bill with 113 provisions without previously consulting any members of Congress constituted a bigger error than any rhetorical missteps he could make. However, Carter's failure to convince the American people that the energy problem was the "moral equivalent of war" was no small failure. With a tough battle in the Senate facing him, Carter needed to amass support wherever he could find it.

Carter started out on the right foot. His first speech concerning energy on April 18, 1977, was widely lauded, even though his message was far from inspiring or uplifting; the *Washington Post* front-page headline read "Outlook Grim for Energy, Carter Warns." In fact, Carter began the speech by calling his address an "unpleasant talk." He then characterized the energy problem in moral terms: "Our decision about energy will test the character of the American people and the ability of the President and the Congress to govern this Nation. This difficult effort will be the 'moral equivalent of war'—except that we will be uniting our efforts to build and not destroy."[74] With this proclamation, Carter explicitly labeled his energy legislation a moral cause. It was now up to the American people to accept this "test of character." Carter staked out his independence in moral terms: as president, his job was to "govern this Nation" in a way that enabled citizens to step up to the moral challenge he outlined. His moral rhetoric gave his leadership a higher purpose than simply solving the energy shortage. According to Carter's words, his job involved guiding the American people through these moral trials and decisions.

Carter's energy address received favorable reviews from the national media. Journalists lauded Carter's attempt to strengthen the presidency by establishing a strong symbolic and moral presence in the White House.[75] In the early months of his term, there was talk that Carter might become a "Great Communicator" with his moderate and moral tone. However, by the end of the summer, the Bert Lance affair severely damaged Carter's ability to emphasize his moral leadership. It was not that Lance's questionable banking practices proved particularly immoral. In comparison to other presidential scandals, the Lance affair was benign. Rather, candidate Carter had promised an honest administration, and Bert Lance's behavior sullied the president's moral reputation. In August and September, Carter's press conferences became consumed by Bert

Lance questions. Carter acknowledged that the Lance affair drastically affected his presidency; in *Keeping Faith,* he reflected, "It is impossible to overestimate the damage inflicted upon on my administration by the charges leveled against Bert Lance."[76]

Journalists began to change their opinion of Carter's rhetorical effectiveness. In a September 30, 1977, editorial in the *Washington Post,* Roland Evans and Robert Novak blasted Carter's moralistic approach: "The President is still inclined to moralize on issues that, far from being moral, are matters of practical politics and to appeal directly to the voters whenever he runs into trouble with Congress. . . . Upgrading conventional political questions to the status of good v. evil is still an ingrained habit for Carter, but one that has not helped his energy program and could do him harm in the future."[77] By the fall of 1977, Carter's political opportunity for moralizing had ended. Assertions that the energy crisis constituted the "moral equivalent of war" could no longer serve as a substitute for Carter's difficulties with Congress.

Scandals involving Hamilton Jordan and U.S. Attorney David Marston continued to plague the Carter administration through 1978, severely damaging Carter's image. In a July 31, 1978, issue of *Newsweek,* Meg Greenfield wrote: "And there sits Jimmy Carter in the White House, Mr. Morality himself having to answer questions over the first nineteen months about his close associates' entanglements with the quest for dough, the use of drugs, boozing, whoop-de-doo and blabber mouthing. An open Administration, they call it. I think he had better close it down, if he can." Through excoriating language, Greenfield expressed the simple observation that Jimmy Carter's image as a moral reformer had been tarnished permanently.

In October of 1977, Carter attempted to sell his energy program in a six-state tour. However, Carter made few speeches on this tour, instead engaging in question-and-answer sessions with audiences. This allowed the "conversation" to stray into all kinds of topics, including farm subsidies, women's rights, foreign aid, civil rights, population growth, nuclear proliferation, and water conservation policy. As a result, Carter talked very little about his energy legislation now languishing in the Senate. Even if the tour had been structured differently, the Bert Lance scandal had dampened Carter's authority to speak moralistically. Journalists now referred to the phrase "moral equivalent of war" as M.E.O.W. in an attempt to poke fun at Carter's defunct characterization of the energy crisis.

On November 8, 1977, Carter gave his second nationally televised speech to the nation on energy policy. The speech avoided using the "moral equivalent of war" terminology. As his energy legislation moved to a conference committee, Carter hoped his speech might generate public support for his proposals. Instead of moralizing, Carter used facts and figures to demonstrate the urgency of the nation's energy problems. Although the tone was appropriate, Carter's new approach failed to garner much attention. Carter's address did not receive harsh criticism, but it did not generate a renewed interest in energy policy. The "crisis" highlighted six months earlier had disappeared from the political memories of most Americans, and even persuasive statistics could not revitalize support for it.

Carter's use of the "moral equivalent of war" phrase illustrates a valuable political lesson about moral leadership. Moral posturing can be risky if political circumstances change drastically and swiftly. In the spring of 1977, framing the energy crisis in moral terms seemed like a smart idea. After all, Carter had just won election based upon his promise to create a more ethical and honest government. During the campaign, Carter's esteemed character played a prominent role. But after Carter endured a political scandal, his moral legitimacy suffered. Declaring that a crisis exists is not equivalent to convincing the American people that widespread mobilization is necessary to solve a problem.[78] The Bert Lance affair removed Carter's reliable weapon of persuasion from his rhetorical arsenal.

Carter's difficulties also demonstrate that switching from a strong moralistic stance to more restrained rhetoric is not an easy task. Carter eased off his moralizing in the November address, but in light of his earlier speeches, a simple presentation of the facts seemed less authoritative and independent. It is problematic for a president to back away from a strong moral stance. Facts and figures about energy consumption appeared weak compared to his earlier declaration that the crisis constituted "the moral equivalent of war."

Carter's use of moral rhetoric in 1977 was not a rousing success. A compromise energy package eventually passed in the fall of 1978 due to Carter's bargaining with Congress but not because the president had successfully persuaded the public or the Washington community with his rhetoric. Rather than exercising restraint for the remainder of his term, Carter eventually returned to moralistic rhetoric, culminating in his July 1979 "malaise" speech.

Carter's "Crisis of Confidence"

In the spring of 1979, lines at gas stations became long and citizens grew impatient with the federal government's inability to solve the nation's fuel shortage. Throughout the spring, the media ridiculed Carter's efforts to solve the crisis, calling his proposals "M.E.O.W. II" and "second-state M.E.O.W." After former Carter speechwriter James Fallows wrote an unflattering piece entitled "The Passionless Presidency" for the May issue of the *Atlantic,* most journalists regarded the Carter presidency as defunct. Carter's political authority had hit a nadir. By June, fewer than 30 percent of the American public approved of Carter's leadership.[79]

Carter planned to give another national speech on energy policy on July 5. While attending an economic summit in Tokyo, OPEC announced its fourth price surge in five months. Under increasing pressure, Carter returned to the United States and began to prepare his televised address. Only a day and a half before the address, Carter cancelled the speech and retreated to Camp David with advisors. For the next eleven days, Carter met with business leaders, economists, religious leaders, political strategists, and academics in an attempt to reconstruct his administration.

Carter listened to discussions concerning a variety of domestic policy issues during his meetings at Camp David, but a rift developed over what type of speech Carter should give after returning to the White House. Domestic policy advisor Stuart Eizenstat and Vice President Mondale argued that Carter should identify OPEC as the source of America's energy troubles, provide concrete solutions to the problems at hand, and attempt to infuse the speech with an optimistic tone. Pat Cadell, Carter's pollster and trusted confidante, pushed Carter to give a broader speech that addressed the nation's crisis of spirit. Cadell, the only non-Georgian to become part of Carter's inner circle, believed that America's most powerful national resource was its "moral creed."[80] Knowing that Carter was most comfortable talking about matters of faith, Cadell encouraged Carter to issue a speech about abstract principles rather than energy policy.

During an oral history interview, Carter's speechwriters recalled the controversy at Camp David, confessing that several advisors believed that "this whole crisis of confidence stuff was mumbly mush and insane and would reinforce the notion of neurosis." Carter's critical staffers realized what he did not: moral posturing at a time of extreme political weakness is ineffectual at best. In an attempt to placate Eizenstat and Mondale, Carter agreed to address both the broader issues of "faith" and the energy shortage in the speech. Eizenstat and Mondale still protested, arguing that rhetoric about a "spiritual crisis" in America would weaken the energy proposals themselves.[81] In the end, nothing could have stopped Carter from issuing a political speech that resembled a church sermon about sin and redemption.

Carter's "crisis of confidence" speech failed for two reasons. First, the substantive message of the speech was incoherent and inconsistent. Musings about a supposed spiritual crisis mixed with a discussion of the nation's energy problems did not fit together tightly, making it unclear how one problem related to the other. More importantly, the speech ultimately failed because Carter attempted to use moral posturing to solve his political woes. A moralistic sermon given at a time of such weakened legitimacy was a recipe for disaster. At this point in his presidency, Carter's leadership options were slim, but moral appeals would not serve as a panacea.

The first part of the speech identified the problem at hand. According to Carter, the nation faced an "erosion of confidence in the future" that threatened to "destroy the social and political fabric of America." This crisis "strikes at the very heart and soul and spirit of our national will." The nation's spiritual problems were driven by its sins, which included self-indulgence, consumption, and ownership. The solution Carter offered to the problem did not involve strengthening the ties between citizens and government. While citizens are looking for "honest answers," Washington, D.C., has "become an island." The only solution, Carter reasoned, was to simply "have faith in each other, faith in our ability to govern ourselves, and faith in the future of this Nation." Carter urged Americans to follow the "path of common purpose and the restoration of American values" to solve the crisis of confidence that plagued the nation.[82]

The path of common purpose would also help the United States solve its energy problem. But the fusion of the abstract principles and energy portion of the speech made little sense. Carter urged Americans to place faith in each other, not in government. This pronouncement was in keeping with Carter's persistent anti-Washington rhetoric, reminiscent of his 1976 campaign speeches. However, the second half of his speech outlined government programs and solutions to the energy crisis, such as setting import quotas for oil, creating an energy security corporation, and enacting a windfall profits tax. It was logically unclear how increasing trust amongst citizens would help the United States lessen dependence on OPEC and foreign oil. Carter stated: "So, the solution of our energy crisis can also help us to conquer the crisis of the spirit in our country. It can rekindle our sense of unity, our confidence in the future, and give our Nation and all of us individually a new sense of purpose." Carter reasoned that solving the energy crisis would also correct the supposed "confidence" crisis, but the earlier parts of his speech suggested that the nation's spiritual problems were the crux of the problem. Carter did not make it clear which crisis caused the other and how the two issues were intimately related.[83]

The immediate reaction to the speech was mixed. David Broder of the *Washington Post* doubted if the speech could rescue Carter's "faltering presidency" but called the address "distinctive." Other journalists condemned Carter's pessimistic tone and disputed his claim that the nation was experiencing a spiritual crisis. The public reaction to the speech, initially positive, gave Carter a boost in approval ratings. However, many Americans were skeptical about Carter's willingness to classify a spiritual crisis as a "public problem" and also resented his condemning tone.[84] The early positive reaction to the speech resulted more from the unique and unusual nature of the address rather than a whole-hearted endorsement of its substantive content.

The temporary lift evaporated when Carter asked for resignations from thirty-four of his top aides and cabinet members only two days after the speech. In the following week, Carter accepted five resignations in total. This action undermined any positive effect of the speech; the media characterized it as a "massacre" and a "public purge" that was reminiscent of Richard Nixon. In the following weeks, the "crisis of confidence" speech became a political liability for Carter, who later admitted publicly that he "frittered away" any initial dividends he had gained.[85] Eventually, it became popularly known as the "malaise speech," a permanent reminder of the grim outlook Carter's leadership projected. A politically damaged president delivering bleak moral assessments did not resonate well with Washington insiders or the American public.

The administrative shake-up after the July speech was evidence of the political weakness and vulnerability of Carter's presidency. The juxtaposition of issuing a moralistic speech and then firing all top-level staffers was damaging for Carter. Moral stances build upon existing political support. By asking for thirty-four resignations, Carter blatantly advertised that his administration possessed no political stability. This demonstration of instability erased any notion that Carter's moral leadership could lead the nation out of its energy and economic crises. A president hoping to serve as a moral leader needs a solid political regime to steady him—and Carter in 1979 possessed no such groundwork.[86] Firing staffers might have been politically necessary, but such a purge was incompatible with Carter's rhetorical attempt to portray himself as the nation's patriot king, who stood above the self-interested Washington establishment. Grasping at straws, Carter tried to reconstruct his presidency using any plausible avenue. However, moral posturing followed by an administrative upheaval only intensified his political vulnerability. Faced with a Democratic Party that rejected him and a Republican Party who opposed him, it is understandable that Carter found comfort in retreating to familiar rhetoric about faith and morality.[87] Instead of crafting a "third way" possibility, Carter's 1979 moral rhetoric erected an even higher wall between himself and his antagonists. After all, every moral critique of the Washington community amounted to another condemnation of his entrenched liberal allies.

Throughout his presidency, Carter attempted to compensate for his political difficulties by taking moral leadership stances. He believed that his "attitude of piety" was the root of his political success in 1976.[88] The problem was that the anti-Washingtonian rhetoric that helped elect him proved unsuitable for governance. With little support from members of his own party or the public at large, Carter's moralistic repudiations of Beltway politics left him politically isolated instead of politically independent.

The irony of Carter's failed moral leadership lies with his successor, Ronald Reagan. While Carter's moral rhetoric did little to bolster his political standing, Reagan's frequent moral appeals helped win him the title of the "Great Communicator." Although Reagan's use of moral rhetoric was considerably more optimistic than Carter's routine pessimism, the difference between the two presidents stemmed more from political circumstances than rhetorical choice. As a Republican, Reagan could use moral stances to critique the defunct New Deal establishment effectively while Carter could not. Applying Skowronek's terms, Reagan's moral affirmations served as both "order-creating" and "order-shattering" tools that aimed to discredit the liberal regime and replace it with the politics of consolidation. Carter could point fingers and make moral declarations, but lacking political support, his claims fell on deaf ears. The time was ripe for a president who could combine political legitimacy with moral strength.

CONCLUSION

From time to time, the American electorate selects individuals with strong moral dispositions for the presidency. This chapter examined how "moralist" presidents advertised their beliefs and principles in their rhetoric in an attempt to enhance the strength of their leadership. Reinforcing moral leaders are potentially advantaged because their authority can draw upon moral principles and political resources for support. However, these two sources of authority can work at cross purposes rather than in concert. The sections on Theodore Roosevelt and Jimmy Carter showed that cultivating political support must take precedence over moral posturing. Even if the public clamors for moralizing rhetoric, other political conditions should be considered before "moralist" presidents showcase their beliefs.

Prudent rhetors emphasize immutable moral principles but not at the expense of imminent political demands. When contradictory circumstances pull presidents in opposing directions, the limitations of prudential rhetoric must be considered. A morally infused approach will not work in every rhetorical situation; *phronesis* demands a balance between the "ideal and the possible." Presidents with a morally infused outlook may find it especially difficult to achieve this mean because they frame their political leadership from a starting point based upon virtue's fulfillment. It is important to remember that *phronesis* is concerned not only with universal moral axioms but also with the particulars of a given political situation. In this chapter, George Washington best embodied the *phronesis* ideal; the varied experience of his military and political career enabled him to choose the right words for the appropriate rhetorical situation. In a description written about Washington in 1814, Thomas Jefferson concluded, "Perhaps the strongest feature in his character was prudence, never acting until every circumstance, every consideration, was maturely weighed."[89]

All three presidents examined in this chapter used moral rhetoric to denounce special interests or faction with limited success. The fulfillment of the patriot king ideal involves creating a morally upright rhetorical position that catapults the president above self-interested concerns. Despite Washington's best efforts, political parties developed in the early nineteenth century. Likewise, Theodore Roosevelt's attempts to ameliorate economic, class-based conflict in the United States failed. Finally, Jimmy Carter's anti-Washingtonian rhetoric only exacerbated his political problems by increasing his political vulnerability. The "special interests" these presidents criticized also grew larger over time. Roosevelt's aspiration to eradicate class warfare was more elaborate than Washington's goal of destroying nascent political parties, while Carter's rhetoric—which characterized the entire Washington establishment as selfish and narrow-minded—exceeded even Roosevelt's ambitions. Presidents who adopt the reinforcing moral leadership approach are drawn to stand "above politics," but the evidence presented in this chapter questions the lasting effectiveness of such a rhetorical stance. As the special interests attacked by reinforcing moral presidents became grander in scope, the plausible efficacy of such a rhetorical approach diminished even further.

The final conclusion of this chapter concerns the broader limitations of reinforcing moral leadership. Teddy Roosevelt's rhetorical characterization of the nation's moral and spiritual strength as a "superstructure" resting upon material prosperity provides an analogous illustration of the relationship between political and moral leadership in the American presidency. The president must cultivate as much political support as possible from members of his own party, Washington insiders, and the American public. Moral posturing through rhetoric is a special tool that presidents can use to enhance or substantiate an existing political base. Moral posturing cannot serve as a substitute for political leadership. Rather, moral leadership is a "superstructure" that rests upon a president's political strength. Without a base from which to emerge, a moral superstructure cannot enhance presidential power.

CHAPTER 4

THE POLITICS OF MORAL RESTRAINT

alvin Coolidge was known for his reticence. When he was president, a woman approached him at a social function and revealed that she bet her friend she could persuade Coolidge to say at least three words during the course of the evening. Coolidge looked at her and simply responded, "You lose." Although the story has become part of presidential folklore, Coolidge understood the broader lesson: sometimes restraint is the better option. Determining the political value of moral rhetoric requires a serious examination of presidents who chose *not* to engage in such posturing. To examine a behavior or phenomenon, the dependent variable must fluctuate. Consequently, we must not only pay attention to presidents who moralized but also to those who avoided it.

This chapter examines three presidents who purposefully refrained from moral and religious appeals in their rhetoric. In these case studies, moral restraint originates from either a philosophical or principled commitment that moralizing in office is inappropriate (Jefferson) or from political concerns (Lincoln and Kennedy). When moral restraint is a strategic choice, leadership capacities are enhanced because the president can respond to changing circumstances and adapt rhetoric to the demands of the situation. However, when moral restraint is a philosophical commitment, the president is boxed in and is unable to capitalize upon moral rhetoric's potential power.

THOMAS JEFFERSON: A PHILOSOPHICAL COMMITMENT TO MORAL RESTRAINT

In his private writings and personal letters, Thomas Jefferson wrote widely about the essence of human nature and man's innate capacity for moral action. Perhaps more than any other Founder, Jefferson's correspondences are filled with musings on morality, virtue, and Christianity. In one of his more creative endeavors, Jefferson took it upon himself to compile the teachings of Jesus into a condensed rendition of the Gospels, formally titled *The Life and Morals of Jesus of Nazareth.*[1] Even Jefferson's political treatises demonstrated his belief in the importance of moral virtue; in his *Notes on the State of Virginia,* Jefferson called American yeoman farmers "the chosen people of God, if ever he had a chosen people, whose breasts he has made his peculiar deposit for substantial and genuine virtue."[2]

However, Jefferson's presidential rhetoric tells us very little, if anything, about his belief in an innate moral sense. He did not, as James Wilson did, give famous law lectures on public morality. Most importantly, unlike his predecessors George Washington and John Adams, Jefferson did not frequently employ moral and religious arguments in his presidential rhetoric. As figure 3 shows, Washington, John Adams, and Madison moralized twice as frequently as Jefferson. Amongst the first four presidents, Jefferson's moral restraint is striking.

Jefferson, a man who invested a significant amount of time thinking and writing about morality and virtue and its relation to political life, chose not to disseminate his moral or religious knowledge to citizens while serving as president. Jefferson exhibited a liberal reluctance to force his moral views on others and also believed in the effectiveness of a wide-reaching social propagation of virtue rather than moralistic platitudes administered from above. Although he wrote about democracy's need to propagate virtue in citizens, Jefferson did not believe it was the statesman's role to encourage such civic-mindedness. Instead, Jefferson thought that citizens would spontaneously realize their moral responsibilities by living under republican institutions, participating in an agrarian economy, and receiving a universal education.[3] Jefferson did not exercise the president's role as the nation's moral educator. Instead, he relied heavily on the ability of citizens to govern themselves, both politically and morally. It is quite possible that Jefferson considered his rhetorical restraint a moral choice and commitment.

Jefferson expressed reluctance to share his moral and religious views publicly in a letter to Dr. Benjamin Rush, written on April 21, 1803. For several years, Jefferson had carried on conversations with Rush about Christianity and philosophy. In this letter, Jefferson offered Dr. Rush a "syllabus or general outline" on Christianity. In his comments, Jefferson called the teachings of Jesus "more pure and perfect than those of the most correct of the philosophers." However, in his letter to Rush, Jefferson made it clear he wanted these reflections to remain private:

> I am moreover averse to the communication of my religious tenets to the public; because it would countenance the presump-

tion of those who have endeavored to draw them before that tribunal, and to seduce public opinion to erect itself into that inquisition over the rights of conscience, which the laws have so justly proscribed. It behooves every man who values liberty of conscience for himself, to resist invasions of it in the case of others; or their case may, by change of circumstances, become his own. It behooves him, too, in his own case, to give no example of concession, betraying the common right of independent opinion, by answering questions of faith, which the laws have left between God and himself.[4]

Even though Jefferson had thought extensively about religion and morality, he did not endorse the president's pedagogical role. Instead, Jefferson believed that an innate moral sense would lead citizens in the right direction. Jefferson further expressed this belief in Query XVIII of his *Notes on the State of Virginia*. In this section, Jefferson acknowledged that slavery was an unjust institution: "Indeed I tremble for my country when I reflect that God is just: that his justice cannot sleep for ever. . . . The Almighty has no attribute which can take side with us in such a contest. But it is impossible to be temperate and to pursue this subject through the various considerations of policy, of morals, of history natural and civil. We must be contented to hope they will force their way into every one's mind."[5] Rejecting the notion that a change in policy or moral exhortations would bring about the abolition of slavery, Jefferson relied instead on a spontaneous manifestation of the innate moral sense. As a slave owner, Jefferson's view is hardly surprising. Nonetheless, his specific rationale for inaction is still illuminating. Citizens would realize eventually that slavery was unjust, but in the meantime, statesmen could do little to eradicate the institution. According to Jefferson, individuals realized their moral capacities through self-discovery, not through a hierarchical pedagogy imposed by politicians.

Jefferson's reluctance to moralize also stemmed more broadly from his political movement's ideological attack on the Federalists. One of the main criticisms Jeffersonians leveled against their opponents was Federalism's tendency to impose one view of the nation upon all citizens. In 1798, the Jeffersonian Virginia legislature issued a public critique of the Federalists that called their regime a "favorite system" they sought to "build up." In contrast, Jeffersonianism opposed the exercise of arbitrary powers, instead advocating a "wise and frugal" government with a narrower scope.[6]

All of the remnants of monarchy needed to be eliminated for a more pluralistic, progressive, and democratic government, which, Jefferson believed, fulfilled the principles of the American Revolution. Jefferson's moral restraint went hand-in-hand with the goals of republican simplicity advocated by the larger political movement he represented.

During most of his presidency, Jefferson's moral restraint did not encumber his leadership. Jefferson's deft control of Congress minimized his need for moralistic rhetoric. The opposition Jefferson faced in his effort to dismantle the Federalist regime was not formidable, and his presidential authority was "singularly disarming and all-encompassing."[7] Jefferson understood that his political situation allowed him to restructure government without sacrificing the appearance of consensus. For example, without any rhetorical justification grounded in high-minded moral principles, Jefferson simply proclaimed in his First Inaugural Address that "we are all federalists; we are all republicans." For the first seven years of his presidency, Jefferson did not need, nor want, to include moral justifications in his rhetoric.

This analysis compares the effectiveness of Jefferson's presidential rhetoric during the Louisiana Purchase and the 1808 shipping embargo. Even though both the Louisiana Purchase and the embargo required sweeping exercises of executive power, Jefferson did not reach for justifications based upon moral principles in his rhetoric. However, the political circumstances surrounding the Louisiana Purchase differed from the political situation of the embargo. While the Louisiana Purchase demonstrated the strength of Jefferson's controlled rhetoric, the embargo controversy demonstrated the weaknesses of his deliberate restraint. Because Jefferson did not change his rhetoric to meet the new political demands dictated by the embargo, support for his policy waned, leading to its eventual repeal six weeks before he left office. At the end of his presidency, Jefferson's inflexible philosophical commitment to avoid moral pronouncements encumbered his independent authority.

The Louisiana Purchase: The Strength of Moral Restraint
On October 1, 1800, France and Spain signed the treaty at San Ildefonso, which gave France control over Louisiana and gave Spain a kingdom in Italy. Before occupying Louisiana, Napoleon attempted to reestablish control in Santo Domingo, a West Indies possession where slaves were waging a revolt. But he did not have enough troops to occupy Santo Domingo and Louisiana at the same time. His wife Josephine owned a

plantation on Santo Domingo, and it is believed that she urged Napoleon to send troops there instead of Louisiana. When Jefferson learned that the troops sent to Santo Domingo were headed eventually to Louisiana, he increased American aid to the slave revolt. The takeover did not go well for the French. Because of the revolts and the breakout of the yellow fever, approximately twenty-four-thousand Frenchmen died in Santo Domingo.[8]

Jefferson instructed Robert Livingston, the American minister to France, to either stop the transfer of Louisiana to France or offer to buy the Floridas and New Orleans from Napoleon. Tensions in the region escalated when Juan Morales, the acting supervisor in Louisiana, ended the American right to deposit goods in the warehouses of New Orleans. Now that England and Spain were at peace, Morales contended that the Americans deserved no special status as neutrals. Even though it was probably untrue, the public believed that Napoleon had directed Morales to stop the right of deposit. Anti-French sentiment grew, and the Federalists called for war—on France, Spain, or both.[9]

Most members of Congress expected that Jefferson's Second Annual Message would contain moralizing rhetoric that alluded to the acquisition of Louisiana as God's will.[10] But his December 15, 1802, message did not live up to these expectations. In a letter to Charles Pinckney, Alexander Hamilton called the presidential message "a lullaby." In the address, Jefferson only mentioned the controversy surrounding Louisiana in passing: "The cession of the Spanish Province of Louisiana to France, which took place in the course of the late war, will, if carried into effect, make a change in the aspect of our foreign relations which will doubtless have just weight in any deliberations of the Legislature connected with that subject."[11] On this occasion, Jefferson's restraint served his political purposes well. Uncertain about how Napoleon's future actions would affect the United States's ability to expand its territory, Jefferson's restrained language kept his options open and gave Napoleon ample time to determine that his expedition in America was imprudent. By March of 1803, war between England and France seemed imminent, and Napoleon's losses in Santo Domingo had grown. Fearing an Anglo-American alliance, Napoleon ceded Louisiana to the United States. Jefferson's rhetorical restraint did not force Napoleon's hand but served the strategic interests of the United States well.

Pleased with the outcome, Jefferson wrote letters to friends about the decision but did not issue a proclamation of any sort. According to the terms of the agreement, the Senate needed to approve the treaty by October 30, 1803. Immediately prior to its deliberation, Jefferson issued his Third Annual Message, in which he discussed the Louisiana Purchase. Within the three paragraphs of the address that concerned the Louisiana treaty, Jefferson did not include any moral or religious justifications to encourage the arrangement. Rather, he concentrated on the interest and advantage provided by the acquisition of such a large piece of land: "Whilst the property and sovereignty of the Mississippi and its waters secure an independent outlet for the produce of the Western States and an uncontrolled navigation through their whole course, free from collision with other powers and the dangers to our peace from that source, the fertility of the country, its climate and extent, promise in due season important aids to our Treasury, an ample provision for our posterity, and a wide spread for the blessings of freedom and equal laws." Even though his executive actions had doubled the size of the country, Jefferson felt no need to make a grand announcement that celebrated the yeoman virtue the Louisiana Purchase had supposedly insured. By acquiring Louisiana, Jefferson believed he had secured a moral way of life for agrarians, but he included none of these thoughts in his official statements.[12]

Jefferson's lack of a moral statement justifying the Louisiana Purchase is not considered a breach of presidential leadership. The popular reaction to the Purchase was "very favorable."[13] The political situation did not require moral argumentation. Since reaction to the Purchase was positive, there was no need to rally the nation. Jefferson's response of rhetorical restraint matched the response anticipated by a calculated assessment of the situation. His 1802 Annual Address actually enhanced his leadership by allowing him to respond to the changing circumstances of the situation. Although Jefferson's rhetoric strengthened his authority in this instance, it is not an example of prudent rhetorical leadership. In the *Ethics*, Aristotle stated: "But it is also possible to attain something good by a false syllogism, to arrive at the right action, but to arrive at it by the wrong means when the middle term is false. Accordingly, this process, which makes us attain the right goal but not by the right means, is still not good deliberation."[14] Aristotle explained that the process of deliberation is more important than the action itself. Prudence is the consistent understanding of the correct means to achieve the best ends, not simply the finished product.

Jefferson never quite fulfilled the demanding requirements of *phronesis* in his rhetorical leadership, which became more evident near the end of his administration. Jefferson continued to employ rhetorical restraint during the implementation of the shipping embargo, but his leadership during this crisis is often considered his greatest presidential miscalculation. When political circumstances changed, Jefferson should have altered his rhetoric to match the new demands placed upon him. Instead, Jefferson held fast to his philosophical commitment not to moralize as president.

The Embargo: The Weakness of Moral Restraint
By 1806, the situation of American sailors on the high seas had grown perilous. British ships routinely stopped American vessels to impress sailors who had abandoned their military posts. Jefferson sent ambassadors to London for negotiations, but the treaty they brought back to the United States did not solve the issue of impressment. Refusing to send a weak treaty to the Senate, Jefferson witnessed the gradual deterioration of Anglo-American relations. To make matters worse, in July of 1807, a British vessel attacked the American warship *Chesapeake*. As a result of the incident, three Americans were killed, and the *Chesapeake* was boarded before it was allowed to return to land. The reaction to the attack was swift and furious; Americans of both parties were outraged and demanded action. Jefferson was faced with three choices: he could wage immediate war with Britain, delay war by enforcing a shipping embargo on foreign trade, or do nothing.[15] As members of both political parties in Congress pressed for action, the latter option quickly disappeared.

Although members were eager for some sort of retaliation to redress British transgressions on the high seas, the Tenth Congress that assembled in October 1807 was a "Jefferson Congress." Nathaniel Macon, who had flirted with joining John Randolph's oppositional radical faction called the Quids, lost his job as Speaker of the House to Jefferson loyalist Joseph Varnum. Additionally, Randolph was replaced by G. W. Campbell as the chairman of the Committee on Ways and Means.[16] Even late in his second term of office, Jefferson possessed firm control and influence over congressional decision-making.

Jefferson, Madison, and Gallatin hoped that the British would issue an apologetic response regarding the *Chesapeake* affair in November. A favorable British proclamation to this effect might calm American indignation and quell the desire for immediate retribution. By the end of November, Jefferson learned that the British remained "uncompromising" on the *Chesapeake* incident, thereby pushing Jefferson to decide on a course of action.[17] Jefferson seemed to be leaning towards economic sanctions, which might delay war with Britain and give the United States time to prepare a stronger military. Jefferson's course seemed apparent when, in early December, Congress allowed a Non-Importation Act against Britain, passed nine months earlier, to take immediate effect.

On December 18, 1807, Jefferson sent a brief message to the Senate to recommend a full shipping embargo. The message, which was only 107 words in length, was direct in its language and offered little explanation for the proposed action:

> The communications now made, showing the great and increasing dangers with which our vessels, our seamen, and merchandise are threatened on the high seas and elsewhere, from the belligerent powers of Europe, and it being of great importance to keep in safety these essential resources, I deem it my duty to recommend the subject to the consideration of Congress, who will doubtless perceive all the advantages which may be expected from an inhibition of the departure of our vessels from the ports of the United States. Their wisdom will also see the necessity of making every preparation for whatever events may grow out of the present crisis.[18]

The terseness of Jefferson's message and Congress's earlier December decision to implement the Non-Importation Act against Britain indicate that Washington insiders were not surprised by the embargo decision. Most likely, congressional leaders anticipated Jefferson's decision. Samuel Smith, the floor leader in the Senate, quickly guided the embargo bill through the Senate on the same day of Jefferson's message. The House approved a similar bill on December 21, and the Senate agreed to the House version the following day. Without offering any public justifications for the implementation of a full embargo, Jefferson managed to persuade Congress of his policy. Indeed, many members did not know the reasons for the enactment of the embargo; they acted on their "blind faith" of the Jefferson administration.[19]

Because Jefferson possessed a comprehensive control of the federal government, he was able to implement the embargo with little opposition. From December 1807 until the end of his second presidential term, Jefferson failed to issue any public statements, declarations, or proclamations that forcefully explained his embargo policy. Jefferson employed no inspirational calls to service or principled language in an attempt to rouse citizens in support. Jefferson's rhetorical defense of the embargo was scant, but the arguments he did make accomplished very little in rousing support for his policies.

Jefferson's moral restraint became problematic when public support for the embargo weakened, and noncompliance threatened to decrease its potential effectiveness. A president less doggedly opposed to moralizing might have benefited from a principled justification of his actions during an imminent national crisis in which public support was divided, but party support was strong. The Republican governor of Massachusetts, James Sullivan, wrote to Jefferson shortly after the announcement of the embargo about the desperate situation in his state, cautioning him, "you are now in a critical situation. . . . The Federalists here openly avow that if a war takes place England will send an army to the Southern states to cause the blacks to cut their masters' throats. They talk of a division between the southern and northern States as a matter of course." Only ten days after the embargo's implementation, Secretary of the Treasury Albert Gallatin began receiving information that "gross evasions" had already occurred.[20] The potential effectiveness of the embargo required all citizens to comply with its regulations. With marginal public support for the embargo, Jefferson needed to rally the country behind the policy. The embargo was a test of endurance for the American people, and Jefferson had to persuade citizens to accept the imposed hardships as a means of avoiding a costly and dangerous war. As opposition to the embargo grew stronger throughout the summer months of 1808, Jefferson's philosophical refusal to moralize increasingly inhibited his leadership.

Jefferson did defend the embargo privately in a number of letters to personal friends, contending that the policy was an issue of moral resolve that the nation must endure. In a January 22, 1808, letter to Gideon Granger, Jefferson wrote that the purpose of the embargo was to "discontinue all intercourse with these nations till they should return again to some sense of moral right."[21] Additionally, Jefferson's reply to the Society of Tammany in New York furnished a succinct moral defense of the embargo. In his short reply to the Society, Jefferson explained that a cessation of all intercourse with Britain must continue until it could be "resumed under the protection of a returning sense of the moral obligations which constitute a law for nations as well individuals." Even though Jefferson's letter to Tammany was not private, replies to memorial addresses did not circulate widely beyond the local group who initiated the correspondence.[22] Despite these indirect communications, Jefferson never issued a nationwide proclamation stressing the embargo's presumably moral obligations.

Circumstances recommending moral argumentation intensified as the embargo's restrictions tightened and public support waned. Initially, the embargo only affected New England and southern shipping towns that depended on trade with the British and the Caribbean. Border states were still free to transport goods over rivers and lakes for trade. As part of the third embargo act, passed into law on March 3, 1808, Jefferson declared a land embargo and ended frontier trade. This action proved extremely unpopular, particularly amongst New Englanders. As a stronghold of the Federalists and commercial interests, the northern seaboard protested Jefferson's intensified policy. Federalists in Congress opposed the restrictive penalties contained in the third embargo act but were unable to voice their opposition when both the tightly controlled Senate and the House leadership did not allow debate on these bills. In addition to New England, parts of the South, New York, and Pennsylvania strongly opposed the embargo.[23]

Before Congress adjourned in the spring, it passed the Enforcement Act of 1808, which required all ships to secure clearance from the president before departing from port. Under the provisions of this act, the president could also employ navy vessels to stop and detain ships under suspicion of a violation. From April until October, Jefferson, with the help of Gallatin, assumed the chief responsibility of embargo enforcement. With Congress adjourned, the president acted with no legislative restraint or guidance. Although each successive embargo act increasingly curtailed individual rights, Jefferson never enacted a program of public education to explain the necessity of the embargo. He also never provided citizens with an estimated timetable for success. Even when Jefferson ordered the regular army to enforce the embargo in August of 1808, he did not issue a proclamation or a decree. Jefferson's advisors encouraged him to issue some sort of public appeal to provide moral inspiration for those adversely affected by the policy. In a letter written to Jefferson on July 29, 1808, Gallatin argued that the people needed their patriotism aroused to withstand the economic hardships precipitated by the embargo.[24] Gallatin's plea fell on deaf ears, and Jefferson refused to issue a public statement in the summer months.

Although it is impossible to know if a strong call for sacrifice would have influenced public opinion, it is unlikely that an attempt by Jefferson to rouse public support would have gone unheeded.[25] On this point, a comparison between Jefferson and Washington is instructive. Both during and after the Whiskey Rebellion, Washington used moral and religious argumentation in his rhetoric to condemn the "insurgents" and also to rally the militia behind his executive decision to quell the disturbance with military force. Washington's effective use of moral and religious rhetoric could have served as a telling example to Jefferson during the embargo. Instead of restraining his rhetoric, Jefferson might have morally chastised the individuals who refused to comply with the embargo's dictates. Furthermore, he might have described the embargo in moral terms, arguing that the sacrifices endured by the restrictions were part of a citizen's moral and patriotic duty. Whereas Washington used rhetoric to enhance his authority, Jefferson's failure to moralize during the embargo handicapped his leadership.

From a political standpoint, moralizing posed little risks for Jefferson. By November of 1808, New England Republicans opposed the continuation of the embargo, but until then, Jefferson's rhetoric was not inhibited by lukewarm or divided support from his party. In the spring and summer of 1808, Republicans supported the embargo wholeheartedly.[26] The only potential risk for moralizing in this situation might have been its inflexibility. Once Jefferson issued a strong statement condemning the disobedient, it would have been difficult to back away from supporting the embargo, much like Teddy Roosevelt's inability to maneuver his position on railroad regulation after moralizing on the stump in 1905. However, Jefferson showed no indication that he intended to change his mind on the embargo. Convinced this was the best possible course of action, Jefferson should have used moral argumentation to rally the nation behind the cause.

If Jefferson was unaware of the embargo's unpopularity, his rhetorical restraint might be considered a strategic response. In light of the information Jefferson received about the embargo, this explanation is not credible. Albert Gallatin consistently informed Jefferson of the strong opposition to the embargo and the damaging effects of noncompliance. In a September 16, 1808, letter to Jefferson that described the situation in Massachusetts, Gallatin wrote, "The systematic opposition connected with the political views which prevails there, renders the execution of the embargo still more difficult." James Bowdoin registered his reservations about the embargo with Jefferson in a July 1808 letter: "[I]t is yet doubtful, whether the country has the disposition, fortitude or virtue to submit its privations, for a sufficient length of time, to procure these advantages which are contemplated from it." In addition to letters from his associates, Jefferson also received a multitude of letters from citizens who informed the president of their opposition to the embargo. One remarkable letter began with the salutation "You Infernal Villain" and went on to inform Jefferson that the author's son had died from hunger because of the embargo.[27] In short, Jefferson was certainly aware that many citizens refused to support the embargo or comply with its regulations.

Jefferson's rhetorical restraint might have constituted an attempt to distance himself from a policy gone awry. In an August 26, 1808, response to three New England port towns that had held public meetings criticizing the embargo, Jefferson reminded them it was Congress who had "passed the laws of which you complain."[28] While still implementing the policy from behind the scenes, Jefferson tried to detach himself as much as possible from the controversies of the embargo. If Jefferson had issued proclamations or special messages concerning the embargo, he would have been intimately associated with its unpopular consequences. Instead, Jefferson relied upon the tightly controlled Congress to provide him with the sweeping license of power he needed for enforcement.

Once again, this leadership strategy was not and could not be effective. Without a principled defense of the embargo, Jefferson was in a no-win situation. An attempt to duck responsibility and shift the blame to Congress not only hurt Jefferson's reputation but also the authority of the government itself. Because of the embargo, lawlessness and disorder swept through the land, eventually undermining the economic strength developed in the past two decades.[29]

Even when he found himself faced with a situation that demanded a more publicly inspirational role for the chief executive, Jefferson's philosophical beliefs about the purpose of executive power continued to influence his presidential rhetoric. Jefferson viewed the United States as an inherently pluralistic nation and remained unwilling to raise the specter of an imposed moral vision, *even when he was in fact imposing one himself.* When pushed to the limits, Jefferson's commitment to reject the president's role as the nation's moral spokesman led to its antithesis. In other words, Jefferson's pronounced reluctance inhibited his rhetorical choices. Undoubtedly, Jefferson believed that his rhetorical restraint actually served as a fulfillment of moral leadership, but his desire to fulfill this conception of moral restraint forced him to neglect the more pressing demands of political leadership.

Jefferson is an excellent example of a president who refused to sideline his philosophical inclinations or moral outlook when political circumstances demanded a different response. Throughout much of his eight years in office, Jefferson did not need to arouse public support for his proposed policies; his rhetorical choices coincided with his philosophical commitments. But when political circumstances changed after the implementation of the embargo, Jefferson refused to deviate from his restrained approach, even when urged by his close advisors to do so. Before Jefferson left office in March of 1809, Congress repealed the embargo and replaced it with a less stringent non-importation act. Jefferson's presidency ended with his political authority weakened and his embargo policy discredited. Jefferson's leadership stands in contrast to the other two presidents discussed in this chapter, Lincoln and Kennedy, who exercised moral restraint because of strategic motivations rather than rigid philosophical beliefs.

ABRAHAM LINCOLN: MORAL RESTRAINT AND THE REPUBLICAN PARTY

Widely considered the most distinguished moral leader to inhabit the executive office, one would expect to find many moral and religious arguments in Lincoln's presidential speeches and statements. Thus, the relative paucity of moral and religious language in Lincoln's presidential

TABLE 7. MORAL AND RELIGIOUS RHETORIC OF THE CIVIL WAR ERA: ANNUAL ADDRESSES

	Total Number of Moral/Religious Appeals	Total Number of Sentences	Percentage of Moral/ Religious Sentences	Average Number of Moral/ Religious Appeals per Address
James Buchanan	71	1356	5.2%	17.8
Abraham Lincoln	30	940	3.2%	6.0
Andrew Johnson	58	1175	4.9%	14.5

rhetoric, illustrated in table 7, requires an explanation. Harold Holzer has called Lincoln an "oratorical enigma."[30] It is true that Lincoln's rhetoric was not one-dimensional or easily understood, but placing his rhetorical choices within a political context helps elucidate the puzzle.

Scholars agree that Lincoln's strong moral beliefs shaped his political creed and persona. David Greenstone argued in *The Lincoln Persuasion* that Lincoln believed the Union was worth saving only if it shared basic moral commitments. According to Greenstone, Lincoln's leadership explicitly directed itself towards correcting the Founders' more relativistic view of *union*.[31] The scholarship that explores the influence of the Bible and Christianity on Lincoln's language is voluminous.[32] But an awareness of the political constraints and pressures Lincoln felt encourages a greater sensitivity concerning the prudent rhetorical choices he made throughout his public career.

In his pre-presidential rhetoric, Lincoln often emphasized the moral arguments surrounding the slavery issue. For example, in a speech given on July 10, 1858, in Chicago, Lincoln stated: "The Savior, I suppose, did not expect that any human creature could be perfect as the Father in Heaven; but He said, 'As your Father in Heaven is perfect, be ye also perfect.' He set that up as a standard, and he who did most towards reaching that standard, attained the highest degree of moral perfection. So I say in relation to the principle that all men are created equal, let it be as nearly reached as we can." In the above passage, Lincoln likened the fulfillment of equality in the United States to the desire of Christians to follow Jesus' instructions. Lincoln also used moral arguments that directly appealed to the ideals the Founders fought for in the Revolution. In his first Senate debate with Stephen Douglas, held in Ottawa, Illinois, on August 21, 1858, Lincoln invoked his hero Clay to emphasize the concluding point: "Henry Clay, my beau ideal of a statesman, the man for whom I fought all my humble life—Henry Clay once said of a class of men who would repress all tendencies to liberty and ultimate emancipation, that they must, if they would do this, go back to the era of our Independence, and muzzle the cannon which thunders its annual joyous return; they must blow out the moral lights around us; they must penetrate the human soul, and eradicate there the love of liberty; and then and not till then, could they perpetuate slavery in this country!" Lincoln argued that only individuals who were willing to ignore morality by blowing out "the moral lights around us" would oppose the eventual eradication of slavery. In a direct statement in a March 1, 1859, speech in Chicago, Lincoln explicitly classified slavery as a moral wrong. Lincoln used such language to underscore what he believed to be a common sentiment shared amongst all Republicans in Illinois: "I say this for the purpose of suggesting that we consider whether it would not be better and wiser, so long as we all agree that this matter of slavery is a moral, political, and social wrong, and ought to be treated as a wrong, not to let anything minor or subsidiary to that main principle and purpose make us fail to cooperate."[33] In every one of these statements, Lincoln advanced arguments that included a moral condemnation of slavery. Not coincidentally, Lincoln gave all of these speeches in the northern region of Illinois, in which abolitionist sentiment prospered. Lincoln carefully tailored his arguments to the audience at hand and avoided moral arguments concerning slavery when he moved to other regions in the state. As a whole, the Lincoln-Douglas debates are not laden with moralistic rhetoric. In fact, a contemporary reader of the debates might be "both disappointed and puzzled" at the lack of attention paid to the moral dimension.[34]

In his presidential rhetoric, Lincoln also relied heavily on non-moralistic arguments. Once again, Jeffrey Tulis's explanation—that Lincoln belonged within the "Old Way" of presidential rhetoric—is not adequate because other nineteenth-century presidents frequently used moralistic language in their rhetoric. As the coding results in figure 3 and table 7 demonstrate, Jackson, Van Buren, Tyler, Buchanan, and Andrew Johnson used moral and religious language more frequently than Lincoln in their Annual Addresses. Previous presidents had spoken moralistically. Given Lincoln's deep ethical beliefs regarding slavery, we might anticipate that he would follow in their footsteps. However, Lincoln's presidential rhetoric contains fewer moral and religious arguments than expected, given the moral nature of the political problems he confronted. In particular, Lincoln refrained from classifying slavery as a moral wrong in his presidential speeches and addresses. This change in rhetorical practices seems puzzling, but when the constraints of Lincoln's particular leadership situation are considered, Lincoln's restrained presidential rhetoric makes sense politically.

Lincoln's Political and Rhetorical Constraints
In the mid-nineteenth century, the United States witnessed a wave of reform movements, such as abolitionism, nativism, and temperance. These movements were all associated, in some way, with organized churches and can be characterized as examples of millennialism, or the utopian

vision of America as the New Jerusalem. While Lincoln was generally sympathetic to the ultimate aims of abolitionism and temperance, he strongly disproved of the movements' extreme rhetoric and moral pretentiousness. Indeed, when moral reform was attempted, Lincoln believed that "unassuming persuasion" was the best rhetorical strategy, stating in an 1842 temperance society speech that if a speaker commands a certain action, the listener will often "retreat within himself."[35]

On the contrary, in the view of mid-century reformers, "it was no longer necessary to restrain one's impatience in dealing with evil." But as a minority "dark horse" president who needed support from Democrats, Republicans, border-states citizens, Northerners, and Westerners alike, Lincoln did not enjoy the luxury of rhetorical license. The diversity of interests and factions contained within the Republican machine posed the greatest challenge to Lincoln's presidency; T. Harry Williams observed, "No polyglot army of an ancient emperor ever exhibited more variety than did the Republican Party in 1860."[36] The partisan restraint Lincoln faced can be sharply contrasted to Jefferson's political position during the embargo. As the unquestioned leader of the dominant Republicans, Jefferson possessed a firm control of his party and the federal government. The homogeneity of Jefferson's political base encouraged moral argumentation whereas the heterogeneity of Lincoln's Republican Party discouraged it.

While the diversity of views within the Republican Party was intense, all Republicans shared antislavery tendencies. Differences arose over the timing and implementation of slavery's eradication. The Conservatives recoiled at the reforming zeal of the Radicals and urged a slow process of emancipation, possibly followed by colonization. On the other hand, the Radicals vowed to drive the "slave traders from the national temple" immediately and urged the confiscation of "rebel" property and the inclusion of freed slaves in the army. When Lincoln became president, he was charged with the challenge of keeping both the Radical and Conservative factions within the Republican Party. The Radicals, or "Jacobins," were a particular problem for Lincoln. Historians disagree about the ideological cohesiveness of the Radicals, but it is clear that all Radicals were stringent and vocal abolitionists. In particular, the Radicals frequently exhibited a moralizing tendency in their public rhetoric. Antislavery militants emphasized the importance of moral purity in their public arguments and wanted to destroy slavery with revenge and passion.[37] As the driving force within the Republican Party, the Radicals possessed a great deal of political power. Lincoln could not ignore them and also could not associate closely with them. All of Lincoln's actions, particularly his public statements and rhetoric, faced careful scrutiny in an effort to determine the relative status of influence enjoyed by the Radicals versus the Conservatives.

Politically, Lincoln had to distance himself from the Radicals as much as possible while still maintaining a working relationship with men such as Charles Sumner and Salmon Chase. Many rumors circulated around Washington that Lincoln was a minion of the Radicals—or, even worse, their leader. To keep the Conservatives within the Republican Party, Lincoln could not risk being too closely associated with the Radical faction. Strategically, Lincoln could not adopt the moralistic rhetoric that was commonly attributed to the Radicals. By speaking too moralistically, Lincoln might have been mistaken as a Radical himself. This would have been a political nightmare for Lincoln—and would have certainly cost him reelection. Lincoln recalled the political, moral, and constitutional imitations of his situation in an April 4, 1864, letter to Albert Hodges:

> It was in the oath I took that I would, to the best of my ability, preserve, protect, and defend the Constitution of the United States. I could not take the office without taking the oath. Nor was it my view that I might take an oath to get power, and break the oath in using the power. I understood, too, that in ordinary civil administration this oath even forbade me to practically indulge my primary abstract judgment on the moral question of slavery. I had publicly declared this many times, and in many ways. And I aver that, to this day, I have done no official act in mere deference to my abstract judgment and feeling on slavery.[38]

In a particularly revealing statement, Lincoln theorized that the oath of office actually restrained him from judging slavery with a moral lens. Lincoln guarded his official actions with great care and paid scrupulous attention to the public justifications he chose to emphasize.

Lincoln faced great pressure from many abolitionist members of his party to infuse his rhetoric with moral condemnations against slavery. In general, the Radicals believed that Lincoln was indifferent to the moral issues of the war. In addition to his constitutional interpretation of the presidential oath, Lincoln had political reasons for holding back on such moral pronouncements. Besides fracturing the Republican Party, moralistic rhetoric could divide the Union further by agitating the border states and eventually driving them away to the Confederacy. It was reported that President Lincoln confessed he would like to have God on his side, but he *must* have Kentucky. Two days after the Union's defeat at Bull Run, Sen. Zachariah Chandler, Sen. Charles Sumner, and Vice Pres. Hannibal Hamlin urged Lincoln to turn the Civil War into a moral contest between freedom and slavery. As always, Lincoln listened but resisted their advice; the timing was grossly inappropriate for such radical statements. During the winter of 1861–62, Lincoln allowed Sumner to lecture him two or three times a week on his moral duty to eradicate slavery. Although Lincoln agreed with Sumner on most issues concerning slavery's eradication, they disagreed about when Lincoln should initiate executive action. Lincoln's interactions with the Radical Republicans adopted this familiar course: the Jacobins agitated for swift action while Lincoln resisted, waiting patiently to react at the opportune moment. As he stated famously in a letter to Hodges: "I claim not to have controlled events, but confess plainly that events have controlled me."[39]

Lincoln's rhetorical calculus was influenced by at least three political conditions. Because Lincoln faced an imminent political crisis in which public support was divided and sacrifice was anticipated, we might expect him to engage in heightened levels of moral appeals to influence opinion. Likewise, the Radical faction of the Republican Party expected Lincoln to denounce slavery as a moral wrong. However, the morally divisive issue of slavery threatened to divide his political party, and Lincoln needed to determine how to hold the diverse Republican factions together. Because of the divisions within the Republican Party, the political circumstances of Lincoln's situation recommended moral restraint. As a mid-nineteenth century president, Lincoln's greatest resource for power and authority rested with his political party. If the Republican Party divided over slavery, Lincoln's 1864 reelection would be unlikely. Throughout his presidency, Lincoln did encounter pressure from Radicals who expected him to characterize the Civil War as a moral crusade against the sins of Southern slaveholders. Despite their critical comments, Lincoln calculated that fracturing his party posed greater risks than not fulfilling the zealous moral expectations of the Radicals.

Lincoln's Rhetorical Restraint
Lincoln exhibited rhetorical restraint immediately after he won the presidency. For three months after the 1860 election, Lincoln did not issue

any public statements and made no formal addresses. Despite growing pressure that urged him to either placate the South or state his views on the Union, Lincoln remained silent, fully aware that the presidential electors did not meet until December 5. Members of his own party urged Lincoln not to speak; Joseph Medill warned Lincoln that giving a rousing "union saving speech" would indicate he was frightened by Southern threats and consequently demoralize the North: "He must keep his feet out of all such wolf traps." Lincoln heeded Medill's advice and did not speak publicly until he began his Inaugural trip to the nation's capital. Harry Jaffa has described Lincoln's silence at this time as "notable" and "impressive."[40]

Even though Lincoln knew he could not speak publicly about the moral injustice of slavery, he continued to evaluate relevant moral arguments in private. Indeed, throughout his presidency, moral considerations were never far from Lincoln's mind. In a note to himself written in early September 1862, now called his "Meditation on the Divine Will," Lincoln grappled with the religious implications of the conflict: "The will of God prevails. In great contests each party claims to act in accordance with the will of God. Both may be, and one must be wrong. God cannot be for, and against the same thing at the same time. . . . I am almost ready to say this is probably true—that God wills this contest, and wills that it shall not end yet. By his mere quiet power, on the minds of the now contestants, He could have either saved or destroyed the Union without a human contest. Yet the contest began. And having begun He could give the final victory to either side any day. Yet the contest proceeds."[41] Lincoln's private musing is remarkable not only because of its foreboding tone but because his religious awareness is so noticeably absent from his presidential rhetoric at this time. Lincoln wondered if God willed the war as a punishment for the American sin of slavery, but due to the deep divisions within his own party, he did not state this interpretation publicly. The meditation also substantiates the notion that Lincoln understood the importance of timing; he was "almost ready to say this is probably true." Until he could make such an important statement with confidence, Lincoln refrained from discussing God's role in the conflict.

On March 6, 1862, Lincoln began the first steps towards preparing the Union for the emancipation of the slaves. In a message to Congress released to the newspapers, Lincoln called for the voluntary abolishment of slavery. According to the details of the plan, if a state wished to participate in emancipation, the federal government would provide financial compensation. The message contained no moral or religious justification for emancipation. Instead, Lincoln hoped that the policy would prevent border states from leaving the Union to join the Southern rebellion: "The leaders of the existing insurrection entertain the hope that this government will ultimately be forced to acknowledge the independence of some part of the disaffected region. . . . To deprive them of this hope, substantially ends the rebellion; and the initiation of emancipation completely deprives them of it, as to all the states initiating it."[42] While some Radical Republicans found the message devoid of any moral purpose and viewed it as a slippery attempt to mollify abolitionists, Congress readily adopted the proposal into law. Because none of the border states accepted Lincoln's offer, no further discussion took place on the matter.

The most obvious piece of Lincoln's presidential rhetoric that is almost completely devoid of moral argumentation is the Emancipation Proclamation. As a document, the Emancipation Proclamation possessed enormous potential as a testimony of Lincoln's moral authority. When he presented the preliminary document to his cabinet before issuing it publicly on September 22, 1862, several members complained that it was dry, impassionate, and mild, utterly failing to reflect the feelings of the people and the moral sentiment of such an action. If not politically pragmatic, these criticisms were indeed accurate.

Lincoln rested his power to emancipate the slaves on his status as commander-in-chief rather than on a claim of moral righteousness or justice. Lincoln summoned his constitutional powers to make his case; he did not appeal to a symbolic, moral, or religious authority. The lack of moral sentiment in the proclamation should not be viewed as evidence that Lincoln issued the proclamation reluctantly. Rather, Lincoln understood that due to his political position, his constitutional authority provided him with a stronger justification for the exercise of power than any moral justification. Radicals, Conservatives, and Democrats readily disagreed about the moral import of emancipation, but Lincoln's constitutional powers to preserve and protect rested on solid ground.

Acknowledging Lincoln's strategic choices should not minimize his legacy as a moral leader. It is likely that Lincoln viewed emancipation as a moral and religious act. During a meeting in which Lincoln presented a draft of the proclamation to his cabinet, Lincoln admitted that he had promised God he would free the slaves if General Lee was driven back from Pennsylvania. Secretary Chase asked Lincoln to repeat his affirmation, and he complied.[43] Lincoln's personal reasons for emancipation differed from the public justification he chose to emphasize in the official document.

Richard Hofstadter recognized the surprising lack of moral argumentation in the Emancipation Proclamation, describing it as a document that possessed "all the moral grandeur of a bill of lading." Hofstadter's observation regarding the lack of moral argumentation is correct, but his implied condemnation of Lincoln is misplaced. In writing the proclamation, Lincoln wisely chose "function over form" and focused on affirming the constitutional justification of his actions. Lincoln had no other choice; Gabor Boritt concluded that Lincoln used "boring legalese language" in writing the proclamation because he correctly judged the "antiblack majorities required it."[44]

In the first draft of the document, originally released to the public on September 22, 1862, no morally based arguments were included. In the original proclamation, Lincoln called the emancipation a "practical measure" to end the rebellion of the slave states and made no mention of justice, morality, or God's will. In the final draft of the Emancipation Proclamation, issued on January 1, 1863, a sentence at the end of the document had been added: "And upon this act, sincerely believed to be an act of justice, warranted by the Constitution, upon military necessity, I invoke the considerate judgment of mankind, and the gracious favor of Almighty God."[45] In the official version of the decree, Lincoln did invoke God and called emancipation an "act of justice" but greatly diminished the overall moral force of the sentence by including the provision of "military necessity." Before Lincoln sent the final proclamation to the printer, he consulted his cabinet on December 30 for any final recommendations or changes. Lincoln ignored almost all of the substantive changes except one. Charles Sumner and Salmon Chase insisted upon the addition of the concluding sentence, calling the emancipation of slaves an "act of justice." Lincoln agreed to the small alteration, and consequently the Radicals felt they had contributed to the moral elevation of the document.[46]

Lincoln knew the proclamation was controversial enough in bland language and that adding too many moralistic or religious statements would only add fuel to the fire. Just six days after he issued the final decree in January, Lincoln wrote to Vice President Hamlin and remarked, "My expectations are not as sanguine as are those of some friends."[47] As a concession, Lincoln allowed the Radicals to include one reference of moral import to the end of the document but made sure the remainder of the decree described emancipation as a military act. The lack of moral argumentation did not go unnoticed. The *New York Times* observed that Lincoln had avoided the impulse to place the proclamation on "high moral grounds" and had instead used the constitutional commander-in-chief clause to substantiate his authority.[48]

Lincoln's qualms about emancipation were not unfounded. While many Northern Republicans lauded Lincoln's action, the mid-term elections in October and November of 1862 gave large victories to the Democrats in Pennsylvania, Ohio, Indiana, New York, New Jersey, Illinois, and Delaware, increasing the Democrats' share in the House of Representatives from 44 to 72. The *Chicago Sun Times,* a Democratic newspaper, called the proclamation a "monstrous usurpation, a criminal wrong, and an act of national suicide."[49] The proclamation helped Lincoln in New England, Michigan, and Kansas but hurt him elsewhere. Because of the Democratic electoral victories, many wondered if Lincoln might change his mind about formally issuing the emancipation decree on January 1, 1863. Lincoln responded not by revoking his promise but by carefully choosing his words in his 1862 Annual Address issued in December.

Lincoln's Second Annual Message served as a complement to the Emancipation Proclamation. Realizing that emancipation did not affect slaves in the border states and that as an act of war the proclamation could be reversed if he was not reelected, Lincoln provided moderate solutions to eradicate slavery. Fearing the demise of the Republican Party, Lincoln tempered emancipation with colonization to appease the fears of white Americans.[50] In his address, Lincoln proposed three constitutional amendments: financial restitution to states that abolished slavery, guaranteed freedom to escaped slaves, and congressional appropriations for the colonization of freed slaves.

The political purpose of the 1862 message was to ameliorate his image as a radical abolitionist. Lincoln was aware that his policy proposals, even if popular, might take years to enact. Despite the unlikelihood of success, Lincoln defended his program with zeal in the Annual Address, encouraged by rumors that Kentucky and Maryland might accept his offer of compensated emancipation. The tone of this address was more passionate than his earlier presidential rhetoric; David Donald compared his 1862 Annual Message to the stronger moral rhetoric he employed in the Senate campaign debates against Douglas.[51] While his language in the 1862 Annual Address contained more eloquence and emotion than his previous presidential efforts, Lincoln still refrained from making moral judgments. Instead, Lincoln's rhetoric offered solutions to eradicate slavery but avoided answering whether such solutions were humane or just. While his arguments transcended the practical dictates of policy, they did not discuss the morality of the issue at hand. Although the conclusion of his 1862 Annual Address was poignant, Lincoln carefully avoided moral judgments:

> Fellow citizens, we cannot escape history. We of this Congress and this administration, will be remembered in spite of ourselves. No personal significance, or insignificance, can spare one or another of us. The fiery trial through which we pass, will light us down, in honor or dishonor, to the latest generation. We say we are for the Union. The world will not forget that we say this. We know how to save the Union. The world knows we do know how to save it. We—even we here—hold the power, and bear the responsibility. In giving freedom to the slave, we assure freedom to the free—honorable alike in what we give, and what we preserve.[52]

In this passage, Lincoln carefully avoided any moral justification for emancipating the slaves and refrained from calling slavery a moral wrong. In support of this reading, David Zarefsky argues that the restrained rhetoric of the 1862 Annual Address showcases Lincoln as a practical politician and that the ringing conclusion is directed towards his political endorsement of proposed amendments advocating colonization.[53] Any moral message contained in the final paragraph is cautiously implied. Lincoln's rhetoric intimated that history will make its own moral judgments. Even when Lincoln spoke inspirationally, he refused to condemn the South. Lincoln's "historical posterity" conclusion in his Second Annual Address differs from an explicit moral argument, which might have emphasized the justice or moral rightness of emancipation. In 1862, as a minority president trying to keep his party together, Lincoln was right not to issue categorical moral verdicts in his public statements.

In 1863, Lincoln began releasing response papers that addressed controversial issues surrounding the war. In protest of curtailments in freedom of speech and the suspension of the writ of habeas corpus, a group of New York Democrats led by Erastus Corning, the president of the New York Central Railroad, adopted resolutions condemning expanded executive actions. Deciding that these resolutions provided him an ample opportunity to defend his actions and shape public opinion, Lincoln took up the pen and responded, sending a copy of his essay to the *New York Tribune*, where it was promptly published and eventually distributed as a pamphlet read by an estimated ten million people. Lincoln's arguments were controlled and even-handed; he justified his suspension of civil liberties on the Constitution itself, which allowed for such measures if the "public safety may require it." Lincoln did not employ any moral or principled arguments beyond his interpretation of the Constitution. Instead, he appealed dispassionately to the force of necessity. Lincoln's paper was received remarkably well by prominent Republicans, who believed his choice of words were appropriate, moderate, and timely. In a subsequent letter to James Conkling, also released widely to newspapers, Lincoln defended the policies of his administration using arguments that appealed to all factions within the party. In the public letter, Lincoln issued a spirited defense of the emancipation of slaves but argued that their release rested on their status as wartime property, which "may be taken when needed."[54] In no instance did Lincoln engage in a moralistic or religious defense of his executive actions.

By the fall of 1863, Lincoln wanted to issue a statement that addressed the broader implications and concerns of the war. Almost all of his public statements had been directed to justifying his specific wartime decisions and policies. Although his mind was never far from the broader and principled implications of the conflict, an opportunity to express these sentiments was elusive. Massachusetts senator Charles Sumner urged Lincoln to accept "any subsequent chance" to speak about the war's aims. Lincoln was more discerning than that. After the 1863 elections, in which the Republicans made a clean sweep in many statewide races, Lincoln saw an opportunity to make a general statement about the rebellion at the dedication of the Gettysburg battlefield. The dedication of the graves at Gettysburg would draw a large crowd, with important Republican Party notables attending, particularly representatives from the two opposing factions in Pennsylvania. Gettysburg provided Lincoln with an appropriate setting for meaningful remarks, and also enabled him to engage in some "political fence-mending."[55]

In this period of Republican control and authority, Lincoln could now afford to speak more broadly about the ideals affected by the Civil War. Lincoln's memorable rhetoric at Gettysburg served the purpose of addressing the deeper causes and ramifications of the war; he did not discuss any timely, controversial issues. Remarks concerning the Emancipation Proclamation, citizenship for African Americans, slavery, and colonization were missing from his brief speech. Instead, Lincoln used the Gettysburg Address as an opportunity to discuss publicly the intangible principles being contested in the war. In keeping with the common rhetorical practices of a eulogy, Lincoln praised the dead in an attempt to inspire the audience.[56] Lincoln's speech at Gettysburg did not concern justice or morality as much as his confirmation of the notion that all men were created equal. The address is primarily concerned with the topic contained in its first and last sentences: the unique political ideals of the United States and the republican government that perpetuates them. According to Edwin Black, Lincoln at Gettysburg focused on "what he knew" rather than reciting "divine intentions" or issuing "cosmic judgments."[57] Lincoln wanted to incorporate the political principles contained within the Declaration of Independence into his reading of the Constitution, thus combining epideictic rhetoric with deliberative arguments.

It would be an exaggeration to describe the Gettysburg Address as completely devoid of moral and religious influence. Ronald White gives a convincing account of the implicit religious and biblical meanings contained in several of the speech's memorable phrases.[58] However, in contrast to his Second Inaugural, Lincoln chose not to emphasize explicit religious or moral argumentation to articulate his points in Gettysburg. Rather than appealing to a symbolic, moral authority, Lincoln relied upon his constitutional authority as president to reinterpret the nation's governing principles through the expanded lens of the Declaration of Independence. The presidential oath to "preserve, protect, and defend" the Constitution provided Lincoln with the requisite authority to substantiate his reading. In particular, the power of the presidential office gave newfound legitimacy to this interpretation of the Declaration as the guiding text of the nation's political principles. Former slaves, women's suffrage activists, abolitionists, and literary authors had already begun to rethink the meaning of the Declaration of Independence prior to Lincoln's speech at Gettysburg.[59] But as Garry Wills notes, it was Lincoln's words that "remade America." Lincoln's ability to reformulate the American canon is testimony to the power of his well-crafted rhetoric. The combination of carefully chosen words and the constitutional authority of the presidential office itself enabled the transformative capacity of Lincoln's rhetoric at Gettysburg.

Lincoln avoided any mention of slavery's immorality in his address. Instead, Lincoln transcended notions of moral righteousness to develop an argument about freedom and equality. Moral arguments often divide citizens into "evil" versus "good" characterizations; Lincoln's purpose at Gettysburg was to place all human beings on the plateau of universal equality. His rhetoric concerning equality certainly applied to the practice of slavery but also implied that both Northerners and Southerners were equal citizens of the perpetual Union.[60] Even when Lincoln discussed first principles in a eulogy, his arguments emphasized unity rather than divisiveness, an appropriate rhetorical response conditioned by the political constraints he faced. His only explicit religious reference in the speech was the extemporaneous addition of the words "under God" in the concluding sentence. Lincoln's mention of God served to emphasize the unifying principles of the nation's creed. Only a nation held together by God could have "a new birth of freedom." Lincoln's careful words at Gettysburg reflected an understanding that overzealous concern for "timeless eulogistic rhetoric" without paying attention to situational demands can result in "meaningless ceremonial prose." Lincoln avoided this trap and adapted his arguments to the political exigencies surrounding him. The Republican newspaper accounts of the address, which were uniformly positive, reflected Lincoln's careful attention to balance and his desire to "mend political fences" with his remarks.[61]

After Gettysburg, rumors began to surface that Salmon Chase, the secretary of the treasury, would challenge Lincoln for the 1864 Republican nomination for president. By November, Lincoln's informants reported that Chase, growing in popularity, had a chance to win all of the Northwest delegates. Radicals at the outer fringes of the Republican Party would certainly support Chase's insurgent candidacy in 1864, but everything in Lincoln's power had to be done to keep the more "moderate" Radicals within the fold. Even the electoral threat from Chase did not entice Lincoln to moralize; his Third Annual Address continued to present the administration's policies in a restrained, legalistic manner that avoided moral argumentation: "The constitutional obligation of the United States to guarantee to every State in the Union a republican form of government and to protect the State in the cases stated is explicit and full." Overall, the address made more policy concessions to the Radical faction.[62] By including emancipation as a stipulation for reconstruction and requiring Southern rebels to pledge an oath of loyalty to receive a full pardon, Lincoln gained approval from the Radicals, which eventually helped him secure the party's nomination.

After the National Committee of the Republican Party met in February of 1864 to discuss the presidential nomination and 80 percent of the attendees, mostly federal officeholders appointed by the president, registered support for Lincoln, Chase withdrew from the contest. Lincoln received his official nomination in June while the extremist radicals orchestrated a "shadow convention" in which they nominated John C. Fremont for president. Radical Republicans of noteworthy stature, such as Greeley, withdrew their support for the poorly attended "alternative" convention. In the late summer, upon hearing that the conservative Republicans were dissatisfied with recent attempts to placate the Radicals, Lincoln replaced several patronage appointees with Conservatives and firmed up additional support for his candidacy.

In September, news came that General Sherman had evacuated Atlanta. The victory in Atlanta made the Democratic political platform, based upon a promise to end the war, look weak. Because of prudent posturing within his own party and the inopportune peace platform adopted by the Democrats, Lincoln's 1864 reelection prospects seemed favorable. He won the election easily, with 55 percent of the popular vote and 212 electoral votes out of a possible 233.

After the election, Lincoln selected Salmon Chase as chief justice of the Supreme Court. Besides believing Chase possessed the best qualifications for the job, Lincoln's appointment of Chase was strategic. In return for the appointment, the president hoped that the Radicals would not object to his future legislative proposals. When the new legislative session opened in December of 1864, Congress responded favorably to Lincoln. The president's critics, from both the conservative and radical wings of the party, seemed to undergo a change of heart. The Radicals were pleased by the appointment of Chase, and the Conservatives did not believe it was "politically expedient" to attack a president who had just won a resounding electoral victory. While not all of the divisions within his party had been erased, it seemed as though Lincoln's leadership had mitigated the tensions that plagued the Republican organization.[63]

The Second Inaugural Address

It is not a coincidence that Lincoln gave the most explicitly moral and religious speech of his presidential career after his political authority had been secured. Ronald C. White described Lincoln's position at the time of the Second Inaugural as politically "vindicated."[64] Free from worrying about the burden of reelection, Lincoln drafted an address that articulated his innermost contemplations about the war. During his first term, the Radicals often urged Lincoln to discuss publicly the true causes of the war. Lincoln finally answered their calls in the Second Inaugural Address, but his response was not what they anticipated. Even when Lincoln chose to speak morally, he kept his distance from those in his party who demanded a condemnation of the South. Like his earlier rhetorical restraint, Lincoln's moralism served his leadership purposes.

In March of 1865, Lincoln looked towards Reconstruction as his next political challenge. The war's end was in sight (General Lee would surrender in only five weeks' time) and slavery had been routed. Lincoln now faced the task of garnering support for his Reconstruction policies. As president, Lincoln could use moral and religious argumentation to transcend difficult circumstances and emphasize more permanent, immutable principles in his rhetoric. The divisions within the Republican Party had not disappeared altogether but had lessened considerably. The Second Inaugural was the most appropriate opportunity for Lincoln to offer a moral and religious interpretation of the war. As detailed below in his letter to Thurlow Weed, Lincoln was aware of the political risks involved in giving a speech addressing "timeless markers."[65] But the message of the speech—that both the North and the South bore the responsibility for the war—served his political purposes quite well. In the address, Lincoln spoke from a strong moral position but did not take sides or condemn the Southern states. He did not seek to exonerate factions or point fingers at the guilty. Rather, Lincoln called the audience not to judge but to *be judged*.[66]

As observed by Edwin Black, Lincoln did not "propose himself" in his rhetoric but relied upon his arguments to make his point. In the Second Inaugural, Lincoln's withdrawal enabled God's role in the force of history to dominate his message. Although every president before Lincoln had invoked God or the Deity in his inaugural address, only John Quincy Adams had chosen to quote directly from the Bible. In the Second Inaugural alone, Lincoln quoted or paraphrased four biblical passages.[67]

Because the North enjoyed the commercial fruits of slavery, blame for the war did not fall squarely upon the shoulders of the South. Both sides willingly engaged in war, but according to Lincoln, the extent and ferocity of the conflict was attributable to a punitive higher power, reminiscent of the Old Testament:

If we shall suppose that American Slavery is one of those of-
fences which, in the providence of God, must needs come, but
which, having continued through His appointed time, He now
wills to remove, and that He gives to both North and South,
this terrible war, as the woe due to those by whom the offence
came, shall we discern therein any departure from those divine
attributes which the believers in a Living God always ascribe
to Him? Fondly do we hope—fervently do we pray—that this
mighty scourge of war may speedily pass away. Yet, if God wills
that it continue, until all the wealth piled by the bond-man's
two hundred and fifty years of unrequited toil shall be sunk, and
until every drop of blood drawn with the lash, shall be paid by
another drawn with the sword, as was said three thousand years
ago, so still it must be said "the judgments of the Lord, are true
and righteous altogether."[68]

Lincoln's intimation—that the Civil War was a battle waged by God to
punish the sin of slavery—puzzled many of the listeners, including the
Radicals. They had urged Lincoln to draw upon God's will as a source of
political persuasion but never imagined he would use the Bible to imply
that the blood of the war was a product of God's retribution. Lincoln's
reasoning in his Second Inaugural originated in his 1862 private note
now commonly entitled "Meditation on the Divine Will." For at least
three years, Lincoln had contemplated the possibility that God "wills
this contest, and wills that it shall not end yet" but waited until the
Second Inaugural to reveal what he believed were the "true causes" of
the interminable war. In the speech, Lincoln spoke about the historical,
religious, and moral impact of the war, subjects he had discussed previously only in private.[69]

In his first term, Lincoln refrained from issuing explicitly moralistic or
religious interpretations of slavery and emancipation. When he finally
did engage in moral argumentation, his rhetoric avoided intensifying
divisiveness by refusing to take sides. Instead of portraying God as tribal
or territorial, Lincoln emphasized the role of God as a unifier.[70] Even
Lincoln's moralism sought to unite the North and the South rather than
condemn one side as evil. According to Lincoln's speech, God gave "both
the North and South this terrible war." Therefore, both are guilty in the
eyes of the Lord, and both have sinned.

While Lincoln did speak in a moralistic tongue, he refused to de-nounce the South as morally responsible for the Civil War. There was no declaration that the "righteous" had conquered the sinners. Rather than assigning blame to one region of the country, Lincoln saw the purposes of a higher power at work. In the Second Inaugural, Lincoln attempted to enhance his authority as president by offering a new interpretation of the war that rose above the narrow-minded, localized concerns of his critics. The Second Inaugural suggested that as president, Lincoln viewed the war in a wholly unique way. Situated above the particular, and representing the entire nation, Lincoln used his speech to assert an independent interpretation of the Civil War. With the war near its end, Lincoln's appeals for strong executive powers based upon his con-stitutional authority to preserve and protect would begin to lose their force.[71] In his Second Inaugural, Lincoln found a new source of authority based on moral and religious principle. This extra-constitutional power resembled the pedagogical authority George Washington summoned in his Farewell Address. In this respect, Lincoln relied upon the presidential role of moral spokesman that had been established seventy-five years earlier by Washington.

Because of his assassination only a month later, it is difficult to assess the political effects of Lincoln's Second Inaugural. Most newspapers responded to the address in a "respectful" yet "somewhat puzzled" manner, probably unsure about how to assess the speech's deeply religious arguments.[72] Overall, the response was mixed. The *New York Times* complained, "He makes no boasts of what he has done, or promises of what he will do," and the *New York Herald* classified the Second Inaugural as a "little speech of glittering generalities used only to fill in the program." Other papers, such as the *Philadelphia Inquirer* and the *Washington Daily National Intelligencer,* offered more positive commentary.[73] Lincoln understood that once the Radicals figured out the meaning of Lincoln's words, it was altogether probable that they would become irritated. In a letter to Thurlow Weed written on March 15, Lincoln reflected on the address: "I expect the latter [Second Inaugural] to wear as well as—perhaps better than—anything I have produced; but I believe it is not immediately popular. Men are not flattered by being shown that there has been a difference of purpose between the Almighty and them. . . . It is a truth which I thought needed to be told; and as whatever of humiliation there is in it, falls most directly on myself, I thought others might afford for me to tell it."[74] Lincoln knew the speech involved some political risks and acknowledged that he might face humiliation because of his frank words. However, with his strong reelection victory and diminished intra-partisan strife, Lincoln reasoned that "others might afford" him the opportunity to discuss "a truth which . . . needed to be told."

Both Lincoln and Jefferson were morally principled politicians whose strong beliefs guided their political leadership. Despite this similarity, Lincoln and Jefferson differed in how they applied their philosophical beliefs to executive leadership. Believing that the president's role as the nation's moral educator was inappropriate, Jefferson refused to adapt his rhetoric to fit the demands of the political situation. Even though Lincoln's deep moral beliefs motivated his actions, he crafted his rhetoric strategically to serve the higher political ends he aimed to accomplish. Lincoln used his rhetoric as a tool to increase his authority in a way that Jefferson did not. Both Lincoln and Jefferson exercised moral leadership, but Lincoln's willingness to accommodate political circumstances ultimately strengthened his political authority to a greater extent than Jefferson's efforts. Lincoln consistently used his rhetoric to enhance his existing position. In contrast, Jefferson's failure to moralize during the embargo was a missed opportunity. Lincoln made the moral possibilities and political constraints of the presidency work together rather than in opposition to one another.

JOHN F. KENNEDY: MORAL RESTRAINT AND CIVIL RIGHTS

John F. Kennedy's presidential rhetoric is known for its inspirational tone and powerful language. While Kennedy emphasized the obligations and responsibilities of citizenship, his presidential rhetoric did not appeal frequently to moral or religious principles. As figure 3 shows, amongst post–New Deal presidents, Kennedy's rate of moral and religious rhetoric ranked second to last—only Bill Clinton moralized less frequently. To examine Kennedy's moral restraint, this analysis focuses on his civil rights rhetoric. During the first two and a half years of his administration, under pressure from southern Democrats, Kennedy refrained from moralizing about civil rights. The strategic restraint of Kennedy's rhetoric from 1961 and 1962 will be explored, as well as his decision to break his "moral silence" in a televised address to the nation after the desegregation of the University of Alabama in June 1963.

Kennedy's 1960 Campaign Rhetoric: The Promise of Moral Leadership

Kennedy's moral restraint in his presidential civil rights rhetoric is pronounced because his 1960 general campaign speeches—especially those given in the North—were decidedly moralistic in tone. In his campaign addresses, Kennedy repeatedly contended that racial discrimination was wrong and that as president, he would act as the moral leader of the nation with regards to civil rights issues. Eisenhower was not popular amongst civil rights leaders, even though his record on race relations was respectable: he oversaw the passage of two civil rights bills and enforced school desegregation. Much of Eisenhower's unpopularity was due to his failure to inspire civil rights leaders rhetorically. Eisenhower's actions indicated that he believed in the cause of black Americans, but his public statements were often dry and legalistic.[75]

In contrast, Kennedy laid out an energized vision of the presidency, motivated by progress, change, and activism. In an address given to the National Press Club on January 14, 1960, candidate Kennedy emphasized the moral components of presidential leadership: "But the White House is not only the center of political leadership. It must be the center of moral leadership—a 'bully pulpit,' as Theodore Roosevelt described it. For only the president represents the national interest. . . . Roosevelt fulfilled the role of moral leadership. So did Wilson and Lincoln, Truman and Jackson and Teddy Roosevelt. They led the people as well as the government—they fought for great ideals as well as bills. And the time has come to demand that leadership again."[76] In other campaign speeches, Kennedy reiterated his dedication to moral leadership. At a stop in Springfield, Ohio, on October 17, Kennedy remarked, "The next president himself must set the moral tone, and I refer not only to his language, but his actions in office. For the Presidency, as Franklin Roosevelt himself has said, is preeminently a place of moral leadership."

Later in his campaign, Kennedy merged his strong opinions about the importance of moral leadership with his statements on civil rights. In a campaign speech in New York City on June 23, 1960, Kennedy asserted, "Moral persuasion by the president can be more effective than force in ending discrimination against Negroes." In Los Angeles on September 9, Kennedy went further in describing the moral responsibilities of the president in the civil rights arena:

> When our next President takes office in January, he must be prepared to move forward in the field of human rights in three

general areas: as legislative leader, as Chief Executive, and as the center of moral power in the United States. . . . He must exert the great moral and educational force of his office to help bring equal access to public facilities from churches to lunch counters, and to support the right of every American to stand up for his rights, even if on occasion he must sit down for them. For only the President, not the Senate and not the House and not the Supreme Court, in a real sense, only the President can create the understanding and tolerance necessary as the spokesman for all the American people, as the symbol of the moral imperative upon which any free society is based.[77]

By stating that the president must exert the "great moral and educational force of his office" in the realm of civil rights, Kennedy intimated that he would continue to engage in inspirational rhetoric once in office. Kennedy also indicated that the president was uniquely situated for this role. He seemed to embrace the moral responsibilities of the office and welcomed the opportunity to elevate civil rights discourse in the United States.

During the 1960 general campaign, Kennedy's motivations for engaging in moralistic rhetoric originated from political concerns. Harris Wofford commented that Kennedy "wanted to win the election and also liked to do the right thing." During the 1960 election, political circumstances enabled Kennedy to achieve both ends. In fact, Kennedy's adoption of the moral leadership role was so pronounced, it may have served the strategic purpose of obscuring the fact that during the campaign, he almost never endorsed specific ideas for new legislation to prevent racial discrimination.[78] The powerful symbolism of Kennedy's moralistic statements overshadowed his anemic policy commitments.

Although initially hesitant about Kennedy's true devotion to the cause and his prior record on race, civil rights leaders seized upon his rhetorical campaign promises and believed they had finally found a candidate who would not only sign executive orders and legislation but also serve as a national spokesman for their cause. Morally based leadership could enable the president to become a national educator on civil rights. After the 1960 election, Martin Luther King Jr. made it clear that civil rights leaders would hold Kennedy to his promises of moral leadership. In a February 4, 1961, article in the *Nation,* King argued that President Kennedy could make a difference in the struggle for civil rights by continuing to lead by "moral persuasion." For most of his presidency, civil rights activists waited for Kennedy to fulfill the moralistic promises he made in his presidential campaign.

The Political Circumstances of Kennedy's Moral Restraint

Because of his campaign rhetoric's moralistic tone, black leaders and liberal activists had high hopes that Kennedy would serve as a moral leader in the civil rights movement. However, during Kennedy's presidency, civil rights remained a divisive issue with moral overtones that threatened to fracture the Democratic Party. For the first two and a half years of his presidential term, political constraints inhibited Kennedy's actions. In particular, a strong moral stance on civil rights ran the risk of jeopardizing his legislative agenda. Like Lincoln, the political circumstances of Kennedy's leadership suggested that moral restraint was the best approach. Martin Luther King Jr. recognized the comparable political limitations of Kennedy's and Lincoln's situations and conceded that the two presidents were "tormented by a similar dilemma."[79] Throughout most of his presidency, Kennedy crafted his rhetoric to meet these strategic considerations. Until June of 1963, Kennedy refrained from moral pronouncements on civil rights. When Kennedy did moralize in 1963, he paid a political price, suffering a loss in public approval that would have made his 1964 reelection campaign an uphill battle.

During the 1960 campaign, Kennedy projected the image of a president who could speak moralistically, but upon reaching the White House, his advisors judged that in the early years of his presidency, aggressive civil rights leadership would divide the country and shatter the Democratic Party. A December 30, 1960, memo from advisor Harris Wofford to Kennedy recommended "little or no legislation this year . . . and a large measure of executive action" regarding civil rights. Given Kennedy's promises in the 1960 campaign, this decision might have been "morally questionable" but was "politically unassailable." Kennedy concurred with these political assessments.[80] Instead of lobbying Congress for comprehensive anti-discrimination legislation, Kennedy pursued civil rights from the executive office by hiring African Americans in federal agencies, establishing a Committee on Equal Employment Opportunity, abolishing the poll tax, and fighting discrimination (in a limited sense) within public housing. None of these unilateral executive actions required strong rhetorical persuasion from the White House. Kennedy could pursue a moderate, yet quiet, civil rights agenda without engaging in strong moral appeals. Kennedy's restraint averted condemnation from southern Democrats and did not alienate northern liberals or moderates. Civil rights leaders were disappointed with the president's lack of moral leadership and believed that Kennedy treated racism more as a political problem rather than a moral struggle. The moral promises of the 1960 campaign raised expectations amongst civil rights supporters that went unfulfilled throughout most of Kennedy's presidency. In particular, Martin Luther King Jr. urged Kennedy to demonstrate his "personal and moral" commitment to civil rights.[81] King's interest in Kennedy's public demonstration of his commitment stemmed from the concept that the president can utilize symbolism in civil rights leadership and serve a pedagogical function. Such symbolism has the power to set the stage for policy innovations and persuade the public.[82]

Kennedy feared that if he pushed Congress on civil rights legislation in 1961 and 1962, his policy program would be received dead on arrival by a conservative coalition of Republicans and southern Democrats, and consequently his legislative leadership on other matters would be stymied. The voting patterns in January 1961 in the Rules Committee indicated that no amount of presidential pressure could persuade Congress to pass a meaningful civil rights package. The president could either fight for bold legislation and lose his entire policy program or subordinate his civil rights promises. By the spring of 1961, Kennedy could not afford to move ahead on civil rights legislation in the near future. Much of his proposed domestic agenda made it through Congress, but with small margins. If he wanted to pursue his New Frontier agenda, no votes could be sacrificed.

In Congress, Kennedy squared off against Sen. James Eastland of Mississippi, chair of the Judiciary Committee, and Rep. Howard W. Smith of Tennessee, the head of the southern-dominated and powerful Rules Committee in the House. The strength of the conservative coalition in Congress was stronger than ever. According to the 1962 edition of the *Congressional Quarterly Almanac*, northern and southern Democrats split on 40 percent of the roll calls in 1960 and 33 percent of the votes in 1961. By the time Kennedy took office, the threat was not that southern Democrats fractured the party but that the Republican Party had become a viable option in the South. As the South changed from a rural to more urban economy, the conservative economic policies of the Republicans began to look more attractive to southerners.[83] Preventing a southern exodus from the Democratic Party became a serious political consideration for Kennedy.

Kennedy's Rhetoric of Moral Restraint

Although the division within the Democratic Party encouraged Kennedy to treat civil rights gingerly, he could not ignore events that demanded his attention. In the spring of 1961, several Freedom Riders encountered violence throughout Alabama. When one of Robert Kennedy's assistants was beaten in Montgomery, the Kennedy administration decided to dispatch federal forces to the city. Despite the fact that five hundred federal marshals were situated in an American city to preserve the peace, Kennedy's only public response to the incident was answering a question at a press conference in which he stated that all individuals who travel "should enjoy the full constitutional protection given to them by the law and by the Constitution."[84] Kennedy's condemnation of the violence rested upon legal, not moral, reasoning. The president made no public address to the nation on the issue, and the failure of the president to serve a pedagogical function disappointed civil rights leaders. Activists came to the White House to press Kennedy to show stronger support for the freedom rides and urged him to "say something about the moral issue." According to advisor Harris Wofford, the impetus to provide moral leadership at this point angered Kennedy, who considered his support on civil rights more aggressive than any previous president in American history.[85]

Due to his fast-approaching foreign trip, Kennedy did not want to take a strong rhetorical stance on civil rights. In preparing for his June meetings with Khrushchev, DeGaulle, and MacMillan, Kennedy thought it best to minimize the violence that had occurred in Alabama. At this point, civil rights was just another political issue for Kennedy, and he feared that the controversy surrounding the Freedom Rides might damage his ability to negotiate international agreements. After the debacle at the Bay of Pigs, Kennedy hoped to use his international trip to reestablish his credibility as a world leader. The Soviet Union still utilized the 1957 image of federal troops in Little Rock as a "propaganda chip," and Kennedy did not want to provide further fuel for Khrushchev.[86]

Kennedy escaped from making a national speech on civil rights in 1961 but found himself forced into a more difficult bind in 1962. Kennedy began the year cautiously with his State of the Union speech. In this address, Kennedy dedicated three paragraphs to civil rights. In comparison to Kennedy's 1961 State of the Union Address, in which he only mentioned civil rights once, his 1962 speech gave considerable attention to the issue. However, the 1962 State of the Union did not contain any moral pronouncements or inspirational rhetoric. Resembling Lincoln, Kennedy appealed to his strong constitutional authority, emphasizing the effectiveness of pursuing civil rights through a strong exercise of executive powers that insured all Americans were afforded their rights: "This administration has shown as never before how much could be done through the full use of Executive powers—through the enforcement of laws already passed by Congress—through persuasion, negotiation, and litigation, to secure the constitutional rights of all: the right to vote, the right to travel without hindrance across State lines, and the right to free public education."[87] In this passage, Kennedy offered a legalistic defense of civil rights and also intimated that Congress had already passed the relevant legislation needed to ensure the individual liberties in question. Kennedy removed himself from the burden of pushing for additional civil rights legislation from a recalcitrant Congress. According to Kennedy, all the pieces were already in place, and as president, he was fulfilling his constitutional duty to execute the laws fairly and justly. The political reality was that large portions of Kennedy's domestic program had not yet passed Congress, thus making any bold statement on civil rights strategically imprudent. Furthermore, in early 1962, Kennedy's proposal to create a Department of Urban Affairs went down in defeat by a resounding 264–150 vote in the House. Without the support of southern Democrats in Congress, Kennedy found his legislative leadership quite ineffectual.[88]

The 1962 elections brought civil rights more attention. Kennedy would have been more than happy to abstain from any public statements on civil rights until after the mid-terms, but a racial controversy at the University of Mississippi concerning the admission of an African American student, James Meredith, prevented Kennedy from complete silence. After months of legal battles, on September 10, 1962, the Supreme Court ordered Meredith's admission to Ole Miss. On the fourth attempt to register Meredith at the university, riots broke out and federal marshals responded with tear gas and sniper fire. The Mississippi National Guard and federal troops finally prevailed, but not before two rioters were killed and hundreds injured.

Before the rioting began in Mississippi, Kennedy gave a televised address to the American people to explain why federal troops had been sent to preserve the peace in Oxford. It was clear from Kennedy's rhetoric that his legalistic arguments were designed to address southern concerns. In the speech, Kennedy did not state that the admission of Meredith to the University of Mississippi was just, moral, or right. Instead, Kennedy argued that even though Mississippians might not like it, the law dictated that they must accept black students on state campuses: "Americans are free, in short, to disagree with the law but not to disobey it. For in a government of laws and not of men, no man, however prominent or powerful, and no mob, however unruly or boisterous, is entitled to defy a court of law." To convince southerners that desegregation was not a northern policy imposed upon them, Kennedy listed all of the U.S. Court of Appeals judges from southern states who ruled that Meredith must be admitted to Ole Miss. At one point in the speech, Kennedy lauded Mississippians for their great "tradition of honor and courage won on the field of battle and on the gridiron as well as the University campus." According to Kennedy's rhetoric, there was no great moral lesson to be learned from this incident. In fact, Kennedy urged the speedy resolution of the crisis, stating, "There is in short no reason why the books on this case cannot now be quickly and quietly closed in the manner directed by the court." During the 1960 campaign, Kennedy disparaged Eisenhower's handling of Little Rock, but his 1962 University of Mississippi speech strongly resembled Eisenhower's rhetorical appeals to the primacy of law and constitutionality. Additionally, Kennedy's speech also strengthened the connection between domestic civil rights and international stability, warning citizens of Mississippi that "the eyes of the Nation and all of the world are upon you and upon all of us."[89] Kennedy had stressed this delicate relationship before in his civil rights rhetoric and seized upon a nationwide audience to make his international concerns known.

While civil rights leaders believed that Kennedy handled the Ole Miss situation well, they criticized his September 30, 1962, speech to the nation. In particular, they were disappointed that Kennedy had confined himself to a "law and order" argument and had not defined the admission of James Meredith as a moral issue. Instead, Kennedy had spoken patronizingly of football stars and war heroes. Martin Luther King Jr. stated that Kennedy's speech "made Negroes feel like pawns in a white man's political game."[90] Furthermore, the fusion of domestic civil rights and international relations angered activists, who believed that Kennedy depreciated the importance of racial discrimination as an issue deserving attention in its own right.

The disappointed reaction of civil rights leaders was understandable. Even though presidents often do not serve as the dominant actors in formulating civil rights policy, they serve an important function of setting the broader governmental agenda and initiating public policy.[91] At this point in his presidency, Kennedy had failed to live up to the rhetorical promises he made during his 1960 campaign. Giving moral weight to the cause of civil rights elevates the president from his constitutional and political roles and can give agenda-setting statements a better chance to instigate legislative action. It also can serve the purpose of transforming public opinion. Civil rights activists undoubtedly wanted to hear Kennedy define civil rights as a moral issue for their own satisfaction, but the primary motivation rested with the calculation that moral arguments could move the issue forward politically and add another potentially powerful dimension to it. The hope that Kennedy could push civil rights to the forefront of the agenda coincided with activists' plea that a public demonstration of moral leadership was needed from the nation's chief executive.

June of 1963: The End of Moral Restraint
During the first two years of his presidency, Kennedy used his constitutional authority and executive powers to promote civil rights quietly. In 1963, the political climate of the civil rights movement began to change. A more aggressive strain of civil rights activists emerged, and they made it clear they had grown tired of waiting for concessions. Even more moderate leaders started to complain that the defense of freedom abroad was futile if the defense for freedom at home remained weak.[92] In response to their disappointment, the organized mainstream civil rights movement promised to increase non-violent demonstrations and protests in 1963 as part of a concentrated effort to secure strong legislation. King conceded that unless racial tensions reached a more dangerous level, the president might never become actively engaged or initiate significant action.[93]

As civil rights leaders grew restless, the 1964 presidential election began to loom in front of Kennedy. With Gov. Nelson Rockefeller of New York as a likely Republican candidate, Kennedy began worrying about losing northern black votes.[94] Furthermore, liberal Republicans in the Senate issued a press release in late January 1963 that criticized Kennedy's lack of attention to civil rights. Even though GOP liberals represented a small faction of the Republican Party, their disparagement indicated that Kennedy was vulnerable to criticism on civil rights as the 1964 election approached. Kennedy began to feel threatened by a likely opponent in the upcoming election and liberal Republican senators who clamored to take the lead on civil rights legislation. As this political threat intensified, the temptation to take a strong stand on the issue increased for Kennedy. This political challenge did not exist in a vacuum. The divisiveness within the Democratic Party had not subsided. Consequently, Kennedy faced a difficult choice in 1963. He could either continue to restrain his rhetoric and risk losing northern votes in 1964 or moralize and face condemnation from the South. Kennedy chose to take a risk and engage in moral argumentation. This decision generated adverse political consequences for Kennedy and his impending reelection bid.

By early February, Kennedy decided to send a civil rights message to Congress, asking them for legislation. The reasons for Kennedy's decision were political and strategic.[95] By sending legislation to Congress, Kennedy could deflect the increasing criticism of both black leaders and liberal Republicans. In his message, Kennedy included his strongest presidential rhetoric to date regarding civil rights: "Race discrimination hampers our economic growth by preventing maximum development and utilization of our manpower. It hampers our world leadership by contradicting at home the message we preach abroad. . . . Above all, it is wrong. Therefore, let it be clear, in our own hearts and minds, that it is not merely because of the Cold War, and not merely because of the economic waste of discrimination, that we are committed to achieving true equality of opportunity. The basic reason is because it is right." For the first time, Kennedy's presidential rhetoric intimated a moral concern. The notion that discrimination is "wrong" and that true equality is "right" was purposefully included by Kennedy to satisfy black leaders. Louis Martin, the highest-ranking black official in the Democratic Party, insisted that Kennedy include these sentences in his message. The administration's strategy only met with partial success. Civil rights leaders liked Kennedy's rhetoric (although they still complained he did not explicitly call civil rights a "moral issue") but disapproved of his specific legislative proposals, which they felt did not go far enough in eradicating discrimination and segregation. In a March 30, 1963, article in the *Nation,* King pushed Kennedy to take an even stronger stance: "The Administration is at a historic crossroad. It has at stake its moral commitment, and with it its political fortunes."[96] As the country soon turned its attention towards Alabama, King's prophecy proved correct.

In April, civil rights activists traveled to Birmingham, confident that by orchestrating an economic boycott and engaging in protests, they could expose the evils of racism in America's most segregated city. During a protest, police dogs and fire hoses were turned on African American children in the streets. Kennedy was reluctant to speak since he had several important meetings coming up with international leaders about Vietnam. Despite the moral import contained in his special message to Congress a few months earlier, Kennedy still sought to keep the civil rights issue "relatively quiet" to protect his relationship with southern Democrats. Instead of expressing moral outrage about the acts in Birmingham, at a press conference on May 8, Kennedy worried about the image of America abroad. Kennedy's hesitation sparked criticism from black civil rights activists. Kennedy did make a brief television and radio address on May 12 after the bombing of Martin Luther King's home, but his statements were still confined to legalistic arguments: "This Government will do whatever must be done to preserve order, to protect the lives of its citizens, and to uphold the law of the land."[97]

Liberal Republicans in Congress responded by introducing legislation to outlaw segregation. More importantly, threatening to steal northern votes away from Kennedy in 1964, presidential hopeful Nelson Rockefeller indicated that he would try to help King raise bail money for Birmingham demonstrators. As his political rivals tried to take the lead on civil rights, Kennedy decided to change his rhetoric in an attempt to reassert his moral authority on the issue. The president began to perceive civil rights legislation as both a "political and moral necessity."[98] This convergence enabled Kennedy to transform the arguments he employed in his civil rights rhetoric. In less than a month, an opportunity presented itself that enabled Kennedy to speak moralistically and create a favorable climate for serious consideration of civil rights legislation.

On June 11, 1963, Gov. George Wallace blocked the entrance to the University of Alabama in an attempt to prevent two black students from registering for classes. After a nonviolent demonstration and the arrival of Kennedy's federalized Alabama National Guard, Wallace stepped aside and the students walked into the university. Wallace's actions were not much more than a symbolic publicity stunt. Nonetheless, he provided Kennedy with an opportunity to address the nation on civil rights and racial discrimination. Kennedy's advisors were not unified behind his decision to make a speech on the evening of June 11. Most of the White House staff opposed Kennedy giving the speech and making civil rights a "moral issue." Robert Kennedy, his attorney general, convinced his brother that an aggressive position on civil rights was necessary, even if it proved to be his "political swan song." The attorney general told President Kennedy that continued civil rights demonstrations in the streets were "bad for the country" and "bad for us around the world." If civil rights legislation was enacted, then the Justice Department could handle the problem in the judicial realm, which might achieve one of the president's chief objectives: eliminating media opportunities that embarrassed the United States abroad with unfavorable publicity.[99]

Surprisingly, Lyndon Johnson also argued that Kennedy should address the moral aspects of civil rights as soon as possible. In a telephone conversation with Ted Sorensen on June 3, Johnson stated that civil rights leaders "want that moral commitment, and that will do more to satisfy them than your bill. He [Kennedy] should stick to the moral issue and he should do it without equivocation. . . . What the Negroes are really seeking is moral force. . . . If he [Kennedy] goes down there and looks them in the eye and states the moral issue and the Christian issue . . . these Southerners will at least respect his courage." Johnson believed that making civil rights a moral issue would help Kennedy with civil rights leaders and might even earn him some respect from skeptical southerners. The response to the speech proved Johnson's first point but disproved the second. Kennedy's rhetoric won accolades from civil rights activists, but his moral posturing resonated poorly with southerners.[100]

In the speech, Kennedy appealed to the nation's founding principles to make his moral argument. In the introductory paragraphs, Kennedy reached back to concrete, immutable ideals in order to project an image of the more just future: "We are confronted primarily with a moral issue. It is as old as the scriptures and is as clear as the American Constitution." Furthermore, Kennedy was careful to distinguish his rhetorical appeals on June 11 from his previous "law and order" speeches: "We face, therefore, a moral crisis as a country and as a people. It cannot be met by repressive police action. It cannot be left to increased demonstrations in the streets. It cannot be quieted by token moves or talk. It is a time to act in the Congress, in your State and local legislative body and, above all, in all of our daily lives." Kennedy also asked every American to "stop and examine his conscience about this and other related incidents." Kennedy had not previously made a personal appeal for American citizens to examine their own moral ethos regarding racial discrimination. Kennedy's recommendation pleased civil rights leaders, who had previously urged the president to challenge the righteousness of southern racism and accept a pedagogical role. Kennedy also avoided a "preachy" tone in the speech by emphasizing a shared moral code. The words Kennedy chose made it seem as though racial discrimination was unconscionable because it violated the common ethos ("the scripture") of the nation. As much as possible, Kennedy minimized division and divergent viewpoints in his arguments, urging white Americans to put themselves in the position of black Americans. He used the vehicle of morality to discuss universal standards that transcended racism and provided Americans with a new lens for understanding the push for civil rights. This interpretation of Kennedy's impact casts doubt upon Bruce Miroff's conclusion that Kennedy "had nothing new to teach the American public." Kennedy's adoption of a pedagogical role may have been delayed, but it did occur.[101]

Civil rights leaders and media outlets lauded Kennedy's rhetoric. Martin Luther King Jr. called the speech "a hallmark in the annals of American history." The *New Yorker* classified the president's proclamation as "surely the most important one he has ever made and perhaps the most important one he will ever make." Supportive editorials also appeared in the *New York Times, Newsweek, Time,* and the *New Republic.* Civil rights leader Roy Wilkins praised Kennedy for finally incorporating the moral issue into his discourse. The speech's intended audience extended beyond the United States; the White House distributed the address to all American diplomatic posts with directions about its importance and how it should be used. While some criticized Kennedy for not giving the speech earlier, Arthur Schlesinger Jr. noted that the "timing" of the speech was its "vindication." If Kennedy had spoken of a moral crisis earlier, it would not have achieved the pedagogical purpose he wanted it to accomplish. If Kennedy had failed to seize the opportunity to provide a moral interpretation of civil rights, he would have risked ceding executive control of the issue. The change in Kennedy's civil rights discourse reflected the political realization that the president must react both offensively and defensively to protect his authority and relevance.[102]

Nonetheless, Kennedy's popularity across the country, particularly in the South, took a nosedive after the speech. In late May, Kennedy maintained a respectable 52 percent approval rating in the South. After the June 11 speech, his popularity decreased to 33 percent amongst southerners. In a national poll administered in May of 1963, 36 percent surveyed believed Kennedy was pushing racial integration "too fast." By July of 1963, that number had risen to 48 percent. The politically damaging effects of Kennedy's rhetoric were undeniable; the precipitous drop in his public approval coincided perfectly with the timing of his speech. Ramifications were also felt immediately in Congress. On June 12, the House voted to increase authorization and funding for the Area

Redevelopment Administration (ARA). The administration and Democratic leadership believed the bill would pass easily, but it failed 209–204 when eighteen southern Democrats and twenty Republicans, who had voted previously to support the ARA, changed their positions.[103] The vote warned the president that aggressively pursuing civil rights would cost him a hefty political price.

Throughout the remainder of the summer, Kennedy did not reassert his moral leadership of civil rights. After June 11, Kennedy never gave another speech focused on civil rights. As much as possible, Kennedy tried to revert back to a position of moral restraint. Even though his proposed civil rights legislation had stalled in Congress, Kennedy seemed unwilling to make another strong, moralistic statement. In an interview with Walter Cronkite in September, Kennedy acknowledged the costs of his strong stance on civil rights: "It has caused a good deal of feeling against the Administration in the South—also, I suppose, in other parts of the country. . . . I lost some southern states in 1960 so I suppose I will lose some, maybe more, in 1964. I am not sure that I am the most popular figure in the country today in the South, but that is all right." In his response to Cronkite, Kennedy's weakened leadership position was palpable. In mid-October, Kennedy trailed possible opponent Barry Goldwater by ten points in southern states. As white backlash swept the nation, Kennedy's moral position on civil rights began to cause him trouble in non-southern regions. Survey results indicated that urban residents of Boston, Philadelphia, and Chicago remained unsupportive of civil rights and school desegregation.[104]

In late October, southern senators decided to delay civil rights legislation as long as possible. Kennedy's strong moral stance in the June 11 speech had amplified his leadership on civil rights, thereby pinning his political success to the legislation's passage. Kennedy understood that his own political future depended upon the passage of his civil rights proposal.[105] By the fall of 1963, Kennedy's dilemma had become clear. With his party deeply divided on civil rights, Kennedy had hoped his strong moral rhetoric might force a consensus on the issue. As Lyndon Johnson observed, if the president looked southerners in the eye and convinced them that civil rights was a moral and religious responsibility, he could perhaps earn their respect and use the independent moral force of the presidency to forge a new coalition. However, his moralizing proved preemptive and only exacerbated the tensions within his party. In this sense, Kennedy is comparable to Theodore Roosevelt, who moralized to promote railway regulation in 1905. Both Kennedy and Roosevelt tried to push their party in progressive directions, but when conservative party leaders resisted their efforts, moralizing left the Roosevelt and Kennedy unable to fulfill their rhetorical promises.

In 1963, both of Kennedy's options—moral restraint and moral argumentation—had potential costs attached to them. Continuing to exercise moral restraint was the more politically advantageous option because it would have allowed Kennedy to modify his position on civil rights more freely as political circumstances changed during the summer of 1963. Moral restraint might have also facilitated the passage of civil rights legislation by allowing Kennedy to push for a moderate bill from the House judiciary subcommittee, which instead redrafted the administration's bill and made it more progressive and, consequently, less likely to pass in the Senate. After his strong rhetoric on June 11, Kennedy was forced to comply with the strengthened legislation. All things considered, it would have been politically expedient for Kennedy to follow Lincoln's example and withhold his moral pronouncements until after he secured reelection.

Throughout most of his presidency, Kennedy practiced moral restraint as a defensive posture that aimed to minimize the deleterious effects of strong tensions within the Democratic Party. Serving as a national educator on an issue that most Americans do not support can impose significant political costs on the president.[106] After changing his rhetoric and adopting a moral stand, Kennedy suffered a loss of public approval, particularly in the South. A large part of Kennedy's 1964 presidential campaign would have involved strategies to undo the damage done in the southern states. Indeed, Kennedy traveled to Texas in late November to ameliorate the sharp differences between the liberal and conservative wings of the state's Democratic Party and to reestablish electoral support in the South.[107] Kennedy demonstrated that when political circumstances recommend moral restraint, moral posturing can be a risky endeavor.

CONCLUSION

The case studies in this chapter demonstrate that it is politically advantageous for presidents to adapt their rhetoric to the contingencies that surround them. With varying success, Lincoln and Kennedy used rhetoric to enhance their political authority, whereas Jefferson did not. Abraham Lincoln molded his rhetoric to fit the circumstances of his complicated leadership situation. To minimize divisiveness within his political party, John Kennedy purposefully restrained his rhetoric throughout most of his presidency but moralized in 1963 to reassert his authority on civil rights and consequently paid an expected political price. Unlike Lincoln and Kennedy, Thomas Jefferson did not use his rhetoric strategically, instead allowing his philosophical beliefs to influence his choices. Jefferson's unwillingness to serve as the nation's moral educator encumbered his leadership and contributed to the failure of the embargo. Once again, the main point to be emphasized is that when moral restraint is a strategic choice, the capacities of the presidency are enhanced, but when moral restraint is a philosophical commitment, presidential leadership is adversely limited. Furthermore, each of these case studies illustrates an important point about moral leadership and the presidency.

Lincoln demonstrates that moral leadership can involve prudent restraint instead of explicit moral judgments. Indeed, Lincoln's rhetoric embodies the concept of *phronesis*. Throughout his presidency, Lincoln never lost sight of the higher moral principles he hoped to fulfill, a requirement of *phronesis*. He treated his rhetoric as a political tool that could potentially enhance his existing authority. In this light, Lincoln expands our notion of moral leadership by detaching it from explicit moral appeals. Lincoln's talent was "his skill in the ability to work from an absolute value position, yet avoid the need to take an absolutist stance in public debate."[108] From their principled rhetoric, it is obvious that the reinforcing leaders analyzed in chapter 3 aspired to moral leadership. Because the political circumstances of his situation were so fragile, Lincoln exercised a more subtle form of moral leadership, recognizing that while he could not escape the moral implications of presidential leadership, the strategic implications of his rhetorical decisions determined the scope of his authority. Lincoln satisfied the demands of political leadership as a means to attain higher moral ends, demonstrating a fusion of the intellectual and practical virtues of political leadership.

Thomas Jefferson also exercised moral leadership as president. Acting from a firm philosophical commitment that presidents should not moralize, Jefferson deliberately restrained his rhetoric. Even when political circumstances required principled leadership, Jefferson insisted on detaching the presidency completely from its moral demands. The inflexibility of Jefferson's moral leadership encumbered his political authority. While Lincoln attended to the strategic implications of his actions, knowing that his political authority enabled him to accomplish his moral ends,

Jefferson pushed his philosophical beliefs to the point of contradiction. By rejecting the president's role as the nation's moral educator, Jefferson fell victim to his own criticisms of the Federalist regime he displaced. Jefferson's austere implementation of the shipping embargo brought the weaknesses of his moral commitment to the fore.

By comparing Lincoln to Jefferson, the concept of *phronesis* becomes even more apparent. Prudence requires flexibility, a willingness to adapt to changing political situations, which Jefferson did not embody. It is difficult to know what type of argument will work effectively in a particular instance, but the prudential rhetor hits the mark consistently and puts his knowledge into practice. One of the characteristics of a prudent leader is the ability to convince citizens to obey the laws.[109] In this regard, Jefferson abdicated his responsibility to persuade citizens that the policy he had chosen was the right course of action. Jefferson's intellectual reasoning and his practical wisdom worked at cross purposes, which inhibited his rhetorical success during the embargo crisis.

From a strategic perspective, John Kennedy shows that presidents pay a political price if they moralize preemptively. In 1963, Kennedy faced a difficult situation in that both moralizing and restraint had political costs attached to them. When circumstances pull presidents in different directions, moral restraint remains the better strategic option because it allows presidents to shape their rhetoric to changing demands. This is not to say, from a normative perspective, that Kennedy should have ignored a historic opportunity to support civil rights. The larger point is that speaking moralistically can be a political risk for presidents. We can never know if Lincoln's moralistic Second Inaugural would have diminished his political authority, but we are certain that Kennedy's moralizing ended up costing him political support.

CHAPTER 5

THE POLITICS OF STRATEGIC

MORAL RHETORIC

I n his 1965 State of the Union Address, Lyndon Johnson confessed, "A president's hardest task is not to do what is right, but to know what is right." Johnson implied that presidents must possess a foresight to guide their decision-making. His observation is directly applicable to moral leadership. For presidents, advertising a moral position is not a complicated matter; several presidents throughout American history have sounded the moral trumpet loudly. The difficulty resides in knowing when political conditions support moral argumentation.

This chapter will examine three presidents whose heightened levels of moral and religious rhetoric ran contrary to their dispositions. Unlike the reinforcing presidents discussed in chapter 3, these presidents are surprising moral leaders. Their political pasts did not indicate that they would engage in heightened levels of moral and religious rhetoric as president, and their rhetoric is not a direct reflection of their persona. Once again, this group of case studies shows that when presidents pay careful attention to the politically contingent nature of rhetoric, it produces political benefits. James Madison and Lyndon Johnson bolstered their political authority with moralistic speech, while James Buchanan's blunt rhetoric did not reflect his fragile political situation.

JAMES MADISON: MORAL JUSTIFICATIONS
AND THE WAR OF 1812

To unite the nation as it faced inevitable war with the British, James Madison used frequent moral and religious appeals in his presidential rhetoric. According to the content analysis in chapter 2, of the forty moral arguments contained in his eight Annual Addresses, twenty-one (53 percent) referred to foreign policy or war-related issues. Madison's frequent use of moral and religious rhetoric is surprising given that scholars portray Madison as soft-spoken, colorless, and lacking a vigorous presence.[1]

Despite his pious training at Princeton, Madison doubted the clarity of religious rhetoric, opining in Federalist 37 that "When the Almighty himself condescends to address mankind in their own language, his meaning, luminous as it must be, is rendered dim and doubtful by the cloudy medium through which it is communicated." Madison's Calvinist influences encouraged the view that human nature was sinful and self-ish and that little could be done or said to overcome mankind's flawed conscience. From experience, Madison believed that mixing religion and politics was abhorrent, given that colonial Virginia's established Anglican Church had become corrupt and misguided. Only religious practice unfettered from governmental intervention and direction could foster true Christian principles. For both Madison and Jefferson, the "removal of theology from politics was essential to protect rights."[2]

There is little in Madison's pre-presidential political career to suggest that he would adopt a moralistic or religious posture. Ralph Ketcham described Madison as an "almost Hobbesian" figure who "was inclined to center his attention on the observable facts of human nature, and leave the moralizing and speculating to less sober and realistic minds." Ketcham's depiction of Madison is supported by his noteworthy writings. Madison is best known for his composition of Federalist 10, in which he portrayed politics as a secular business driven by economic factions and self-interest. In his famous *Federalist* essay, Madison wrote, "If the impulse and opportunity be suffered to coincide, we well know that neither moral nor religious motives can be relied upon as an adequate control." Furthermore, recent scholarship has reclassified Madison's 1785 "Memorial and Remonstrance Against Religious Assessments" as strategically motivated political rhetoric rather than a true expression of belief that politics is subordinate to religion. Lastly, Madison was the hand-picked successor of Thomas Jefferson, who refrained in principle from moralistic platitudes in his own presidential addresses and did not view the role of the president as a moral educator as appropriate or necessary.[3] And yet, Madison proved a strategic rhetorician who utilized the power of moral and religious arguments in his presidential rhetoric to unite the nation as it faced war with the British.

Madison's Rhetorical Situation

Approximately halfway through Madison's first term, it became apparent that war with the British was, in all likelihood, unavoidable. The politics of Madison's first administration were shaped by the fact that Jefferson's embargo policy needed to be replaced with a stronger alternative. By the fall of 1811, Madison acknowledged that the United States had reached a diplomatic impasse with Britain, and he began to prepare the nation for war. From 1811 until 1814, Madison's leadership situation encouraged strong, moralistic rhetoric. First, Madison was faced with the imminent task of rallying the nation around a war in which public support was mixed. War rhetoric encourages listeners to unite in support of a policy that will end the crisis. As the War of 1812 began, national unity was still elusive. While southerners and westerners strongly favored the war, New Englanders remained critical of its necessity. One way Madison and the Republicans could unite the country behind the war was to "convince the people that the war was necessary and just." Second, the reasons for entering a war with England were complicated and detailed, involving over a decade of British transgressions. Describing the war using moral and religious language was a succinct way of justifying the war to a diverse, national audience. War rhetoric often contains a "dramatic narrative" that simplifies the events leading to conflict. This enables the president to recast the arguments for initiating war in a manner that stresses the threat to national values and principles. Third, Federalists threatened to undermine Madison's leadership of the war effort. In particular, the Federalists disputed Madison's contention that the war was just and sanctioned by God, thereby questioning Madison's authority as commander-in-chief and his ability to interpret moral principles correctly.[4]

No conditions recommending moral restraint existed. A small faction of Republicans did oppose the war, but by the time the conflict began, the party was largely unified behind the decision to go to war with the British. Several of Madison's political decisions enabled this partisan comity. First, Madison implemented a number of personnel and patronage changes in 1811 that ameliorated rising tensions. He also shifted his foreign policy to a more aggressive position adopted by the power center of the party. Madison knew that these actions would help curb any existing partisan dissension and pave the way for strengthening his political position before the nation went to war. Madison's political efforts had their intended effect. An analysis of the voting records of Republicans in the Twelfth Congress shows that the party voted cohesively to maintain momentum for the war.[5] Madison's leadership situation suggested that moral argumentation was the best option.

To meet the conditions of his political situation, Madison needed to change his rhetorical practices. Madison's early presidential addresses were far from inspiring; Henry Adams characterized his 1809 message as "colorless." However, as America moved closer to war with Britain, Madison shifted his rhetorical stance to garner more support for it. Garrett Ward Sheldon observed that Madison's "New Light theology" permeated his rhetoric and writing during the War of 1812, but Sheldon did not explain why Madison gravitated towards this type of argumentation so abruptly.[6]

Madison's Rhetoric during the War of 1812

As president, Madison needed not only to justify the war in his rhetoric but also to unite citizens behind the cause. According to Madison's personal secretary, Edward Coles, Madison aimed to "moderate the zeal and impatience of the ultra belligerent men and to stimulate the more moderate and forbearing" so that the war would be supported by a "large and influential majority." Unlike the "saber-rattling" speeches given by the bellicose congressional "War Hawks," Madison chose rhetoric that would unify the country without instilling fear in citizens.[7]

Madison's 1811 Annual Message began a two-month period in which his administration enjoyed powerful influence over congressional opinion and action. His bold rhetoric awakened the Washington community to the possibility of war and demonstrated, perhaps for the first time, that Madison possessed enough initiative to lead the country in a time of crisis. Realizing that citizens of all political persuasions would read his message in the newspaper, Madison crafted his message carefully.[8] Madison moved the nation towards war in his address, which urged Congress to increase military preparations:

> Notwithstanding the scrupulous justice, the protracted moderation, and the multiplied efforts on the part of the United States to substitute, for the accumulating dangers to the peace of the two Countries, all the mutual advantages, of re-established friendship and confidence; we have seen that the British Cabinet perseveres . . . in the execution . . . of war on our lawful commerce. With this evidence of hostile inflexibility in trampling on rights which no Independent Nation can relinquish; Congress will feel the duty of putting the United States into an armour, and an attitude demanded by the crisis, and corresponding with the national spirit and expectations.[9]

First, in an explicit attempt to distinguish American policies from the course pursued by the British, Madison described U.S. diplomacy as moderate and just. In addition to the passage cited above, Madison labeled American foreign policy as "just" in three other paragraphs in the address. This appeal to justice legitimized and substantiated Madison's defense of the war. Second, Madison instructed Congress to engage in military preparedness that would complement the "national spirit and expectations," stressing the importance of patriotic unity.

Madison's address was well received and earned praise from his opponents and supporters. William Plumer, a former Federalist senator, called the address "manly and energetic." Philadelphia newspaper editor Francis Bailey wrote to Madison that the "raptures" of his message have "almost universally diffused through this city." Bailey noticed that Madison's more inspirational manner marked a change in his rhetorical choices and stated that "sooner or later, than the present, might have been perhaps an improper time, to assume the tone and attitude recommended in your Message." Although Madison made less use of the partisan press than his predecessor Jefferson, he did rely upon its ability to generate support for the impending war with Great Britain.[10] Bailey's favorable response signaled a willingness to provide Madison with an enthusiastic endorsement of the war effort and the president's rhetorical defense of it.

In a letter to Madison, Henry Lee applauded the tone of the message and observed that it reminded him of George Washington. It is interesting to note that Lee compared Madison's address to Washington's rhetoric and not Jefferson's presidential prose.[11] Since Jefferson rarely engaged in inspirational or moralistic speech, a comparison of Madison and Jefferson's rhetoric would have been inaccurate. More than Jefferson, Madison exercised a pedagogical role in molding public opinion. This can be illustrated historically by Madison's insistence after the Philadelphia convention that the nation's leaders must stand firmly behind the Constitution. According to Madison, most men did not apply their own reasoning to the document; instead, they looked to the "positions taken by their social betters whose reputations they knew and could therefore judge."[12] As president, Madison exhibited a greater willingness than Jefferson to influence public sentiment, which contributed to his frequent use of moralistic, inspirational rhetoric.

Madison's stronger rhetoric encouraged legislative action. Congress considered Madison's Annual Address carefully; James Monroe visited the House three times to explain Madison's views regarding British aggression as representatives reconsidered his message. Six measures, which increased the army, alerted the militia, and armed merchant ships, passed the House in December with only token opposition from dissident John Randolph and the Federalists.

As it became evident that Britain would not back down, the United States moved closer to war. The winter of 1812 proved uneventful, but on March 21, Madison received communications indicating that the British refused to rescind their Orders in Council. In an April 3 letter to Jefferson, Madison reported, "It appears . . . that they [the British] prefer war with us, to a repeal of their orders in Council. We have nothing left therefore, but to make ready for it."[13] On June 1, 1812, Madison sent Congress a war message, arguing that because of previous transgressions, a state of war already existed between Great Britain and the United States. The majority of the message consisted of a historical summary of the wrongs inflicted upon the United States by England. While Madison acknowledged that Congress alone possessed the power to declare war, he argued in the conclusion of his address that the proposed war was just, endorsed by God, and worthy of a moral people. For the next several years of his presidency, Madison repeated variations of these three moral and religious arguments in his public messages:

Whether the United States shall continue passive under these progressive usurpations, and these accumulating wrongs; or, opposing force in defence of their national rights, shall commit a just cause into the hands of the Almighty disposer of events . . . is a solemn question, which the Constitution wisely confides to the Legislative Department of the Government. In recommending it to their early deliberations, I am happy in the assurance, that the decision will be worthy the enlightened and patriotic Councils, of a virtuous, a free, and a powerful Nation.[14]

According to Madison's arguments, an attention to justice and rights demanded war. Nothing less than immediate action could be expected from a "virtuous" nation such as the United States. The initiation of war is, after all, a violent act. The inclusion of moral and religious arguments fosters the belief that such actions are justified to preserve the nation's continued virtuous existence. Madison's rhetoric achieved its desired goal. After limited debate, a declaration of war passed 79 to 49 in the House and 19 to 13 in the Senate. In a public effort to justify the war, Madison's message was printed in the *National Intelligencer* on June 20, 1812, next to his official "War Proclamation." While the proclamation was much shorter in length than his message to Congress, it did contain similar moral and religious arguments, emphasizing the just nature of the war and the blessing of "Divine Providence" regarding American action.

Madison took the nation into war knowing that it was divided and poorly prepared. One of the administration's main problems after declaring war was figuring out how to arouse sufficient public support for its implementation. Madison had no choice but to depend on the nation's ability to rise to the challenge. As president, Madison tried to rally the nation behind the war through more inspiring and moralistic addresses. Leading in this fashion allowed Madison to act forcefully but also remain true to his republican ideals.[15]

The summer of 1812 was not a pleasant one for the president. The Federalists in Congress had voted unanimously against a declaration of war, but their small numbers were unable to sway the outcome. After Congress adjourned in July, the Federalists began a "media blitz" to undermine public support for the war. First, Gov. Caleb Strong of Massachusetts told citizens they must "lament a war against the nation from which we are descended, and which for many generations has been the bulwark of the Religion we profess." The governor proclaimed a day of fasting and prayer within Massachusetts to ask the "Divine Providence" to protect Americans from "entangling and fatal alliances with foreign powers."[16]

In the second part of their media blitz, Federalist members of Congress published an address to their constituents, calling upon them to frustrate the execution of the war. Entitled "The Address of the Minority to their Constituents," the Federalists employed several moral arguments to illustrate their anti-war position and criticisms of the Madison administration:

> In addition to the many moral and prudential considerations, which should deter thoughtful men from hastening into the perils of such a war, there were some peculiar to the United States, resulting from the texture of the Government and the political relations of the people. A form of government, in no small degree experimental, composed of powerful and independent sovereignty, associated in relations . . . should not be hastily precipitated into situations, calculated to put to trial the strength of

the moral bond by which they are united. . . . Before a resort to war for such interests, a moral nation will consider what is just, and a wise nation, what is expedient. If the exercise of any right to the full extent of its abstract nature, be inconsistent with the safety of another nation, morality seems to require that, in practice, its exercise should, in this respect, be modified. . . . Moral duty requires that a nation, before it appeals to arms, should have been not only true to itself, but that it should have failed in no duty to others.[17]

The "Address of the Minority" is filled with arguments questioning the morality of the war against England. Besides doubting the expediency of the conflict, the Federalists attempted to undermine any moral justification for the war. By weakening Madison's rhetorical claims of a just war with England, the Federalists paved the way for their constituents to resist the war's prosecution. In the above passage, the Federalists argued that Madison's rationale for the war did not take moral considerations into account. According to the Federalists, all war requires careful moral consideration before it is engaged. The United States shoulders a particular burden in this regard, due to the "strength of the moral bond" that unifies the nation. Madison's failure to appreciate the depth of the moral argument resulted in the nation's failure to be "true to itself" and its "duty to others." Thus, the Federalists implied that Madison's moral judgment was shallow and flawed. Simply proclaiming the war to be "just" did not make it so. In that light, the Federalists attempted to challenge directly any moral authority Madison claimed as president.

In another rhetorical criticism of Madison and his administration, John Lowell wrote a treatise entitled "Mr. Madison's War" that was distributed as a pamphlet and then reprinted in a *Boston Evening Post* serial. Lowell used several religious and moral arguments to debase the war and Madison's leadership. In one passage, he questioned why the United States waged war with Britain and not France: "All men who value the protestant religion—all men who love freedom, and all impartial men acquainted with the moral character and political conduct of the two governments, must admit, that it would be safer for a free and protestant state to have the power in the hands of Great Britain than in that of France." After arguing that war with Britain was fundamentally unjust and religiously misplaced, Lowell then argued that participating in such a military conflict was immoral and against God's wishes. He also questioned the administration's discussion of the war against Britain in moral terms: "In a war offensive and unjust, the citizens are not only not obliged to take part, but, by the laws of God, and of civil society, they are bound to abstain. . . . If a government can lawfully plunge the people in an unjust, offensive war and if they are as much bound to support such a war as a just and defensive one, then the discussion of its justice would be nugatory, and indeed injurious, and the government might very fairly suppress all examination into its merits."[18] Lowell gave moral validation to the opposition of the war by questioning the use of the term "just." Not all wars are just, and a uniform appeal to justice in times of war diminishes any true discussion of justice. The questions posed by Lowell sought to undermine Madison's previous appeals to moral principle as a justification for war. The Federalists sought to weaken the administration's "moral high ground" for action. By questioning the just nature of the war and implying that participating in an unjust conflict was sinful, the Federalists attempted to undercut Madison's moral legitimacy as president. Unlike Lincoln, who based his strong wartime leadership on his constitutional duty to "preserve and protect," Madison emphasized the moral dimensions of the office to justify his executive actions. This rhetorical posture made Madison more vulnerable to questions of moral interpretation. The Federalists did not attack the constitutionality of Madison's wartime powers but his specific claim that the war was moral and just. To respond to these criticisms in his 1812 Annual Message, Madison needed to reassert his moral, not constitutional, authority.

After his 128 to 89 Electoral College victory in the fall of 1812, Madison turned towards writing his Fourth Annual Address. Richard Rush urged Madison not to write the address in a pedantic fashion. Instead, Rush urged Madison that a "blast of war against England" was needed in the public message.[19] The country was in a state of confusion, and an inspiring presidential statement might prove influential. Furthermore, Madison needed to combat the Federalists' rhetorical claims that the war was unjust and immoral. Madison's Fourth Annual Message, issued in November of 1812, was filled with moral and religious appeals. In this passage, Madison described the rationale behind the war's declaration:

> To have shrunk under such circumstances from manly resistance would have been a degradation blasting our best and proudest hopes; it would have struck us from the high rank where the virtuous struggles of our fathers had placed us. . . . The appeal was

accordingly made, in a just cause, to the Just and All-Powerful Being who holds in his hand the chain of events and destiny of nations. It remains only that, faithful to ourselves, entangled in no connections with the views of other powers, and ever ready to accept peace from the hand of justice, we prosecute the war with united counsels and with the ample faculties of the nation until peace be so obtained and as the only means under the Divine blessing of speedily obtaining it.[20]

Madison's Fourth Annual Message challenged the Federalists' use of moral and religious rhetoric. In their public addresses and pamphlets, the Federalists repeatedly asserted that religious and moral principles guided their anti-war position. In the Fourth Annual Address, Madison explicitly challenged the Federalist monopoly of moral justification by asserting that the war effort had a "Divine blessing." Additionally, Madison tried to link the war with the American Revolution, arguing that avoiding war tainted the "virtuous" example of the Founding Fathers.

Madison continued his rhetorical assault on moralistic Federalist propaganda in his Second Inaugural Address, issued on March 4, 1813. In the early months of 1813, Madison suffered sharp criticisms from the Federalists. The criticisms sparked long debates in the House. On January 8 and 9, Henry Clay spoke for two days to defend Madison and his policies. In an attempt to describe the unreasonableness of the anti-war faction, Clay contended, "No Matter with what sincerity the Administration cultivates peace, the opposition will insist that it alone is culpable for any breach between the two countries." Madison certainly felt pressure in his Inaugural to answer the charges being leveled against his administration. The early part of the Second Inaugural was a clear reaction to criticisms leveled by the Federalists regarding the just nature of the war: "From the weight and magnitude now belonging to it I should be compelled to shrink if I had less reliance on the support of an enlightened and generous people, and felt less deeply a conviction that the war with a powerful nation, which forms so prominent a feature in our situation, is stamped with that justice which invites the smiles of Heaven on the means of conducting it to a successful termination." The speech generated quite a response. The Federalists correctly surmised that Madison had strategically directed his remarks towards them. In particular, Federalist newspapers across the country took great offense to Madison's lofty claim that the war invited the "smiles of Heaven."[21] In the above sentence,

Madison also revealed that strong moral and religious convictions enabled his continued prosecution of the war. Madison reiterated that his moral and religious beliefs substantiated and reinforced the political positions he espoused.

Later in the address, Madison contended that Great Britain, not the United States, acted as the aggressor in the conflict. In juxtaposition to the British, whom Madison described as bloodthirsty ("they have let loose the savages armed with cruel instruments"), the citizens of the United States are "a brave, a free, a virtuous" people.[22] According to Madison's reasoning in the Second Inaugural, if critics believed the war was unjust, they must also doubt his laudatory description of American character. If the war was unjust, Madison concluded that Federalists must be prepared to make a moral distinction between the United States and Great Britain. Madison contended that the war was just because the immoral British persecuted innocent Americans on the high seas. Thus, the Federalist condemnation of the war was tantamount to a moral condemnation of America itself. Just as the Federalists questioned Madison's rhetorical use of justice, Madison in turn attacked the Federalists' criticisms. Instead of arguing about the principles themselves, Madison took the debate to the next level in the Second Inaugural and the 1812 Annual Address by linking opinions about the just nature of the war to moral evaluations of America, its Founders, and the British. According to Madison's strong rhetoric, anti-war sentiment was not a principled belief but an egregious violation of patriotism. Instead of basing his arguments on immediate circumstance, Madison elevated his discourse to first principles in an attempt to stigmatize his opponents. The strength of Madison's rhetorical position as president is evident in his moral rebuttal of the Federalists. Although not all presidents succeed at crisis rhetoric (Jimmy Carter and the hostage crisis is a case in point), it is clear that chief executives possess an advantage over their political adversaries.[23] Instead of backing away from the moral arguments concerning the war, Madison countered them, displaying the true force of independence embodied by the executive office.

In this light, Madison's rhetoric strongly resembled George Washington's moral and religious argumentation during the Whiskey Rebellion. Like Madison, Washington employed moral and religious language to chastise the immoral "insurgents" who led the domestic disturbance in Pennsylvania. On the other hand, Madison's wartime rhetoric can be contrasted to Lincoln's moralism. When Lincoln did moralize in the Second Inaugural, he refrained from condemning his adversaries, instead placing the South and the North on the same moral plane of judgment. In contrast, Madison used moral and religious argumentation to "shout down" his Federalist opponents, who threatened to undermine his authority to prosecute the war. While Lincoln stood above the fray, Madison moralized to take sides and denounce his enemies. This difference can be attributed to the fact that Madison's critics were *outside* his party, whereas Lincoln had to remain mindful of dissension *within* his party. Moral and religious rhetoric can intensify and exacerbate political disputes, which is helpful when a president (such as Madison) wants to distinguish his position from the opposition. Such a rhetorical posture proves damaging when the desired outcome is to minimize differences within a political party.

Madison continued to moralize in his 1813 Annual Address. Under other circumstances, the public might have perceived Madison's language of moral inspiration as mere rhetoric with little political meaning. However, by December 1813, the country was in deep peril. Many prominent individuals wondered if the nation could survive the conflict. In a letter to former president John Adams, Richard Rush confessed, "The prospect looks bleak." In his reply, Adams concurred, telling Rush that the "times are too serious to write." Madison knew that confidence had slumped to a dangerously low level and that the American public needed a strong pledge of faith in the union to allay fears. In his 1813 message, his most moralistic Annual Address, Madison not only proclaimed the war a "righteous cause" but also stressed "Heaven's approval" of it. Madison urged citizens to consider that "the justice and necessity of resisting wrongs and usurpations no longer to be borne will sufficiently outweigh the privations and sacrifices inseparable from a state of war." Madison argued that the necessary burdens of war had a positive effect on American virtue by strengthening the "national character" and generating a "greater respect for our rights." Finally, Madison condemned the British cause as immoral, calling their course of action "most afflicting to humanity."[24] Madison's moral rhetoric served a political purpose. At a time when many prominent figures doubted the future of the nation's sovereignty, Madison's rhetoric remained strong. Through his rhetoric, Madison distinguished himself from those who questioned the strength and longevity of the American republic.

Madison's Sixth Annual Address marked a change in his rhetorical practices. By the fall of 1814, a turning point in the war had occurred. After the attack on Washington, American forces began to defeat the

British offensive. Baltimore successfully defended itself in early September, and a powerful British force moving from Montreal to Albany was repelled a week later.[25] Madison stressed these military successes in his 1814 message, but did not engage in moralistic argumentation. The end of the war was in sight; thus Madison's repeated appeals to justice and the "Heavens" disappeared from his rhetoric.

Finally, the Seventh Annual Address in 1815 signaled a complete change in Madison's rhetorical leadership. This message was unlike any of his earlier presidential addresses. Confident that the nation's republican ideals had been secured, Madison advocated new, forward-looking domestic policies such as a national university, a recharter of the national bank, and internal improvements. Madison no longer needed to defend his administration against powerful Federalist criticisms; thus he returned to his more restrained and less moralistic rhetoric.

As the content analysis from chapter 2 demonstrated, war-time presidents do not exhibit increased levels of moralistic and religious rhetoric in their Annual Addresses. Likewise, the War of 1812 alone did not precipitate Madison's moralistic rhetoric. If the nation and Congress had been united behind the war, Madison would not have needed to resort to arguments about moral principle. Madison's moralistic rhetoric was a strategic reaction to the critical arguments leveled at him. Madison opted for a moderate rhetorical solution that he believed had the most potential for unifying the nation behind his administration.

Madison's presidential addresses and messages may not contain many memorable phrases, but they are examples of carefully crafted political rhetoric aimed to elevate and educate the national conscience in a time of peril. Although Madison's rhetoric did not influence Federalists to become strong supporters of the war, his sharp rebuttals confined anti-war sentiment to the New England states. Through his strong rhetoric, Madison prevented the Federalists in Congress from encumbering his authority. Furthermore, after the war ended, Madison stood victorious over those who had opposed the war. As his presidential rhetoric shows, Madison did not succumb to the Federalists or even cede ground to them. Because their lack of support for the war made them appear unpatriotic after Britain and the United States signed the Treaty of Ghent, the Federalist Party committed "political suicide" while Madison was left standing.[26]

In sharp contrast to Thomas Jefferson's weak leadership during the embargo, Madison used his rhetoric to boost his authority. In particular, Madison's willingness to shape his rhetoric to meet the political circumstances of the situation can be contrasted to the philosophical reluctance that fueled Jefferson's rhetorical rigidity. While Jefferson refused to justify the policy he imposed from above, Madison actually engaged in rhetoric that defended his leadership position, fought off allegations made by the opposition, and tried to unite the country behind his cause. Unlike his predecessor, Madison used his rhetoric to augment and protect his political authority. Madison's presidency may never be considered a pinnacle of executive leadership, but his use of moral and religious argumentation should, at the very least, generate respect for his prudential understanding of rhetoric as a powerful political tool.

JAMES BUCHANAN: THE RHETORIC OF MORAL CONTRADICTION

In the previous chapter, the examination of Lincoln's rhetoric suggested that when a president faces the task of keeping his party together as a moral issue threatens to divide it, practicing moral restraint is the best strategic option. Finding his Democratic Party divided between southerners and Stephen Douglas northerners, James Buchanan faced similar circumstances in his presidency. However, rather than adopt the Jeffersonian practice of moral restraint, Buchanan moralized haphazardly in his presidential rhetoric.[27]

Besides moralizing inopportunely, Buchanan also used moral and religious rhetoric in a contradictory fashion. He provided confusing moral arguments that condoned both sides of the slavery issue and used moral arguments to support the proslavery South. In an 1857 public reply to Connecticut citizens, Buchanan chastised the antislavery movement, which angered northerners who opposed the extension of slavery into western territories. Since Buchanan, a known southern sympathizer, needed to placate the northern faction of his party, his moral condemnation of the antislavery movement was quite imprudent. Furthermore, in two of his Annual Addresses, Buchanan employed moral argumentation to substantiate *both* proslavery and antislavery positions. This attempt to moralize on both sides of the issue was also a failure. At the end of his term, Buchanan left the presidency with no political support whatsoever—both antislavery and proslavery factions of the Democratic Party deserted him.

Buchanan's confusing moral rhetoric reflected his own views on slavery, which can be distilled into two propositions. First, Buchanan

viewed slavery as a moral evil, but as a political and constitutional issue, he cast himself on the side of slaveholders. Even though Buchanan
believed slavery was immoral, he considered an attack on the Constitution an "immorality of grosser proportions." In a floor speech given in
the House of Representatives in 1826, Buchanan explained his political
convictions:

> I believe it [slavery] to be a great political and a great moral evil.
> I thank God, my lot has been cast in a State where it does not
> exist. But while I entertain these opinions, I know it as an evil
> at present without remedy. . . . It is, however, one of those moral
> evils, from which it is impossible for us to escape, without the
> introduction of evils infinitely greater. There are portions of this
> Union, in which, if you emancipate your slaves, they will be-
> come masters. . . . Is there any man in this Union who could, for
> a moment, indulge in the horrible idea of abolishing slavery by
> the massacre of the high-minded, and the chivalrous race of men
> in the South? I trust there is not one. . . . I am willing to con-
> sider slavery as a question entirely domestic, and leave it to those
> States in which it exists. The Constitution of the United States
> shall be my rule of conduct upon this subject.

Buchanan viewed slavery as a moral, but politically tolerable, evil. According to Buchanan's public rationale, slavery's immorality did not
mean that the institution was not sanctioned by the Constitution. His
attitude towards slavery did not change drastically throughout his life.
As president, Buchanan believed that the Constitution represented the
"highest moral judgment" of the Founding Fathers. Since the Constitution recognized the rights of slaveholders, Buchanan condoned the
perpetuation of the institution and did not support political or military
intervention to facilitate its suppression.[28]

Second, even though Buchanan believed slavery was immoral, he
disliked abolitionists. He believed their activism did more evil than good
by encouraging insurrection, violence, and disunion. For Buchanan,
abolitionists threatened a tenuous national stability and frustrated his
impulse to affirm the existing political order. In the first two chapters of
his 1866 presidential autobiography, Buchanan blamed the abolitionists
for igniting the conflict between the North and the South. Strident abolitionists aroused the indignation of the South, which led to a polarized

standoff on slavery. According to Buchanan, antislavery crusaders actually prolonged slavery by arresting "the natural progress of emancipation under legitimate State authority." In Buchanan's eyes, northern agitation made disunion a credible threat.[29]

As an individual, Buchanan thought slavery was immoral and evil, but as a politician, he condoned it and actively opposed the abolitionists. Buchanan might not have been a "proslavery" president, yet he was clearly "anti-antislavery."[30] Other politicians may be able to resolve divergences between their personal beliefs and political convictions, but Buchanan's ambivalence plagued his presidency: he refused to bow to southern demands, such as reopening the slave trade, but also could not bring himself to placate antislavery northerners. Buchanan needed to unify his party, but he took no steps as president towards fulfilling this political demand. As a politician, Buchanan stood squarely with the proslavery faction while his conscience wavered. Buchanan's uncertainty about slavery complicated his rhetoric, making many of his arguments convoluted and contradictory. Rather than strengthening his political authority, Buchanan's confusing rhetoric weakened it.

Buchanan's Political Situation

When Buchanan began his term in 1857, his greatest political challenge was to dampen the sectional conflict over slavery and minimize the growth of the suddenly robust Republican Party. Besides reassuring proslavery southerners, Buchanan needed to pacify Stephen Douglas's wing of the Democratic Party, who clamored for Buchanan's attention. The Democratic Party could not win the presidency or Congress in 1860 without the support of some northern states. To remain competitive, the image of the Democratic Party as "southern-dominated" needed to be eradicated. Buchanan's political task was clear: appease the northern faction of the party without driving the southern contingent towards secession.[31]

Even though Buchanan hailed from the northern state of Pennsylvania, his own political support rested primarily with the southern faction of the Democratic Party. In the 1856 election, Buchanan lost every New England electoral vote. This lack of support from northerners should have alerted president-elect Buchanan to the weaknesses of his leadership situation. Buchanan was known as a "dough face" politician—a northerner with southern political principles. For thirty years as an elected politician in Washington, Buchanan's closest friends were southerners; he professed a "strong emotional attachment to the South."[32] If President Buchanan favored the South without conceding anything to the North, fears about the growing southern slave power would intensify. On the other hand, if Buchanan favored the North at the expense of the South, he might alienate the faction of the Democratic Party in which his support was the strongest and most reliable.

All elements of Buchanan's political situation recommended moral restraint. First, Buchanan had to deal with an explosive moral issue that divided his political party. Second, Buchanan's administration suffered accusations of corruption, thus weakening his ability to stand publicly as a moral leader. Third, resembling Jimmy Carter, Buchanan found himself in an extremely weak position of political authority as president. By 1860, Buchanan's southern political support had largely eroded because he refused to condone secession. Buchanan never attempted to foster any northern support within his party, and his bitter personal feud with Stephen Douglas prevented any possible alliances. Lastly, Buchanan was not elected on the premise that he would provide strong moral leadership. As a candidate, Buchanan was known for his restraint. In the 1856 election, John Fremont, the nominee from the newly formed Republican Party, ran on a platform that promised extensive moral reform. In juxtaposition to Fremont, Buchanan won his party's support due to his silence on slavery; the Democrats wanted a candidate who could mollify, not intensify, tensions within the party.[33]

Lacking strong political support for moralizing, Buchanan would have been wise to refrain from it. Instead, he continually employed moral and religious argumentation in his public messages. Before Buchanan assumed office, John Forney, the editor of the *Washington Union* newspaper, wrote to the president-elect in 1856 and offered some eloquent words of advice: "Pause before yielding to new demands upon your opinions about slavery. Your life is an assurance; your record a bond; your word a truth. Pause before you go beyond them upon the slavery question. Mr. Buchanan, there is a North as well as a South."[34] Forney recommended that Buchanan should choose his words carefully. Statements designed to appease his southern supporters might alienate the northern faction of his party, and vice versa. The best rhetorical strategy available to Buchanan was careful restraint. Buchanan's failure to adapt his rhetoric to the limitations of his particular leadership situation exacerbated his already weak authority. Buchanan's moralizing made a bad situation worse.

*Moralizing on the Wrong Side of the Issue: The 1857 Reply
to the Connecticut Citizens*

Buchanan penned his public statements without seriously considering
that reassuring or supportive statements directed towards the North
might help his own political standing.[35] This section will describe how
Buchanan's dislike of northern abolitionists adversely influenced his 1857
reply to Connecticut citizens by infusing his statements with proslavery,
southern sentiment.

Buchanan used his August 1857 reply to a memorial written by Connecticut citizens as an opportunity to issue an invective against abolitionists. To bolster his own authority, Buchanan attempted to stigmatize
the "extreme" position of abolitionism by chastising it in his rhetoric.
Buchanan's reply to the memorial was a public message, reprinted in
many newspapers, that addressed arguments contained in a letter sent
to him by forty-three prominent antislavery Connecticut residents,
including clergymen and Yale professors. After the Dred Scott decision,
northerners from both parties feared that many western territories would
enter the Union as slave states. By supporting a fair democratic process
that would lead to Kansas being admitted as a free state, Buchanan might
have capitalized on an opportunity to placate northern fears. However,
Buchanan vacillated on the issue and eventually supported the proslavery Lecompton Constitution in Kansas, which was written by delegates
selected in a fraudulent election.[36] To support proslavery Democrats in
the territory, Buchanan ordered the army to occupy Kansas and provide
assistance to the governor he appointed.

Buchanan's actions agitated antislavery northerners who opposed
slavery's expansion. These sentiments were expressed in the 1857 Connecticut memorial addressed to Buchanan. Upon receiving the memorial, Buchanan decided to compose a public reply to clarify his views
regarding Kansas. With his reply, Buchanan hoped to draw upon his
presidential authority to dampen the continual agitation over slavery. He
also thought that his message might persuade the Stephen Douglas faction of the Democratic Party that the LeCompton Constitution was fair.
Fueled by his personal distaste for New England abolitionists, Buchanan
issued the statement with little regard to the political implications of his
words. The reply ended with a moralizing statement: "I thank you for
the assurances that you will not 'refrain from the prayer that Almighty
God will make my administration an example of justice and beneficence.'
You can greatly assist me in arriving at this blessed consummation by

exerting your influence in allaying the existing sectional excitement on the subject of slavery, which has been productive of much evil and no good, and which, if it could succeed in attaining its object, would ruin the slave as well as the master." Amongst his southern proslavery supporters, Buchanan's reply gathered very favorable reviews. The editor of the *Philadelphia Press* concluded that Buchanan had used "the language of simple truth" to show his "superior patriotism and piety." Buchanan's southern friends applauded his reply; Secretary of the Treasury Howell Cobb thought it was a "great document" that would "tell powerfully" in his home state of Georgia. Howell's brother went even further, stating, "Buchanan's letter to the Forty Fools from Connecticut is the greatest state paper for the South that has ever emanated from the executive chair since the days of Washington." However, antislavery northerners took offense to Buchanan's concluding remarks, which openly mocked the pious beliefs of abolitionists by suggesting that their prayers would be better suited towards allaying sectional fears than abolishing slavery. In his reply, Buchanan claimed that his executive actions were motivated by God's influence, further inciting those who believed that the spread of slavery to western lands was abominable and evil. Buchanan's reply was ineffective in its attempt to persuade northern Democrats that the LeCompton Constitution was just.[37] In December of 1857, Stephen Douglas officially broke with the Buchanan administration and joined forces with Republicans to repudiate the LeCompton Constitution.

Less than a year into his presidency, Buchanan had forgotten Forney's reminder that "there is a North as well as a South." By condemning the antislavery movement in his 1857 reply, Buchanan tried to bolster his own authority. But his weak political authority made his efforts futile. Unlike James Madison, Buchanan did not have the unified support of his own party to condemn his opponents. By dismissing the efforts of northerners to limit slavery in the western states, Buchanan pushed Stephen Douglas's faction further away and intensified the split within his own party.

The Rhetoric of Contradiction: Moralizing on Both Sides of the Issue
Buchanan's 1859 Annual Address was even more inappropriate than his 1857 reply to the Connecticut citizens. In his 1859 Annual Message, Buchanan used moral arguments to substantiate both antislavery and proslavery positions. Buchanan issued his address two months after John Brown's raid on Harper's Ferry. The uprising had two effects on the politi-

cal landscape. First, it hardened and intensified southerners against the newly strengthened Republican Party. Harper's Ferry brought the moral dimensions of slavery to the fore; antislavery Republicans exploited John Brown as a "latter-day Christ" and portrayed him as a martyr. After the raid, more southerners began to view the Republican Party as moral extremists who would stop at nothing to eradicate slavery. Secondly, Harper's Ferry further widened the rift within the Democratic Party. In the previous congressional session, Stephen Douglas allied his northern Democratic contingent with Republicans on the issue of slavery in Kansas by refusing to accept the proslavery LeCompton Constitution. After John Brown's raid, southern Democrats felt an increased animosity towards the northern contingent of the party, calling the antislavery northern Democrats the "Black Republican Reserve."[38] Congress convened on December 5 but found itself immobilized by sectional strife. It took two months of bitter fighting for members to select the Stephen Douglas Democrats and moderate Republicans as the new leadership.

In the midst of this intensified controversy and strife, Buchanan issued his 1859 Annual Address. The political situation demanded that the address exhibit two characteristics. First, Buchanan needed to try, as much as possible, to ameliorate the divisiveness between the northern and southern factions of his party. Second, Buchanan had to speak forcefully and independently to mute calls for southern secession. Given the intense divisions within his party and throughout the country, Buchanan should have avoided contentious moral and religious language altogether and, like Lincoln, used the supple rhetoric of moral restraint to establish an independent source of authority.

In particular, it was not prudent for Buchanan to discuss slavery in moral or religious terms. After Harper's Ferry, the moral dimensions of slavery had intensified, making it an even more explosive issue in the Democratic Party. However, in his 1859 Annual Address, Buchanan used moral and religious arguments to support both proslavery and antislavery positions. Furthermore, he did not use his rhetoric to stake out an independent stand on secession. Buchanan's use of moral and religious rhetoric was completely misplaced in his 1859 Address, thereby further weakening any political authority he still possessed. Without doubt, Buchanan's 1859 Address is one of the most poorly crafted pieces of rhetoric in presidential history.

First, Buchanan used moral rhetoric to support the idea that slaves are property. He stated, "It is a striking proof to the sense of justice which is inherent in our people that the property in slaves has never been disturbed, to my knowledge, in any of the Territories. . . . Had it been decided that either Congress or the Territorial legislature possess the power to annul or impair the right to property in slaves, the evil would be intolerable."[39] Buchanan's statement was surprising in that he completely denied Douglas's doctrine of popular sovereignty. According to Buchanan's interpretation, the Dred Scott decision insured the right to own slaves, and that right was protected further by a "sense of justice." The justice Buchanan referenced was not a legal justice imposed by the courts. Instead, it was a justice "inherent in our people," a natural justice that arises from a shared interpretation of the nation's governing principles. In contradiction to previous statements, Buchanan stated here that slavery was not a moral wrong, but threatening the right to own slaves was an "intolerable evil."

Buchanan then went on to discuss the reopening of the slave trade. Buchanan opposed such a reopening, but the reasons he gave for his position were convoluted. His first argument stressed that reopening the slave trade would have deleterious effects on the existing slave population. He argued that the slaves currently owned in the United States had been uplifted by their captivity, implying that slavery was a morally beneficial institution: "For a period of more than a half a century there has been no perceptible addition to the number of our domestic slaves. During this period their advancement in civilization has far surpassed any other portion of the African race. The light and the blessings of Christianity have been extended to them, and both their moral and physical condition has been greatly improved."[40] Buchanan clearly directed the above passage at slave owners, contending that reopening the slave trade might cause more harm than good. In the process of trying to convince slave owners that a reopening of the slave trade would be problematic, Buchanan angered antislavery forces by arguing that slavery actually improved the moral condition of the "African race." Buchanan contended that slavery was not immoral—rather, it was a morally uplifting institution. By doing this, Buchanan allied himself with the most radical faction of southerners within the Democratic Party who believed that the laws of God and nature condoned slavery. This radical proslavery faction, led by William Lowndes Yancey of Alabama, demanded not only that northerners tolerate slavery but also give it their moral stamp of approval.[41] If anything, the power center of the Democratic Party had moved away from the proslavery southern faction and towards the moderate northern component. In his address, Buchanan did not acknowledge this shift of power and instead paid lip service to the most extreme elements of his party.

Buchanan then directed his rhetoric towards those who opposed the slave trade on moral and religious grounds: "But we are obliged, as a Christian and moral nation, to consider what would be the effect upon unhappy Africa itself if we should reopen the slave trade. . . . The numerous victims required to supply it would convert the whole slave coast into a perfect pandemonium, for which this country would be held responsible in the eyes both of God and man."[42] Buchanan's latter remarks intimated that slavery was a vicious institution, calling Africans the "victims" of slavery. Indeed, God would hold the United States responsible for the "perfect pandemonium" created by the reopening of the slave trade. This argument makes little sense when juxtaposed with his earlier sentences in the address that discussed the morally uplifting benefits of Christianity and the abolition of slavery as an "intolerable evil."

Because political support for reopening the slave trade was weak, Buchanan did not need to mention the issue for strategic reasons. Only extremist proslavery southerners, mostly from South Carolina and Louisiana, advocated a change in the policy. Since serving as secretary of state, Buchanan aggressively opposed the slave trade. As a matter of personal belief, Buchanan abhorred the slave trade and thought it immoral. The slave trade was also against the law, which gave Buchanan the unique opportunity to stand forcefully against slavery without compromising his higher moral belief in the sanctity of the Constitution.[43]

The movement to reopen the slave trade in the United States never generated enough support to jeopardize the trade's illegal status, so Buchanan's long-winded arguments in the 1859 Annual Address were politically unnecessary as well as imprudent. However clumsy, his remarks condemning the slave trade were most likely a strategic overture to the North. At a time in which the moral dimensions of slavery had escalated, instead of placating antislavery and proslavery forces, Buchanan agitated them further by filling his Annual Address with gratuitous ruminations on slavery. Buchanan's attempt to justify his opposition to the slave trade did not convince extremist proslavery southerners of his position, and antislavery proponents did not appreciate his rhetorical ploy to bestow moral legitimacy upon slavery. Buchanan's moral arguments neither consoled nor satisfied either faction of the Democratic Party or, more broadly, the sectional tensions that had intensified across the country.[44]

Buchanan could have used his rhetoric to establish a strong leadership rationale that opposed secession. Instead, Buchanan recklessly described the events at Harper's Ferry as perpetuating an "apprehension" that resulted from the "symptoms of an incurable disease in the public mind." Buchanan concluded the address with the pronouncement there was nothing he could do to prevent a civil war. Goodwill was the only possible solution: "Let me implore my countrymen, North and South, to cultivate the ancient feelings of mutual forbearance and goodwill toward each other, and strive to allay the demon-spirit of sectional hatred and strife now alive in the land." Notice that Buchanan did not indicate that he, as president, would facilitate any "mutual forbearance" between the North and South. Buchanan rejected any independent authority, instead shifting all responsibility onto the shoulders of Congress.[45] Even as his political standing evaporated and moral pedagogy was the only resource left in his arsenal, Buchanan refused to interject himself into the process. Unlike his predecessors Washington and Madison, Buchanan did not appreciate the potentially powerful interplay that exists between a president's constitutional and moral authority.

Without a doubt, Buchanan's leadership situation was undesirable; by 1859, he maintained little support from the Washington community or the American people. However, Buchanan did not even *attempt* to construct a rationale for presidential leadership. The 1859 Annual Address was a strategic opportunity for Buchanan to develop some plan of action that could potentially improve his position within the fracturing political environment. Of course, there is no guarantee that even perfectly crafted rhetoric would have catapulted Buchanan's authority and prestige, but by failing to project an independent leadership stance from which to address the issues he confronted, he certainly did not help his situation. Instead of constructing his own sphere of influence (like Lincoln's constitutional claim to "preserve and protect") Buchanan straddled a middle position between the North and the South that did nothing to enhance his authority or ameliorate the conflict. In this light, Buchanan's rhetoric can be contrasted to Madison's moralizing. Madison used moral and religious rhetoric to defend his executive actions; Madison's strong statements argued *for* his policy decisions *against* Federalist criticisms. Unlike Madison, Buchanan did not moralize to defend his policy positions in the 1859 Annual Address. Rather, Buchanan's moral rhetoric wavered between the two contradictory sides of the issue, demonstrating ambivalence rather than strength and independence.

Buchanan's last Annual Address in 1860 proved as disappointing as his 1859 effort. When writing his 1860 Annual, Buchanan decided to deny any right to secession while making an appeal to the North for "justice" in the South. Buchanan widely distributed his message. Although he issued the address before any state had seceded, it was not well designed to prevent secession. Instead of potentially mollifying northerners and southerners, the address generated more antipathy than unity. Northerners believed the message confirmed their worst fears: southern sympathizers ran the country. On the other side of the coin, southerners strongly disapproved of the address because Buchanan did not admit the legal right to secession.[46]

Buchanan's moralizing was more inappropriate in 1860 than any other year of his presidency. In addition to dealing with a morally charged issue that divided his party, Buchanan had recently endured a long congressional investigation that charged the president's administration with corruption. During the summer of 1860, the Covode Committee issued a detailed report, collected from testimony of both Republicans and northern Democrats, that made Buchanan and his entire administration appear weak and dishonest. The testimony implied that patronage rewards and threats had been involved in lobbying for the proslavery Lecompton Constitution in Kansas. The report portrayed Buchanan as a puppet of the slave power, willing to sell votes to extend southern principles. Buchanan repudiated the committee's findings and challenged Congress to gather enough votes for impeachment. When Covode decided not to press for removal, Buchanan declared victory over his accusers. However, Buchanan's victory was not as simple as he might have liked. Over one hundred thousand copies of the thirty-page Covode Committee report were distributed throughout the country to discredit Buchanan and weaken his authority even further. Buchanan had always considered himself a "paragon of virtue," and these accusations sullied his moral reputation.[47] Even though the congressional investigation never resulted in any official censure, Covode's purpose—to portray Buchanan and the Democratic Party as immoral and corrupt—had been achieved.

Despite his weakened moral image, Buchanan used religiously based arguments in his 1860 Address to persuade the North that the sins of slave states did not extend to them: "All for which the slave States have ever contended, is to be let alone and permitted to manage their domestic institutions in their own way. As sovereign States, they, and they alone, are responsible before God and the world for the slavery existing among them. For this the people of the North are not responsible and have no more right to interfere than with similar institutions in Russia or in Brazil."[48] Once again, Buchanan's rhetoric can only be interpreted as passive acceptance of the irresolvable moral division that plagued the nation. Buchanan's remarks can be contrasted to Lincoln's Second Inaugural, in which Lincoln argued that the North and the South collectively bore responsibility for the Civil War. While Lincoln assigned blame to both sides of the conflict, Buchanan urged the North to leave the South alone. According to Buchanan's 1860 Address, the South was solely responsible for its actions and decisions, and the North was not culpable for those transgressions. Instead of mitigating sectional conflict, Buchanan's rhetoric intensified existing divisions. The prudential even-handedness exhibited by Lincoln was altogether absent in Buchanan's polarizing rhetoric. Buchanan's complete abdication of constitutional authority is also blatantly apparent. By comparing the North's interest in southern practices to Russia or Brazil, Buchanan made it clear that he did not stand before the nation as a constitutional officer representing the whole polity. His rhetoric articulated his anemic view of the Union and the ties that bound it together.

Buchanan also used religious argumentation to dissuade southern states from seceding. He explained that no congressional act had ever been passed that impaired the rights of the South to own slaves. He continued, "Surely under these circumstances we ought to be restrained from present action by the precept of Him who spake as man never spoke, that 'sufficient unto the day is the evil thereof.' The day of evil may never come unless we shall rashly bring it upon ourselves."[49] Although the meaning behind his rhetoric was opaque, Buchanan seemed to urge the South to imitate God's restraint and caution. The Bible quotation Buchanan included appears in the New Testament's Book of Matthew. Its full text reads: "Take therefore no thought for the morrow: for the morrow shall take thought for the things of itself. Sufficient unto the day is the evil thereof" (Matthew 6:34). In this passage, Buchanan implied that the real evil to be endured was not slavery but northern abolitionism. According to Buchanan, burdened southerners were the real martyrs deserving of sympathy, and the antislavery crusaders were the "evil thereof." This argument conflicted with his earlier rhetoric in the 1860 Annual Address, which speculated that the South was morally responsible before God for its continued perpetuation of slavery. Furthermore, a close reading of the biblical passage Buchanan quoted also revealed his inability to understand the political seriousness of the situation at hand; it was altogether unlikely that the slavery controversy and the threatened dissolution of the Union would resolve itself. By 1860, Buchanan's "middle position" had become untenable. Condemning southern slaveholders as morally culpable in one breath and exonerating them in another only deepened the growing divisions between proslavery and antislavery forces.

In conclusion, Buchanan did not carefully adapt his presidential rhetoric to accommodate the political circumstances of his leadership situation. As president, Buchanan faced the difficult task of trying to ease sectional strife regarding slavery. Buchanan needed to ameliorate the divisions existing within his own party and, if possible, the nation at large. Such a challenge required, at the very least, skillful political maneuvering and restrained rhetoric. Rather than having a unifying effect, Buchanan's rhetoric polarized proslavery and antislavery forces. Buchanan should have tried to strengthen the Democratic Party in the northern states, but instead of allaying sectional fears, he intensified them by either blaming northerners for the growing conflict (1857 Reply to Connecticut Citizens) or appealing to extreme proslavery sentiment (1859 Annual Address). Buchanan's public statements highlighted the ugly and divisive disagreements about slavery. Buchanan's rhetoric proved useful in only one sense: it provided Lincoln with stark examples of presidential rhetoric *not* to imitate as president.

LYNDON JOHNSON: THE STRATEGIC MORALIST

If an unbiased observer read a biographical summary of Lyndon Johnson's pre-presidential political career and his 1965 Voting Rights speech, it is unlikely that he or she would believe that this was the same person. The man who voted against anti-lynching legislation twice as a member of Congress also gave the most inspiring presidential speech on racial discrimination in American history. Both Johnson's legislative record on race and his lack of rhetorical prowess made him an unlikely moral spokesman for the civil rights movement.

Prior to ascending to the presidency, Lyndon Johnson was thought of as a secular, southern, strategizing politico but certainly not an inspirational rhetor. As a member of Congress, Johnson usually gave dry speeches that lacked eloquent or high-minded rhetoric. In fact, Johnson disdained flowery oratory. Famous for his ability to make deals and forge compromises, Johnson never concentrated on developing his rhetorical skills. Garth Pauley described Johnson's pre-presidential rhetoric as "flat and hackneyed."[50]

Furthermore, Johnson's legislative record on race was questionable, at best. As a member of Congress, Johnson did support numerous anti-poverty programs that benefited both blacks and whites. Despite his commitment to the poor, Johnson voted against every piece of civil rights legislation that came to the House floor from 1938 through 1946, including an anti-discrimination amendment to the federal school lunch program. When he ran for the Senate in 1948, Johnson described himself as a proud segregationist who opposed Truman's proposed civil rights initiatives. Throughout the 1950s, Johnson continued to vote against civil rights legislation in an attempt to ally himself strongly with Georgia's Richard Russell, the leader of the southern contingent in the Senate. After becoming Senate majority leader, Johnson did manage to secure passage for the 1957 Civil Rights Act but only after weakening the legislation significantly. Although not the most vocal segregationist in Congress, Johnson's record on civil rights was dubious, at best.

How might we reconcile these two Lyndon Johnsons—the civil rights opponent and the inspirational moral rhetor of 1965? This analysis contends that as president, Johnson continued to act as a strategist by using moral rhetoric as a politically motivated tactic to enhance his authority and secure passage of civil rights legislation. Political circumstances dictated how and when he would include moralistic argumentation in his speeches. In 1964, Johnson refrained from strong rhetorical pronouncements, instead using moral suasion only to invoke Kennedy's legacy on civil rights. On the other hand, with a solid liberal majority in Congress behind him, Johnson felt confident in his ability to label passage of the 1965 Voting Rights Act as a moral cause. In both situations, Johnson crafted his rhetoric to suit his political position vis-à-vis Congress and public opinion.

As president, Johnson became a prominent leader on civil rights, but such leadership was more a response to the evolving political situation and institutional capacities than a conscious philosophical epiphany or personal transformation. Throughout his political career, Johnson exercised strong public leadership on civil rights and racial issues when it suited his political purposes. Unlike many of his southern colleagues in Congress, Johnson never wholeheartedly believed in segregation or racial discrimination. However, Johnson strategically chose when and how to support civil rights policies. In particular, Johnson's strategizing influenced his presidential rhetoric concerning civil rights.

1964 Civil Rights Act

After Kennedy's assassination, Lyndon Johnson inherited many of Kennedy's domestic initiatives, with civil rights legislation at the top of the list. In the summer and fall of 1963, Kennedy's proposed civil rights package bounced from committee to committee without much firm support. To insure a strong bill, Kennedy needed to throw all of his energy and support behind the legislation, yet he remained reluctant to do so. Despite his strong rhetoric in the summer of 1963, Kennedy feared it would take a "crusade" to pass civil rights legislation, and he wasn't sure if that type of struggle was appropriate as the 1964 election loomed before him.[51]

Kennedy's assassination turned the controversy concerning civil rights into a moral battle. In his televised Thanksgiving address, Johnson depicted the passage of Kennedy's civil rights legislation as a moral duty. The speech combined the elements of a eulogy with the broad policy pronouncements contained in an Inaugural, making the inclusion of moral and religious language an expected component: "Let us today renew our dedication to the ideals that are American. Let us pray for His divine wisdom in banishing from our land any injustice and intolerance or oppression to any of our fellow Americans whatsoever their opinion, whatever the color of their skins—for God made all of us, not some of us, in His image. All of us, not just some of us, are His children."[52] Johnson's rhetoric emphasized the introspective and religious mood generated by the recent tragedy. As the nation searched for a greater purpose, Johnson intimated that turning attention towards civil rights could help Americans make sense of Kennedy's death.

Johnson also used moral arguments to legitimize his new presidential role.[53] His call to "renew our dedication to the ideals that are American" emphasized that now Johnson possessed the executive authority to ask for such a rededication of American values. This rhetorical acknowledgement catapulted Johnson from the dependency of the vice-presidency to the independent stature of the presidency. It also helped Johnson carve out a new political orientation. To establish legitimacy within the Democratic Party, Johnson had to convince northern liberals that he could lead effectively on civil rights, despite the fact that civil rights still remained a contentious issue within the party. Johnson wanted to secure passage of the legislation but hoped his leadership on the bill would not alienate him from his southern political base. Johnson needed to pass strong civil rights legislation but also did not want the remainder of his domestic program to fail because of southern retribution.

Kennedy's death gave Johnson a limited lever to speak in his own voice about the morality of civil rights. In his State of the Union Address, Johnson reiterated his moral duty to continue his predecessor's legislative initiatives: "Let us carry forward the plans and programs of John Fitzgerald Kennedy—not because of our sorrow or sympathy, but because they are right." Later in the speech, Johnson specifically addressed the passage of civil rights legislation, calling it a "moral issue" that must be resolved by Congress.[54] However, once Johnson linked Kennedy's legacy to the passage of civil rights legislation, he did not moralize any more on the issue in 1964.

Even though the House of Representatives appeared eager to pass civil rights legislation, Johnson knew his former colleagues in the Senate exhibited less enthusiasm for the measure. Still facing a much divided Democratic Party in the Senate, Johnson had to proceed cautiously. If possible, Johnson hoped to avoid engaging in public persuasion to force the bill's passage.[55]

In 1964, senators could be divided into three categories: pro–civil rights Republicans and Democrats, anti–civil rights southern Democrats and far-right Republicans, and moderate Republicans. The pro–civil rights coalition possessed the fifty-one votes to pass the legislation but fell short of the sixty-seven votes needed for cloture. Of the Senate's thirty-three Republicans, approximately two-thirds were moderate legislators from the Midwest and the West. To invoke cloture, pro–civil rights forces had to persuade moderate Republicans to join their coalition. Such persuasion would not be an easy task—in forty-seven years, civil rights supporters had never successfully ended a southern filibuster.[56]

Majority Whip Hubert Humphrey served as the administration's floor leader on the legislation. Afraid of a liberal backlash, Johnson did not want a compromise bill that watered down the legislation's provisions. Humphrey needed to convince moderate Republicans of the bill's merits as it stood. With few options, Humphrey enlisted the help of civil rights groups and labor organizers to lobby on-the-fence senators. However, civil rights groups were relatively ineffective in convincing moderate Republican senators to support their cause, because western and midwestern constituencies were vastly white. Labor groups also had little effect since most Republicans received little or no money from unions. Humphrey eventually decided to address civil rights legislation as a "moral question."[57] The strategic question became how to frame the passage of civil rights in moral terms. Most importantly, who could deliver a forceful, moral message without generating a massive political backlash?

While Johnson had set the tone of the debate months earlier by fusing Kennedy's legacy with civil rights legislation, the president could not become the bill's moral spokesman without incurring significant political costs. Civil rights still divided the Democratic Party, making moral restraint the best option for the president. Similar to the circumstances endured by Abraham Lincoln, bold moral pronouncements were politically inappropriate for Johnson at this time. In particular, Johnson needed to avoid antagonizing southern senators as much as possible. Johnson's southern mentor, Sen. Richard Russell, warned the president that if he pushed civil rights too aggressively, it would "by God" cost him the South and the election. The South's support was vital to the remainder of Johnson's domestic program, which he hoped to pass during the summer of 1964. Johnson's success as a presidential candidate depended heavily on his ability to deliver his entire legislative package. If Johnson exasperated southerners on civil rights, he might find their support waning for his other legislative initiatives.[58]

Kennedy's assassination gave Johnson more leverage to pursue civil rights, but he still had to deal with the same reluctant members of Congress that had plagued Kennedy during his presidency. It was unlikely that moderate Republicans would listen to high-minded moral pronouncements from Johnson, a southerner with a questionable civil rights record facing a fast-approaching election. Rather than appearing genuine, any moral appeals issued by Johnson might sound fulsome and politically expedient. Moral persuasion would be an effective political tactic, but in the spring of 1964, the president could not vocalize this type of leadership. Johnson understood that passing civil rights legislation might require a moral crusade, made evident by an earlier phone conversation with Ted Sorenson in which Vice President Johnson argued that President Kennedy should "stick to the moral issue . . . without equivocation." Johnson recognized the powerful moral arguments favoring civil rights legislation, but, facing reelection, he did not want to lead the public fight. It is possible that the southern backlash against Kennedy during the summer of 1963 encouraged Johnson to exercise moral restraint and proceed cautiously. Attorney General Robert Kennedy remarked that

President Johnson took a backseat on civil rights legislation in 1964 because he didn't want to shoulder "sole responsibility" if the bill failed.[59] In this light, Johnson in 1964 can be compared to Thomas Jefferson, who avoided a strong moral defense of the embargo in a preemptive attempt to distance himself publicly from its possible failure.

To generate moral suasion from a source other than the presidency, Humphrey turned to the nation's religious leaders, recruiting ministers, priests, and rabbis to lobby undecided senators to invoke cloture and support the 1964 Civil Rights Act. The strategy was brilliant—it allowed Humphrey to continue Johnson's theme of the Kennedy legacy without forcing Johnson to moralize. After recruiting religious leaders to the lobbying task, Humphrey confided to a fellow Democratic senator, "The key to passing the bill is the prayer groups. Just wait until senators start hearing from church people."[60]

Humphrey's political intuitions were correct. While moderate Republicans represented few black citizens in their home states, religious leaders created a pro–civil rights constituency for them. During their weekend sermons, enlisted religious leaders urged attendees to support civil rights and to contact undecided senators. As a result, key senators, mostly midwestern and western Republicans, received thousands of calls from churchgoers asking them to break the southern filibuster.[61] Additionally, religious supporters engaged in public demonstrations to draw wide public attention to their support for civil rights. As the Senate entered its fourth week of the southern filibuster, religious leaders began a vigil at the Lincoln Memorial they vowed to continue until the Senate passed civil rights legislation. Although Johnson chose not to use the bully pulpit in 1964, others fulfilled the task of moral persuasion for him. On June 10, 1964, the Senate voted to invoke cloture by a vote of 71–29 after a fifty-seven-day filibuster. Although it is impossible to measure the exact effect of the pressure exerted by religious leaders on moderate Republicans, Senator Russell remarked that cloture would have never occurred if the nation's clergy hadn't influenced the votes of key western and midwestern GOP senators.[62]

Johnson managed to mute his public role in the controversy and still achieve his strategic objective of establishing himself as a certified liberal. Southern Democrats blamed Humphrey, not Johnson, for implementing the pro–civil rights tactics of "shameless religious fervor."[63] Throughout the filibuster, Johnson skillfully avoided any highly charged political confrontation with southern Democrats and also managed to display his mettle to northern liberals by refusing to accept weakened civil rights legislation. Johnson restrained his rhetoric as much as possible, engaging in moral argumentation only when he was able to attach his arguments to the unassailable Kennedy legacy. After signing the Civil Rights Act of 1964 into law, Johnson became a national leader on civil rights. Seizing upon a new liberal majority in 1965, Johnson expanded his newly found leadership role by giving his rhetoric a strong moral dimension.

The 1965 Voting Rights Act: "We Shall Overcome"
After the 1964 electoral landslide, Johnson's political position within the Democratic Party changed fundamentally. Strengthened by a new liberal majority in Congress, Johnson no longer faced the wrath of southern Democrats who disapproved of civil rights legislation. In his autobiography *Vantage Point,* Johnson described his 1964 electoral victory as a mandate to "move forward" on civil rights. By securing the passage of the 1964 Civil Rights Act, Johnson had already moved beyond Kennedy's legislative achievements. With a liberal consensus behind him in Congress, the newly elected Johnson now wanted to transcend Kennedy's moral commitment to civil rights. The words Johnson chose for his 1965 Inaugural were testimony to his political independence: "Is our world gone? We say farewell. Is a new world coming? We welcome it, and we will bend it to the hopes of man."[64] The entire Inaugural, which focused on the idea of "rapid and fantastic change," aimed to establish Johnson as the leader of a new era heralding consensual liberal politics. Johnson's optimistic rhetoric signaled the end of political divisions that frustrated change and development. His Inaugural language suggested that the restrictions Kennedy faced as president had been replaced by a new and less encumbered leadership opportunity.

Johnson's attempt to fulfill both the rhetorical and legislative demands of civil rights leadership culminated in his 1965 Voting Rights speech. The unique political circumstances of 1965 allowed Johnson to speak more forcefully on civil rights than his presidential predecessors. After the violence in Selma, in which state troopers assaulted demonstrators and released tear gas upon the crowd, Johnson knew he had to move quickly on voting rights legislation. The opportunity for strong rhetorical leadership presented itself, and Johnson seized the chance to enhance his political authority and power.

After the 1964 election, political circumstances encouraged moral argumentation. Civil rights still divided the Democratic Party, but the division no longer circumscribed Johnson's actions or decisions. After the 1964 passage of the Civil Rights Act and the landslide election, the southern anti–civil rights contingent of the Democratic Party lost its political leverage. Unlike Franklin Roosevelt, Harry Truman, or John Kennedy, Johnson had a liberal majority in both houses. Upon hearing the 1964 election results, Senator Russell of Georgia concluded, "They [civil rights supporters] have overtaken and overwhelmed us."[65] In 1965, Johnson's political authority reached its pinnacle—he was not in a weak position that prevented him from moralizing.

Several circumstances encouraged Johnson to engage in moral argumentation. First, Johnson's newfound liberal allies from the Republican Party threatened to assume stronger leadership on civil rights. If Johnson balked at serving as the nation's leader on racial issues, Republicans anxiously hoped to steal the issue away from the Democratic Party in 1965 and make it their own. Secondly, Johnson hoped to use the violent, transitory images in Selma to argue for a permanent change in voting rights.[66] Johnson's rhetoric stemmed from circumstance, but through his rhetoric, he wanted to transcend the violence in Selma to make a more principled argument about civil rights. By using moral and religious argumentation, Johnson rose above the conception that he was simply engaging in "crisis management" leadership. In his March 1965 speech, Johnson did not want to revert to "law and order" arguments that assured American citizens the violence in Selma would stop. Instead, Johnson's goal of the speech was to reach higher and surpass previous presidential rhetoric on civil rights by taking a morally principled stand. Johnson wanted to use strong moral language to carve out a new sphere of authority for the presidency that would put him at the forefront of a nationwide social movement.

Immediately following his election, Johnson instructed the Justice Department to begin working on a draft of voting rights legislation. Johnson planned to move slowly on the measure, gathering support from Washington insiders, particularly moderate Republicans. But after the violence in Selma, Johnson knew he had to move quickly on the proposed bill. Members of Congress began to clamor for a legal solution; thirty-one congressional Republicans signed a petition demanding that Johnson introduce voting legislation in response to the violence in Alabama. If Johnson hesitated to move forward on voting rights, liberal Republicans made it clear they would step up to the plate and assume leadership on the legislation. As Johnson decided how to handle the looming crisis, six hundred angry protestors, frustrated by the president's failure to issue a strong statement about Selma and dispatch federal troops, picketed the White House, chanting, "LBJ, just you wait. See what happens in '68." Lastly, a group of national religious leaders denounced LBJ for his "unbelievable lack of action" immediately following Selma.[67]

The political situation at hand welcomed a strong and inspirational rhetorical response. Nonetheless, appearing in front of a joint session of Congress to push for voting rights had its risks. By giving such a speech, Johnson would place his considerable popularity behind one piece of legislation whose passage was likely but not completely guaranteed. Since Harry Truman appeared before a joint session in 1946 to ask for authority to end the railway strike, no president had gone before Congress to push a single piece of legislation.[68] Johnson knew that the prospects of passage were high, but such a bold rhetorical stand on a single bill was a risky endeavor. In this light, Johnson's situation resembled Theodore Roosevelt's campaign for the Hepburn Act. Moralizing to sell one piece of legislation can be precarious, but in 1965, the southern Democrats maintained less influence and power than the "Old Guard" that haunted Roosevelt. Like Johnson, Roosevelt hoped his strong rhetorical stance would place him at the cusp of a burgeoning social movement. In contrast to Roosevelt, however, Johnson prudently waited until party divisions lessened before engaging in moral rhetoric.

With public and congressional pressure mounting, Johnson concluded that he would lose too much credibility and independent authority if he failed to address the issue directly. Comforted by the knowledge that over 90 percent of the Americans polled in January supported the concept of voting rights legislation, Johnson prepared to deliver a major television address concerning the violence in Selma and voting discrimination. After a March 14 meeting with advisors, Johnson instructed his speechwriter Richard Goodwin that he wanted to "use every ounce of moral persuasion the presidency held" to show that he would condone "no hedging, no equivocation."[69] If he was going to stick his neck out for a single piece of legislation, Johnson wanted to make sure his speech gave members of Congress little choice but to support his proposals. In 1964, Johnson allowed religious leaders to make morally driven arguments for him, whereas in 1965, Johnson assumed the role of national moral spokesman.

Johnson's speech, formally entitled "The American Promise," rested its arguments on one underlying assumption: the purpose of the United States is to fulfill a greater moral mission. In his opening paragraphs,

Johnson introduced this premise: "Our mission is at once the oldest and the most basic of our country: to right wrong, to do justice, to serve man. . . . Rarely are we met with a challenge, not to our growth or abundance, our welfare or our security, but rather to the values and the purposes and the meaning of our beloved Nation. The issue of equal rights for American Negroes is such an issue." In these sentences, Johnson embedded his arguments about voting rights within a broad moral context. The immediate issue at hand involved voting rights while the larger issue, according to Johnson, concerned the fulfillment of America's moral purpose. The very fact that the identity of the United States is based upon moral convictions is a remarkable insight.[70] Due to the fact that he could acknowledge old political orders while also creating new ones, Johnson's ability to articulate this powerful interpretation strengthened his constitutional position as president.

After briefly describing the legislation he planned to send to Congress the following day, Johnson minimized the divisiveness usually associated with civil rights legislation: "There is no constitutional issue here. The command of the Constitution is plain. There is no moral issue. It is wrong—deadly wrong—to deny any of your fellow Americans to the right to vote in this country."[71] Johnson's contention that voting rights legislation failed to constitute a "moral issue" did not mean he wanted to diminish its moral importance. Instead, Johnson challenged the notion that a moral alternative to civil rights existed. In his rhetoric, Johnson defined a "moral issue" as a debatable proposition with competing, valid arguments. By stating that "no moral issue" existed, Johnson created a rhetorical immutability that was beyond question or equivocation. Only a president with a solid liberal majority behind him could have made such a firm pronouncement that wholly repudiated southern sentiment and opinion.

Finally, in an attempt to rise above mere crisis management, Johnson used moral language to transcend the imminent circumstances in Selma: "For at the real heart of the battle for equality is a deep-seated belief in the democratic process. Equality depends not on the force of arms or tear gas but upon the force of moral right; not on recourse to violence but on respect for law and order." In these lines of the speech, Johnson established a connection between the transitory violence in Selma and the permanent moral principles emphasized in the address.[72] The tear gas and armed soldiers were only incidental to the struggle for civil rights while its moral component was everlasting.

Other parts of Johnson's speech, which did not explicitly utilize moral and religious argumentation, were also revolutionary and unprecedented. In the middle of the speech, Johnson shocked listeners by repeating the words from the civil rights anthem "We Shall Overcome." This pronouncement catapulted Johnson's status within the movement. In a subsequent part of the speech, Johnson also valorized the "American Negro" as the "real hero in this struggle." Because Johnson's speech eventually became known for the "We Shall Overcome" phrase, his characterization of black Americans has often been forgotten, even though this line was just as remarkable as anything else in the address.

Over seventy million people watched the speech on television. Newspapers and media outlets praised Johnson's rhetoric for its strong and timely message. The *New York Times* commented, "No other President has made the issue of equality for Negroes so frankly a moral cause for himself and all Americans." Johnson's speech found favor with white liberals and the moderate civil rights movement, but black militants dismissed the address, believing it had come too late after the violence in Selma.[73]

Despite the criticisms of extremists, the 1965 Voting Rights speech helped Johnson achieve several political goals. First, Johnson believed his strong words made him an established, influential leader within the civil rights movement. Southern blacks had cast pivotal votes in the 1964 election, and Johnson recognized that any leader of the new Democratic Party needed to demonstrate his strong commitment to racial issues. By 1965, the Democratic Party had changed, and Johnson knew that by virtue of political necessity, he needed to change with it. A successful president must stay at the forefront of the civil rights movement and try to influence its agenda as much as possible.[74] Johnson's well-received Voting Rights speech put him in a good position for such leadership. Throughout the summer of 1965, Johnson continued to ally himself with the civil rights movement, most notably in his June 4 commencement address at Howard University in which he spoke about the more subtle problems of de facto segregation.

Second, the wide popularity of his address virtually guaranteed passage of the administration's voting rights legislation. After Johnson's speech, Washington insiders anticipated immediate bipartisan support for the bill in Congress. Southern senators were still worn out from the 1964 filibuster battle, and Johnson's speech only energized supporters of strong voting rights legislation. A liberal senator compared the situation of anti–civil rights southerners in 1965 to the Civil War South after Grant conquered Richmond: "The southern generals are brilliant, but their troops are old and tired, and there simply aren't enough to go around."[75]

After only four months of deliberation, Johnson's voting rights bill passed both the Senate and the House by wide margins. The 1964 election contributed to the bill's easy passage; the House Democrats who won formerly Republican seats in 1964 voted 44–0 in favor of the legislation. As anticipated, in the Senate, the bill only encountered token resistance from southerners. On the final vote, five southerners (Bass, Gore, Harris, Monroney, and Yarborough) decided to support Johnson's legislation.[76] The law, which was not weakened by legislative compromises, gave the Justice Department significant power to insure voting rights. Under the law's provisions, state literacy tests faced careful scrutiny, and the attorney general gained the authority to dispatch registrars to southern counties who refused to extend voting rights to African Americans. It also provided a three-judge panel to review cases of alleged voting rights violations.

Johnson's 1965 Voting Rights Act marked the pinnacle of his rhetorical and legislative leadership on civil rights. Only four days after Johnson signed the bill into law, race riots broke out in the Watts section of Los Angeles. Johnson never regained the political consensus and authority he enjoyed after his voting rights speech. After the summer of 1965, three factors recommended moral restraint. First, white backlash against civil rights grew more intense. As violence and riots swept through numerous cities, the white population lost sympathy for the civil rights movement. The 1966 election, in which Republicans gained forty-seven seats in the House and six in the Senate, was considered to have a "white backlash" component to it. Second, Johnson parted ways with many mainstream civil rights leaders when they refused to support the war in Vietnam. Caught in the middle with little room to maneuver, Johnson felt the pressure of "white backlash" on one hand and the force of anti-war civil rights activists on the other. The rhetoric of restraint was the better option for Johnson, who felt boxed in from both the right and the left. Third, the Johnson administration became less willing to associate itself with an increasingly militant black power movement. Civil rights was no longer a divisive issue that threatened to tear the Democratic Party apart, but black activism had become more controversial nationwide, thus dampening public support for civil rights initiatives. After Johnson's Voting Rights speech in 1965, a Gallup poll showed that 55 percent of the American public believed Johnson was pushing integration at the "right pace" or "not fast enough." At this point, Johnson had the support of more than half the nation to continue his work on civil rights or even increase his efforts. By August of 1967, only 38 percent believed that Johnson's pace was appropriate or too slow while 44 percent of those surveyed thought he was moving "too fast."[77] In contrast to his unencumbered leadership position in 1965, Johnson's political authority on civil rights weakened as his term progressed, thus making moral restraint the best option.

Despite these adverse conditions, Johnson did muster support for the 1968 Civil Rights Act, which prohibited discrimination in the sale or rental of approximately 80 percent of the nation's housing units. Because of decreased white support for civil rights, Republicans were reluctant in 1968 to jump on Johnson's bandwagon. In the wake of Martin Luther King's assassination, Johnson managed to secure passage for the bill but only after agreeing to a significant GOP compromise. After 1965, Johnson spoke publicly about civil rights much less frequently. While Johnson did continue to issue a special written message to Congress every year on the subject of civil rights, his role as the movement's moral spokesman faded. Instead of waging a public speaking campaign in 1968, Johnson wrote letters to Speaker McCormack and Senate minority leader Gerald Ford after King's death to urge support for the civil rights legislation.[78]

The political circumstances of 1965—the congruence of societal demands and the Democratic Party's liberal agenda—never surfaced again in Johnson's presidency. A rare window to exercise moral leadership on civil rights opened, and Johnson, the consummate political strategist, capitalized upon the opportunity. David Zarefsky, a scholar of Johnson's rhetoric, praised his Voting Rights speech because it "conveyed the eloquence he often shielded."[79] Johnson "shielded" his rhetoric on civil rights because of political considerations. Even though Johnson was sympathetic to the difficulties experienced by black Americans, he chose to support civil rights policies when it was politically advantageous to do so. By circumscribing his rhetoric when the political situation recommended restraint and employing strong language when the threat of divisiveness was minimal, Johnson used rhetoric as a strategic tool to enhance his independent leadership. This fact does not diminish Johnson's distinguished presidential record on civil rights or his rhetorical achievement in 1965. However, Johnson's moral leadership on civil rights must be viewed within the context of political exigency and opportunity. This is, of course, how Johnson—the quintessential politico—viewed it himself.

This chapter demonstrates that when moral rhetoric is a purposeful, political choice, it can enhance the president's leadership and authority. Both Madison and Johnson shaped their rhetoric according to the political circumstances they encountered. In contrast, Buchanan allowed his personal beliefs to complicate his rhetoric, making any strategic overtures damaging rather than empowering. While Madison and Johnson benefited from their rhetorical choices, Buchanan's moralizing encumbered his leadership.

Presidents can use moral appeals to either defend a position they have taken (Madison) or to enhance their existing authority (Johnson). To resist the rhetorical criticisms leveled by the Federalists during the War of 1812, Madison engaged in moral discourse that elevated his arguments about the war to unassailable first principles. Madison's position of authority was neither extremely weak nor strong. He used moral argumentation as a defensive mechanism to deflect threats to his leadership. Madison did not have the political authority to reconstruct new governing norms or principles, but he was able to use moral argumentation to affirm his own independence. In Madison's case, moral rhetoric can be viewed as a competitive mechanism used by presidents to "shout down" other institutional actors who threaten to assume leadership on an issue or frame it according to their own perceptions.

On the other hand, Lyndon Johnson moralized to enhance his leadership situation. In 1965, Johnson's authority was robust. Johnson used his moral stance to assume a commanding position in the nation's leading social movement. Unlike Madison, Johnson did not need to defend his political position and instead used moral rhetoric to establish a new sphere of presidential authority. Rather than reacting to the civil rights movement, Johnson's moral posturing gave him the power to initiate action and leadership. Because of urban race riots and white backlash, Johnson's opportunity to capitalize upon his strengthened role was shorter than he anticipated, but his enhanced position did facilitate quick passage of the 1965 Voting Rights Act.

Both Madison and Johnson exemplified qualities of *phronesis* in their rhetorical choices. In particular, Madison and Johnson illustrate prudence's status as practical intelligence. As Leroy Dorsey explained, prudence is about "human concerns" and working to achieve the best possible good with appropriate actions.[80] Madison and Johnson attended to the expediencies of their political situations and used moral and religious appeals to make their political arguments stronger. Madison understood that war was the best, and perhaps only, option for the nation's survival, and Johnson became a believer in the moral cause of civil rights. To achieve the political goals they desired, Madison and Johnson allowed the circumstances of their political situations guide their rhetorical choices. When *phronesis* combines deliberation with an appropriate rhetorical response, the result is a powerful argument that strengthens political authority and commands persuasion.

While moral argumentation served the strategic purposes of both Madison and Johnson, James Buchanan suffered because of his inopportune rhetoric. Like Jimmy Carter, Buchanan's weak political authority recommended moral restraint. Instead of heeding the political demands of the situation, Buchanan allowed his rhetoric to reflect his own contradictory views on slavery. Buchanan did not use his rhetoric as a strategic tool to enhance his authority. Consequently, he issued convoluted rhetoric that exacerbated existing divisions within his party and the country. Buchanan demonstrated that moralizing on both sides of a contentious issue is counterproductive. Moral rhetoric is too blunt for a "balancing act."

This chapter reinforces the observation illustrated in the previous chapter: moral leadership can be risky. When used to enhance power and authority, moral leadership is motivated more by politics and strategy than pure idealism. Despite the strategic possibilities of moral leadership, principled leadership stances are not a panacea for all presidents who face a political crisis. Moral stances cannot make political weaknesses disappear, but when used strategically, moral leadership can enhance the president's power. As the case of Lyndon Johnson demonstrated, moral leadership is most advantageous when the political risks surrounding such a principled stand are minimal.

As the case studies in this chapter demonstrated, presidents who adopt the moral spokesman role are not always paragons of virtue. The personal moral inclinations of the president matter less than the political and institutional circumstances that encapsulate his rhetorical message. When presidents issue eloquent and inspirational words that challenge the moral beliefs of listeners, the political context of such rhetoric must be analyzed as much as the arguments themselves. Moral leadership requires presidents to gamble that their existing political legitimacy will support their idealism. Without such an assurance, the blunt language of moral pronouncements can damage a president's strategic position rather than improve it.

CHAPTER 6

THE FUTURE OF RHETORICAL

MORALISM IN THE PRESIDENCY

W hen campaigning for the presidency in 1932, Franklin Roosevelt concluded that the office he sought was not merely administrative but "preeminently a place of moral leadership." At the National Press Club several decades later, presidential candidate John Kennedy reiterated Roosevelt's observation, stating that the "White House is not only the center of political leadership. It must be the center of moral leadership—a 'bully pulpit,' as Theodore Roosevelt described it." Above all, this book reaffirms what Teddy Roosevelt, FDR, and Kennedy realized: the moral possibilities and political realities of presidential leadership are inextricably linked. Presidents use rhetoric to forge a concrete connection between possibilities and realities. When used to strengthen a president's constitutional position, rhetoric reflects political legitimacy and elucidates the type of authority a president claims to possess. In this sense, the strategic component of moral and religious rhetoric cannot be ignored.

Emphasizing the strategic nature of moral and religious rhetoric is not a calculated attempt to "politicize" or "secularize" the ethical dimensions of leadership. Rather, choices about rhetoric should be perceived as exciting political opportunities for presidents and their administrations. Due to the "deep structure" and vast institutional layering of the executive office, the modern presidency exercises limited influence over legislative programs and bureaucratic management.[1] In comparison, presidents have greater autonomy in crafting their rhetoric, and these decisions can generate a powerful political impact. Rhetorical choices affect individual presidents and their political authority and also, on a larger scale, influence the governing capacities of the office itself.

The case studies contained in chapters 3, 4, and 5 make it abundantly clear that some presidents derive more political benefits than others from their rhetoric. Presidents who have viewed rhetoric as a unique executive resource for augmenting, defending, or maintaining their political authority have profited from its application. I have used the concept of Aristotelian *phronesis* to illustrate the most effective engagement of moral and religious rhetoric. The presidents I discuss who embody *phronesis*—Washington, Madison, Lincoln, and Lyndon Johnson—exhibited a practical wisdom in their rhetorical decisions. However, the pragmatism of their rhetorical choices is not enough to fulfill the dictates of *phronesis*, which also requires an attention to "moral nobility" that reflects an encouragement for humans to "live better." Washington's rhetoric concerning the dangers of faction certainly aimed to fulfill this higher purpose. While Madison's rhetoric stemmed from necessity, it embodied *phronesis* due to the nature of the ends he pursued. Political prudence is concerned with "guiding and sustaining the city," and Madison's rhetoric geared itself towards the latter.[2] Both Lincoln's and Johnson's rhetoric aspired to extend the nation's founding principles to African Americans. Lincoln pursued this goal with a scrupulous attention to the potential divisiveness of rhetoric, and Johnson waited patiently for the most appropriate political circumstances that would support the use of powerful moral and religious arguments as an executive tool for enlightening the American citizenry about civil rights. Washington, Madison, Lincoln, and Johnson constitute a disparate grouping of presidents, each of whom arrived to the executive office with different historical expectations. Despite such dissimilarities, these four presidents took advantage of rhetoric's political capacity and treated it as a valuable resource for the protection or augmentation of their authority.

In this chapter, I outline the general lessons concerning rhetoric and moral leadership drawn from the nine case studies and the quantitative evidence. First, I consider the historical development of presidential rhetoric and how changes in speech affect the political capacities of modern presidential leadership. I then provide a response to recent research that argues rhetorical choices have little political impact upon presidential leadership and the polity. I conclude with an analysis of Pres. George W. Bush's rhetoric and its future political implications.

ORDER AND CHANGE: STRATEGIC CHOICES AND RHETORICAL DEVELOPMENT

In chapter 2, the content analysis showed that American presidents have always used moral and religious argumentation, but modern presidential moralizing is distinctive for its detachment from specific policy concerns.

Woodrow Wilson began the twentieth-century tendency of non-policy moralizing, which initiated a new type of modern presidential rhetoric. Open-ended moralizing has now become a prevalent mode of presidential rhetoric. When presidents speak moralistically, they often pontificate about abstract concepts such as the spiritual health of the nation or the character of the citizenry. The detachment of policy concerns and moral rhetoric has wrought several problematic effects on the development of the presidency and its institutional capacities.

First, exalted rhetoric fosters the notion that modern presidents have the power to accomplish tasks that no executive embedded within a separated power system possesses. Presidents cannot single-handedly change the entire moral ethos of the nation or alter cultural standards. Quite simply, non-policy moralizing encourages expectations to exceed capacities for action. This is an endemic problem of the plebiscitary presidency, and the modern changes in moral rhetoric exacerbate the issues at hand concerning governance and leadership. When presidents are unable to live up to the moralistic promises they make in their rhetoric, their ability to function as political leaders is diminished. Presidents increase their political authority through a skillful use of rhetoric, not haphazardly employing grandiose claims that cannot be fulfilled.

Second, the prevalence of non-policy moralizing implies that modern presidents labor uniformly under the requirement that they must formulate some sort of moral outlook for the nation. Presidents of both parties cannot escape the duty of formulating a broad moral message. Moral symbolism has become as institutionalized as the modern president's administrative management or legislative roles. This development suggests that modern presidents are under more pressure to ignore the strategic capabilities of rhetoric and that moral restraint is quickly disappearing as a viable rhetorical option. George H. W. Bush understood the importance of prudence but suffered politically because he lacked the ability to articulate "the vision thing." Bush fell victim to the plebiscitary expectation that presidents must inspire the citizenry and provide a moral direction for the country, even though no evidence suggests that such a "vision" would have changed the substance of Bush's policies.

Thus, rhetoric's historical development rests uneasily upon its impervious contingencies, exemplifying the intersection of "order and change."[3] The nine case studies substantiate the existence of a stable rhetorical order. Thomas Jefferson's decisions about rhetoric bear insights that prove fruitful when we study John Kennedy almost 150 years later.

We can compare the rhetorical approaches of Theodore Roosevelt and Jimmy Carter, or James Buchanan and Lyndon Johnson. Regardless of time period, the strategic component of presidential moral rhetoric remains pervasive and constant. When used appropriately, moral rhetoric enhances a president's constitutional position, allowing him to build political authority and legitimacy. But in a separate dimension, we know that the content of moral rhetoric itself has changed, becoming increasingly non-policy specific. The effect of rhetoric's development on its strategic capacities poses debilitating consequences for executive governance; the collision of order and change gives rise to new tensions and inconsistencies in presidential leadership.

If rhetorical trends continue along their current path, we face the danger of moral rhetoric losing its political clout. When contemporary presidents moralize, Americans are often left with empty and vacuous phrases.[4] For example, in his 1980 State of the Union Address, Jimmy Carter stated, "We can thrive in a world of change if we remain true to our values." However, he never explained what values required maintenance or why he believed they required preservation. Ronald Reagan called to "strengthen our community of shared values" (1984 State of the Union) and implored citizens to become a "force of good in the world" (1985 State of the Union). In a prophetic and slightly ironic turn of phrase, Bill Clinton observed in his 1995 State of the Union, "All of us have made our mistakes, and none of us can change our yesterdays. But every one of us can change our tomorrows." All of these statements are fuzzy proclamations that suffer from a lack of specificity and political purpose. No doubt, all Americans want to reach their "God-given potential" (Clinton 1995 State of the Union), but it is unclear what these rhetorical assertions mean politically. Presidential rhetoric of this vein lends credence to the supposition that modern presidential leadership has increasingly become a spectacle designed to foster awe or tacit acceptance rather than generate productive political debate.[5]

The presidency continues to persist as an institution that thrives on its ability to perpetuate change. When used strategically, moral rhetoric has served as an effective tool for justifying independent policy pronouncements. Presidents have also used moral arguments to fulfill a pedagogical role, enabling them to capitalize upon widely held views and beliefs to elucidate complicated policy decisions. But if moralistic rhetoric loses the bite of a potentially disruptive force, its ability to supplant a president's authority will diminish. If moralizing is expected rather than strategic, it runs the danger of becoming a purely institutional function, another hoop that the president must jump through to fulfill the modern demands of the office. Even when moral leadership is encouraged by the contingencies of a political situation, it is still up to the president to issue moral and religious rhetoric that constitutes a well-developed, meaningful argument. Simply paying lip service to morals and ideals is amorphous political leadership with little potential for rhetorical guidance or direction. This book has demonstrated that several presidents throughout American history have done better than this. Presidents have used moral and religious arguments in their rhetoric to make meaningful points about critical decisions concerning policy and governance. It would behoove contemporary presidents not to lose sight of the great capacity of this potentially powerful executive resource.

Finally, this rhetorical development adds another layer to the bifurcated ambivalence recognized by Jeffrey Tulis in *The Rhetorical Presidency*. According to Tulis, the arguments contained in presidential rhetoric have changed fundamentally, evolving from a principled discussion of the Constitution to routinized crisis discourse. The ambivalence resides in the inability of presidents to keep pace with the promises they purport to make. The upswing in non-policy moralizing further complicates the prospects of governance. Not only do modern presidents attempt to persuade citizens about programmatic matters, they also use rhetoric to construct a world based upon their own moral principles. The modern rhetorical presidency is not limited to policy concerns. Instead, the rhetorical purview for modern presidents is all-encompassing; every aspect of democratic life becomes worthy of a moral pronouncement. Once again, the danger of this development is the legitimacy problem confronting the contemporary presidency, which sets expectations beyond the capacities of the office. Moral rhetoric can enhance the president's constitutional position, but it cannot supercede it. These observations beg the question: are presidents better off remaining silent rather than engaging in rhetorical leadership at all?

Evaluating "Staying Private"

An examination of the rhetorical choices presidents make can offer important scholarly insights to the study of institutionalism but only if the political effects of such decisions can be outlined. George Edwards argues this point forcefully in *On Deaf Ears*, observing that most scholarly examinations of presidential speech and the rhetorical presidency ignore the question of whether rhetorical strategies actually achieve a measurable political impact. Using public opinion data, Edwards contends that presidents routinely fail to persuade citizens to support the policies they espouse in their rhetoric. The bully pulpit is not a particularly strong component of presidential leadership, and a continued focus on rhetorical strategies directed towards changing public opinion is politically futile. The overall message is clear: presidential rhetoric generates a weaker political impact than conventional wisdom suggests, and presidents should spend more time trying to formulate behind-the-scenes compromises that follow a strategy of "staying private" rather than "going public."[6]

Edwards's emphasis on the limits of presidential rhetoric is a lesson underscored by several case studies contained in this book. Not all circumstances call for presidents to articulate moral stances, and sometimes rhetorical restraint is the better political option. But as Edwards acknowledges, presidential rhetoric is not always motivated by a desire to change public opinion on a particular issue.[7] As this book has shown, when presidents choose their rhetorical arguments carefully, they can have the power to send signals to Congress, contribute vital public support to a burgeoning social movement, make important connections between policy decisions and ethical concerns, enhance their constitutional role, oppose political adversaries, or engage in party leadership. In other words, rhetorical leadership in the presidency is not limited to moving public opinion polls.

Instead, the rhetorical choices a president makes are important to his standing as a political leader in a democratic republic. Rhetoric that takes political circumstances into account can help presidents shape the political universe that surrounds them. In other instances, presidents choose appropriate rhetorical arguments to fulfill a pedagogical function of the office. The end of presidential pedagogy is not limited to policy persuasion. Rather, such pedagogy concerns itself with the republican nature of the executive office, the president's representative duty to explain his decisions and positions. "Going public" may pose political challenges for presidents at times, but silencing presidential rhetoric requires a warning akin to Madison's cautionary tale in Federalist 10: "Liberty is to faction what air is to fire, an ailment without which it instantly expires." Removing air and liberty eliminates the potentially damaging effects of fire and faction, while also destroying life and democratic liberalism in the process. Likewise, an overall reduction in presidential communications may reduce roadblocks to policy change but also might simultaneously diminish an important tool of the office that enables presidents to enhance their constitutional role, transform public discourse, and fulfill a representative function.

The problems of the "public presidency" will not be solved with a blanket recommendation of increased rhetorical silence. Rhetoric will always prove tempting for presidents, because the ambiguous structure of the presidency motivates the constant desire for cultivating political support. Rather than urging presidents to "stay private," it is more realistic to encourage careful attention to the specific arguments presidents employ in their rhetoric. Moralistic rhetoric that lacks policy specificity or pedagogical purpose can become vacuous, weakening its potentially powerful effect. Even more important, as the case studies in this book have demonstrated, the politically contingent nature of rhetorical choice is vitally important to an evaluation of its potentially powerful effects. George W. Bush's rhetorical choices illustrate the robust connection between rhetoric and political authority, as well as the constraints, risks, and benefits of presidential moral speech.

GEORGE W. BUSH'S RHETORIC: RIGHT MAKES MIGHT

No recent president has defined his leadership authority with moral and religious overtones as aggressively as George W. Bush. He has spoken repeatedly about the "moral purpose" of his presidency and believes that God has chosen him to fulfill a specific leadership role in American history. More precisely, Bush has used his moralistic rhetoric to define the War on Terror and craft his political authority as a wartime president.[8]

President Bush spoke moralistically prior to September 11, but his earlier use of morality and religion was nuanced, careful, and balanced. Before the terrorist attacks, the most anticipated speech of George W. Bush's first term discussed the future of stem cell research. Since the controversy over stem cell research is steeped in ethical questions, the president could not avoid discussing the moral implications of the course he chose. Nonetheless, the manner in which Bush discussed the relevant moral arguments was noteworthy and reflected the potentially divisive nature of the issue at hand.

Bush's speech sought to elucidate the issue and highlight its complexity, portraying stem cell research as a "difficult moral intersection" and the "leading edge of a series of moral hazards." By considering the arguments on both sides of the issue, Bush paid lip service to both research scientists and pro-life activists by stating, "I'm a strong supporter of science and technology. . . . I also believe life is a sacred gift from our creator."[9] Although Bush did reference the role of morality and religion in his decision-making process, the speech carefully avoided labeling opinions as morally right or wrong, instead concentrating on the advantages and limitations of stem cell research. The speech portrayed Bush as an earnest observer who had been forced, almost unwillingly, to make a choice and implied that the president shared the moral confusions of the citizens he addressed. Bush's rhetoric did not strengthen his position with the pro-life community, but it did foster the image of the president as a thoughtful arbiter who was aware of the moral ramifications of his decision. The rhetorical goal of the speech was to minimize political divisiveness and illustrate moral complexity, and its controlled language demonstrated that Bush understood the delicate nature of the issue at hand.

The terrorist attacks on September 11 profoundly transformed Bush's use of moral and religious rhetoric. In his speeches after September 11, Bush embraced the moral certainty he had avoided in his stem cell speech. In particular, Bush's September 20, 2001, speech before a joint session of Congress has been widely touted by former speechwriters and academics as a remarkable rhetorical effort.[10] The political circumstances after the terrorist attacks certainly affirmed that his use of moral and religious argumentation was an appropriate rhetorical choice. Bush used moral and religious arguments to demonstrate resolve for a confused and devastated American public. With Congress and both parties unified to take action, Bush's political authority was unquestioned and formidable. No intervening circumstances impeded the moral force of his rhetorical claims and observations. The joint session speech used moral and religious arguments to reassure, educate, caution, and inspire its listeners. In particular, the address's conclusion emphasizing the decisiveness and resoluteness of Bush's leadership posture shored up confidence that the demands made on the Taliban possessed both moral and political legitimacy.

Bush's rhetorical moralism entered murkier waters when the War on Terror shifted from Afghanistan to Iraq. In several speeches, Bush attempted to translate the moral cause of September 11 to the impending war with Iraq, applying the morally condemning language of "evil" to the administration's expanding foreign policy territory. Bush's justification for war in Iraq rested upon his assertion that morality transcends both location and time. In earlier speeches, the president had already established the evil nature of the al Qaeda terrorist network. In his October 7, 2002, speech at the Cincinnati Museum Center, Bush extended the description to Iraq, stating that "Terror cells and outlaw regimes building weapons of mass destruction are different faces of the same evil."[11]

Bush's most aggressive pronouncement of a morality-based foreign policy appeared in a June 1, 2002, speech at West Point. Chief speechwriter Michael Gerson believed the West Point speech was "the most important speech he had ever worked on." In the address, President Bush stated: "Some worry that it is somehow undiplomatic or impolite to speak the language of right and wrong. I disagree. Different circumstances require different methods, but not different moralities. Moral truth is the same in every culture, in every time, and in every place . . . We are in a conflict between good and evil, and America will call evil by its name. By confronting evil and lawless regimes, we do not create a problem, we reveal a problem. And we will lead the world in opposing it." Similar to the speeches given immediately after September 11, Bush's rhetoric capitalized upon a charged certainty that asserted moral truth is impervious to cultural interpretation, historical framework, or even religious influences. The firmness of his pronouncement undoubtedly boosted support amongst his most faithful followers, who agree that the language of right and wrong is not simply politically appropriate, but morally necessary.[12]

During the 2004 presidential campaign, Bush used moralistic appeals skillfully to avoid a mired discussion about the messy details of the Iraq War. In an April 13, 2004, nationally televised press conference, Bush focused on the rhetorical argument that the Iraqi occupation was morally right and that "freedom is the Almighty's gift to every man and woman in this world." The president's rhetoric clearly spelled out his vision but offered few details about the administration's policies and plans for instituting a new government in Iraq. As the search for weapons of mass destruction in Iraq faded, Bush's rhetorical defense of the war changed. The invasion no longer rested on the Bush doctrine of preemption but on a moral duty to bestow freedom upon the Iraqi people. With dissension within his own party effectively squelched, Bush successfully relied upon a moral defense of the war during the presidential campaign.[13] It was a political victory, and the strategic utility of moral and religious rhetoric was undoubtedly sustained. Nonetheless, the story of George W. Bush's presidency does not end with the results of the 2004 election. Bush's leadership must be considered in a larger historical and political context, which may complicate the impact of the electoral gains achieved by his rhetorical moralism.

President Bush is not equivocal, either rhetorically or politically. The advantage of his moralistic rhetoric is that everyone knows what he means. Opponents, supporters, and skeptics are not left guessing the direction of the Bush administration. The problem is that Bush's rhetoric situates itself to serve the primary function of *informing* the public of his decisions. Bush's moralism is open for everyone to see, and his rhetoric reflects the fact that he is not afraid to showcase his religious and moral influences. Bush's categorical certainty bolsters his already existing political coalitions, because he is often literally preaching to the choir. But this approach limits Bush's rhetorical reach. The listener must accept Bush's basic moral premises before considering his policy pronouncements or recommendations. Instead of using moral and religious arguments to support his policies, Bush's rhetoric implies the reverse: his policies are an articulation and extension of his existing moral vision. The political effect of this type of sequencing is that there is no room for vacillation or questioning; even Secretary of State Condoleezza Rice learned from her previous job as National Security Advisor that Bush only entertains the essence of a question and disdains complexity.[14] The deliberative component of *phronesis* is missing in Bush's post–September 11 rhetoric. Its absence in the immediate aftermath of the terrorist attacks was warranted and even welcomed, but since then, the rhetorical goal of reassurance has been replaced by the harder tasks of persuasion and education, which require an attention to deliberation and flexibility. The pedagogical focus in Lyndon Johnson's presidential rhetoric—the attempt to enlighten and enlarge the views of Americans—is absent in Bush's speeches. Rather than encouraging listeners to learn from his rhetoric, Bush asks citizens to accept the policies that follow from his own moral vision.

Ironically, the strength of Bush's rhetoric also contributes to its weaknesses. The reinforcing authority Bush emanates is due to the boldness of his moral pronouncements. This boldness may limit the breadth of his political coalition and could also contribute to fractures within it.[15] Bush's political goal is to build upon the Reagan juggernaut—to extend Republican loyalties beyond what existed previously. Bush's aims are corroborated by his often-quoted promise that he wants to serve as a "uniter" rather than a "divider." But because Bush's authority is tied so strongly to his resolute and unwavering moral commitments, it is unclear how he can enlarge the political coalition he seeks to build without placing a rhetorical premium on persuasion. In fact, Bush's rhetoric invites an assault from within the fold. Without a presidential election to hold the Republicans together, it is uncertain whether Bush's principled rhetoric can accomplish this task. Bush has put himself in a difficult situation. Although he has admitted publicly that he struggles with speaking and articulating his arguments, his leadership now depends upon his rhetoric.

With Bush, the acceptable definition of presidential character has evolved into an expression of certainty above all else. Consistency and "staying the course" must be maintained for Bush's seamless moralism to make sense. If the moral legitimacy of Bush's claims is challenged in any significant way, it is unclear where Bush will turn. His rhetorical choices have wedded him to a leadership strategy that does not provide him with room to maneuver or the ability to change direction. Since his defining speech on September 20, 2001, Bush has found a "rhetorical dwelling place" to house his Manichaean moralism, and he refuses to deviate from the course.[16] Because of this rigid rhetorical stance, an internal assault has the power to devastate Bush's authority, in that factional strife makes moral posturing politically disastrous.

Beyond the United States, Bush's moral posturing has failed to change public opinion amongst most European allies and three of the permanent U.N. Security Council members. According to a Pew Global Attitudes survey conducted in 2003, European disapproval of the United States stems largely from Bush's leadership, not from a more "general problem with America." In a 2004 follow-up survey, large majorities in nine nations, except the United States, had a negative opinion of President Bush. Furthermore, the gulf between Americans and Europeans on issues regarding religion and morality is quite large. While most Americans (58 percent) believe in the importance of religion in establishing morality, less than a third of both Western and Eastern Europeans accept this link. It is likely that American and European perspectives concerning the "morality of power" are diverging. Even though President Bush has emphasized the global nature of the War on Terror, a majority of citizens in all major European countries favor a more distant relationship with the United States.[17]

Lastly, Bush's categorical pronouncements have also generated polarizing effects in the Islamic world. When asked why he included Iran in the infamous "axis of evil," Bush responded that it was part of a strategy "to inspire those who love freedom inside the country." He went on to comment that he doubted that the democratic reformers within Iran were upset with the "axis of evil" remark, stating, "I made the calculation that they would be pleased." Instead, Bush's rhetoric has generated the opposite effect: all evidence suggests that the "axis of evil" remark has radicalized Iran further, emboldening its repressive Islamic militants and making the work of democratic reformers and moderates much more difficult, if not impossible.[18]

As the War on Terror and democratization in the Middle East enters situations where the lines between "good" and "evil" are less starkly drawn, Bush's categorical moralism may inhibit international diplomacy efforts. Countries such as Saudi Arabia, Egypt, Sudan, Indonesia, Syria, and Pakistan do not fall neatly within Bush's moral dichotomy. Domestic resolve to fight terrorism must be maintained, but the utility of categorical moral language diminishes as international relationships evolve into intricate commitments that demand diplomatic subtlety rather than moralistic bravado. In his June 1, 2002, speech at West Point, Bush acknowledged the main thesis of this book. He stated that rhetorical articulations of morality are complicated, reflecting the reality that "different circumstances require different methods." However, his continued use of the same moral arguments without an attention to wider international constraints implies that although Bush spoke these words at West Point, he never truly understood the full impact of their meaning.

The projection of a strident moral ideology, even a coherent one, is a risky rhetorical strategy because it creates considerable policy limitations that inevitably lead to political complications. Thus far, with regards to his domestic political standing, Bush has rolled the dice and won. However, any seasoned gambler or student of probability will attest to the fact that past fortune is not always an indicator of future success. It might behoove Bush to consider the rhetorical history of two fellow Republican presidents, Theodore Roosevelt and Abraham Lincoln. Both Roosevelt and Bush are "reinforcing" moral leaders; they advertised their strong ethical and religious beliefs in their rhetoric and emphasized the moral dimensions of their personas. Roosevelt used moral and religious rhetoric to sell his domestic and international policies but did not restrain his speech when his political support fractured. Consequently, Roosevelt found himself politically isolated and boxed into a corner, unable to back away from the bold statements he had issued earlier. Bush should consider Roosevelt's quandary, which demonstrates that the boldness of moral and religious rhetoric can inhibit future political maneuvering.

Lincoln's example is also instructive for Bush. Given that his advisors have recently attested to the fact that Bush admires Lincoln more than any other president, the comparison is particularly suitable.[19] Lincoln understood that complicated political conditions demanded moral restraint. Basing his rhetorical choices on contingent sources of authority, Lincoln is the rhetorical exemplar of prudence, or *phronesis*. Exercising a more subtle form of moral leadership than Theodore Roosevelt, Lincoln's skillful rhetoric illustrates the interdependency of political demands, deliberation, and principled idealism, the embodiment of *phronesis* as a rhetorical concept. When Lincoln did engage in moral and religious argumentation in the Second Inaugural, he avoided divisive language that might threaten the construction of future political coalitions and alliances. In the early aftermath of the Civil War, Lincoln acknowledged that God has His own purposes but admitted that humans do not fully understand them.

As international and domestic politics change, Lincoln's nuanced rhetoric may provide Bush with an instructive template.[20] After all, the ability to demonstrate *phronesis* depends heavily upon the willingness to imitate preceding demonstrations of excellence. Lincoln's recognition of rhetoric as a political tool augmented his authority, which ultimately enabled him to fulfill the moral requirements of his constitutional office. The lesson learned from Lincoln is a valuable one: moral restraint can be a powerful rhetorical option available to presidents. Unfortunately, even if the wisdom of Lincoln's approach is realized, it will be difficult, if not impossible, for Bush to distance himself from the committed moral stances he has already taken.

Lincoln also illustrates a powerful lesson about the modern prospects of political leadership in the United States. To a certain extent, all contemporary presidents now labor under the demands of lofty presidential rhetoric and moral leadership. This expectation constrains the range of rhetoric acceptable for modern presidential leadership. This development ensures that we will never encounter secular dullness in presidential rhetoric again, but we must consider whether the potential loss of a prudently restrained Lincoln is an even trade.

AFTERWORD

The 2006 Election: The Rhetoric of Before and After

The day after the 2006 midterm elections, President Bush held a press conference to announce the resignation of Secretary of Defense, Donald Rumsfeld. The President's personnel change grabbed the headlines, yet the most interesting revelation concerned Bush's demeanor. His entire presentation stood in striking contrast to the image described in the opening pages of this book. The swagger was gone. The chief executive who had once enjoyed a 90 percent approval rating was reduced to pleading for his continued relevancy and leadership, culminating in the admission that he and his party had been the recipients of a cumulative "thumping." The results of the 2006 midterm can be considered another example of the tangible political ramifications of rhetorical choice.

Even President Bush's detractors winced at his performance on November 8. The awkwardness of the Rumsfeld announcement was almost painful to watch. The discomfort arose not from the substantive rationale for Rumsfeld's removal; the time had clearly come for a new Secretary of Defense. What made the event stick out like a sore thumb was the fact that the country had never witnessed Bush's resoluteness and confidence shaken to the core. The results of the election forced Bush to change direction and alter his course of action—something his rhetoric did not encourage. The entire spectacle of the press conference rested awkwardly on the superstructure of moral righteousness Bush had built for himself. If firing the Secretary of Defense proved difficult, Bush's executive leadership did not possess the flexibility to make even more drastic policy changes in the prosecution of the global war on terror.

Rhetoric wasn't the sole cause of Bush's political troubles in 2006, but the language he used to justify the war in Iraq became emblematic of the failed course he chose to pursue. One of the main strategic advantages of moral rhetoric is its potential for eliminating political opposition. Bush's moral justification for the war in Iraq began to have the opposite effect: it emboldened his detractors instead of defeating them. The image of Jim Webb lifting his son's combat boots high above his head is one of the most powerful and lasting images of the 2006 election. This reality is a hard pill for Bush to swallow. Webb, a political novice, found a way to seize the moral high ground from the President of the United States in one meaningful gesture. The ability of a relatively unknown senator-elect to achieve this status is indicative of Bush's weakened political condition.

During the 2006 campaign, Bush continued to use the same moral and religious arguments he had employed earlier in his presidency. With deaths of American soldiers mounting, the effectiveness of Bush's rhetoric diminished. At a September 29, 2006 speech in Washington, D.C., President Bush stated, "I believe deep within the soul of every man, woman, and child on the face of the Earth is a desire to live in freedom." Bush's statement—that the love of freedom is universal—is a familiar rallying cry. Nonetheless, a degree of corroboration is required for such abstract pronouncements to ring true. When Bush stated his belief in freedom's universal appeal years earlier, Americans accepted his premise because they saw evidence of his claims. Most notably, the image of millions of proud Iraqis, raising their inked fingers in the air, gave credence to Bush's claim that freedom and democracy had won the day. In 2006, it was much harder for Americans to reconcile Bush's rhetoric with what they saw every night on the evening news. If freedom's appeal is universal, then why weren't Iraqis fighting for it? Why were coalition forces still facing the threat of improvised explosive devices and random kidnappings if Iraqis truly wanted democracy? Due to the growing weight of countervailing evidence, the categorical nature of Bush's arguments couldn't hold their water.

Despite the rhetorical fallacies that grew around him like ivy, Bush pressed forward, seemingly undeterred. Sometimes the contradiction of Bush's untenable arguments was so stark, it is almost remarkable the President actually spoke the words attributed to him. In the same September 2006 speech, Bush advocated the continued practice of wiretapping in one breath, and two sentences later, stated that we must "help our children and grandchildren live in a peaceful world by encouraging the spread of liberty." Bush's arguments had become routine to the point that such a contradiction in terms—or at least a blatant tension in juxtaposition—went unnoticed by the President and his speechwriters.

His arguments about freedom, values, and morals had become rote to the point that their meaning was almost vacuous. His moral rhetoric had lost its sharp edge. Instead of using moral arguments as a culminating crescendo, Bush incorporated them as his standard vernacular. The contrast with Lincoln illustrates Bush's deficiencies so well, it cannot be avoided. When Lincoln invoked a moral or religious argument, it solicited the anticipated political effect: listeners paid attention. Bush's overkill turned into rhetorical hypnosis with very little political punch.

Throughout the midterm campaign, Bush argued that Iraq was more than a military struggle. At the American Legion National Convention on August 31, 2006, in Salt Lake City, the President described Iraq as the cornerstone of the "decisive ideological struggle of the 21st century." According to Bush, the dividing lines of the struggle are clear. One side are those "who believe in the values of freedom and moderation." On the other side are "those driven by the values of tyranny and extremism." Iraq is an important battle in the wider ideological struggle, but U.S. military tactics in Iraq, which had come under considerable scrutiny, are almost a secondary presidential concern. Focusing on the details has not been a hallmark of George W. Bush's presidency. Conservatives accused his father of missing the "vision thing" during his term, yet the younger Bush never suffered from that shortcoming.

As several case studies in this book have demonstrated, the problem with relying too heavily on strongly held moral beliefs is that stubborn resoluteness often masks the pesky political realities percolating beneath the surface. The battle between the liberal West and radical Islam may become the decisive battle of this century, as President Bush has repeatedly argued. But a persistent and consistent wholesale reliance upon moral justification with little attention to strategic particulars almost always results in failed presidential leadership.

Bush's post-election rhetoric implies the President understood that business as usual was not a viable option. In a move reminiscent of Jimmy Carter's 1979 retreat to Camp David, Bush and his war advisers engaged in extended consultation about Iraq. Throughout December, Bush met with a wide range of experts to consider all strategic options. After allowing the suspense to build for several weeks, the President announced the course he had chosen in a January 10, 2007, televised address to the nation.

Bush's speech reflected his new political situation. Much like his post-election press conference, he shelved his familiar moral confidence. The policy prescription in Iraq had not changed much, but the President's justification for the continued prosecution of the war altered its emphasis. According to the President's speech, the bottom line was "failure in Iraq would be a disaster for the United States." The broad ideological struggle Bush had talked about in numerous speeches before the midterm election had been replaced with an opening argument about national self-interest. The bulk of Bush's speech consisted of a detailed exegesis concerning the military's ground plan for recapturing Baghdad. The broader moral struggle between the moral moderates and the evil extremists made an appearance near the end of the speech, but lost its marquee status. The President had heard loud and clear the message of the American people, and he responded with nuts and bolts rather than ideological warfare.

The President continued his new approach in a follow-up speech the next day at Fort Benning, Georgia. The contrast between Bush's pre-election speech at the American Legion National Convention and his address at Fort Benning is noticeable. In the Legion speech, the President spoke about the wider "ideological struggle" early in his remarks, using that trope as his framing argument. At Fort Benning, he asked his listeners to imagine what would happen if our enemy "gained control of energy reserves." With rising gas prices, the impact of such a consequence is much more tangible than the amorphous implications of losing a struggle between moderation and extremism. Indeed, Bush promised the military families at Fort Benning that a "well-defined mission" would guide the forthcoming surge in Iraq.

President Bush's altered rhetorical script is a step in the right direction. After having the moral wind knocked out of him, Bush refocused his rhetorical justifications for Iraq and the larger global war on terror. The resource that no one can take away from him—neither Harry Reid nor Nancy Pelosi—is the constitutional authority granted to the President as commander-in-chief. Lincoln based his wartime leadership on its premise. Bush might also consider another constitutional resource to substantiate his post-election rhetorical emphasis on national self-interest and security: the oath of office. The oath states that the President must swear to "preserve, protect, and defend the Constitution of the United States." Members of Congress are not constitutionally obligated to take a prescribed oath of office, which makes the oath a unique resource for executive power. Only a few presidents (Jackson, Lincoln, Andrew Johnson) have invoked the oath as justification for their actions. With diminished political resources in his arsenal, Bush might consider shifting his rationale for leadership away from moral and religious justifications and back to the most reliable structure now available to him, the Constitution itself.

LOOKING AHEAD TO 2008: MOVING BEYOND CATEGORICAL MORALITY

With no heir apparent in sight, 2008 may turn into the most volatile election cycle in recent history. The American electorate is faced with a choice between familiar faces of the past (Hillary Clinton, John McCain, Newt Gingrich, John Edwards) and unpredictable newcomers (Barack Obama, Rudy Giuliani, Mitt Romney). As both parties try to settle on a nominee, the political landscape is anything but smooth sailing. Despite all the uncertainty, there is one prediction that is almost guaranteed: none of the presidential candidates will adopt George W. Bush's moralistic rhetoric.

Yes, there will be moralizing. As this book has shown, no president has completely shunned moral and religious language in his public addresses. Since presidential campaigns are nothing more than marathon auditions for the Oval Office, all candidates will try to sound presidential on the stump. No matter who becomes Bush's successor, the new president will change the manner in which moral and religious arguments are articulated. As his second term winds up, it has become abundantly clear that Bush's persistent categorical rhetoric inhibited his political choices. The rigidity of his moral pronouncements proved more costly than beneficial, and the political reality of Bush's constraint should serve as a lesson for the next president.

The Democratic candidates must navigate a potential political minefield in 2008. A complete refusal to engage the electorate morally or spiritually is a dangerous strategy to pursue. The 2008 election will be won and lost in the suburban neighborhoods of states like Florida, Ohio, Pennsylvania, Colorado, Michigan, Wisconsin, and Virginia. Church attendance is high in these areas of the country; morality and religion are not dirty words. Ceding the famous "values voters" in the past two presidential elections, the Democrats have found themselves on the short end of the stick both times. As chapter 2 demonstrated, Democratic presidents are no less moralistic in their rhetoric than Republican presidents. The 2008 Democratic hopefuls need to channel the rhetoric of Woodrow Wilson, Franklin Roosevelt, John Kennedy, Lyndon Johnson, and even

Bill Clinton to point them in the right direction. In this respect, each of the frontrunners shows rhetorical promise.

Something more than a natural talent for public speaking, a powerful presence, and self-confidence makes Barack Obama a capable orator. Obama's speech garners attention because his spoken message closely resembles the Democratic rhetorical tradition of the twentieth century. Obama's message is rooted in the progressive belief of change. In his announcement speech in Springfield, Illinois, Obama described his unyielding faith as his belief that "in the face of impossible odds, people who love their country can change it." Obama's moral imperative is to finish the work that needs to be done in America—the work that will move the nation towards a more perfect model of justice and equality.

Obama understands that Democrats must figure out an effective way to address "religious America." In a June 28, 2006, address at the Call to Renewal conference, Obama called for members of his party to "tackle head-on the mutual suspicion that sometimes exists between religious America and secular America." According to Obama, it is a "mistake when we fail to acknowledge the power of faith in people's lives—in the lives of the American people—and I think it's time that we join a serious debate about how to reconcile faith with our modern, pluralistic democracy."

Obama's rhetoric is supplanted by his own personal story of religious awakening. After college, Obama traveled to Chicago to work as a community organizer for a group of Christian churches. After several months, Obama felt drawn "not just to work with the church, but to be in the church." His own journey of embracing religion is an important narrative; John Kerry had no similar story of faith in 2004. For Obama, religion is both a spiritual and community exercise. The church is an agent of social change, and should be embraced as such. His articulation of religion's intricate relationship with politics elevates his discourse, and enables him to replicate the rhetorical message of previous Democratic presidents. His rhetoric enables him to communicate effectively with millions of church-going Americans who respond to moral and religious arguments, and it also bolsters his credibility among the left-wing of the party, which admires his message of reform. In this sense, Obama's ability to employ moral and religious rhetoric with ease has the potential to boost his political credibility with disparate electoral populations—namely the centrist "swing voters" and the liberals. Obama has found a broad moral framework for his rhetoric. He needs to focus his efforts on providing the policy details and proposals to supplant the morals and principles he advocates.

Without a doubt, John Edwards's rhetoric helped him earn the Democratic vice-presidential nomination in 2004. His "two Americas" speech won him notoriety in a field of lackluster Democratic challengers. Edwards's 2008 rhetoric closely resembles Obama's message. Edwards's conception of American morality is similarly progressive, with a strong emphasis on the eradication of poverty. At a National Press Club event on June 22, 2006, Edwards called poverty the "great moral issue of our time." His legitimacy stems from his recent stint as director of a research center on poverty at the University of North Carolina. Edwards has found a niche in the horse race, and believes that his rhetorical success in the 2004 primary validates his focus on poverty.

Edwards demonstrated his ability to resonate with Democratic voters four years ago, although it is unclear that his elevation of poverty's moral status will generate widespread traction amongst the electorate. Eradicating poverty can be described as a legitimate moral issue, but Edwards's declaration that it is the "great moral issue of our time" may make him vulnerable to criticism among voters who believe that the global war on terror is the nation's most important moral challenge. Edwards differs from Obama in this respect. Avoiding superlatives, Obama speaks in general terms about the moral and religious importance of economic progress and American renewal.

Edwards must be mindful of George W. Bush's pitfalls, and avoid painting himself into a corner. With America's international stature uncertain and the perceived threat of a terrorist attack always imminent, Edwards might reconsider his narrow focus. The strength of Edwards's rhetoric is its capacity to demonstrate empathy, an important Democratic ideal. It is up to Edwards to figure out a way to expand the breadth of his strong Democratic message and make it applicable to other salient policy issues.

Hillary Clinton's speeches prove she understands the weaknesses of Bush's rhetorical choices. Clinton lacks the oratorical flair of Obama and Edwards. Instead, her strength lies in her uncanny ability to cut to the chase of an argument. Her rhetoric is direct, analytical, and uncomplicated. She is also the Democratic candidate who appears the most ambitious in articulating criticisms of the Bush administration.

At an October 31, 2006, speech before the Council on Foreign Relations, Clinton criticized the Bush administration for promoting a "simplistic division of the world into good and evil." She continued:

At the end of the day, you have to question whether this administration has led with our values or used our values as a cloak to justify its ideology and unilateralism. Something is wrong when our pursuit of idealistic goals has turned a good portion of the world against us.

In the same speech, she went on to invoke Protestant theologian Reinhold Niebuhr, cautioning America against believing wholeheartedly "that God was on our side." No other Democratic candidate has nailed this criticism of Bush as squarely as Clinton. Her public critique of Bush can only lead to the assumption that she will not repeat his rhetorical mistakes if elected to the White House.

It is more likely that Clinton's rhetoric will adopt a blend of moralism and pragmatism. Her rhetorical tendency is to gravitate towards the wonky end of the spectrum; she likes quoting data in her speeches and citing specific sections of public law. It would be foolish for Clinton to try to keep up with Obama and Edwards's inspirational verses and rhetorical flourish. Clinton's challenge will be to figure out how she can infuse enough moral and religious language into her speeches to make her sound presidential rather than intellectual. If she includes too much, her rhetoric runs the risk of appearing forced. There is a delicate balance for Clinton that will enable her to reach the occasional lofty platitudes of presidential rhetorical discourse without sounding overly contrived. Her political test will be to find that voice and maintain it throughout a long, protracted campaign.

Republican presidential contenders must traverse a thornier path than Democrats in 2008. Bush's unpopularity puts them in the awkward situation of trying to figure out how to distance themselves from the sitting president while also wooing voters from the party's conservative base. Rudy Giuliani has tried to split the difference in his rhetoric. In his 2004 speech at the Republican National Convention, Giuliani lauded President Bush's leadership style, remarking that "Some call it stubbornness. I call it principled leadership." He contrasted Bush to John Kerry, who Giuliani claimed did not exhibit a "clear, precise, and consistent vision." According to Giuliani, Bush is a "leader who is willing to stick with difficult decisions even as public opinion shifts."

As far as executive leadership style is concerned, Giuliani is the candidate that most closely resembles Bush. Giuliani values persistence, steadfastness, and decisive action. Despite their shared persona, Giuliani will not express these personal characteristics in the same way Bush has articulated them. Because of his checkered past, Giuliani will avoid moralistic and religious platitudes and will instead adopt a secular leadership style. His personal transgressions are only part of his problem. In disagreement with moral conservatives on many social issues, Giuliani needs to minimize reminders of his independence. Whereas Bush cannot and will not separate moral leadership from decisiveness, Giuliani will attempt to sever those two elements.

The other Republican frontrunner, John McCain, has established a unique message of moral leadership. Taking cues from his self-professed hero, Theodore Roosevelt, McCain often adopts the role of the "reformer" to demonstrate his moral commitment. McCain's efforts to clean up the system, including his crusade to change campaign finance laws and eliminate wasteful pork barrel spending—provide him with his "straight talk" script that became popular during the 2000 campaign.

McCain's rhetorical moralism is understated. His speeches are not laden with moral and religious references, and he rarely employs soaring platitudes from above. Instead, McCain's moral leadership comes from who he is—his own personal experiences and history. In this sense, McCain's rhetorical circumstances are vastly different from George W. Bush's. McCain's moral qualifications are self-evidentiary, which gives him more rhetorical latitude than Bush. Even though McCain has supported the war in Iraq, he has not resorted to framing the war in starkly moral terms like Bush. Instead, McCain has focused primarily on national security, and why winning in Iraq is essential for America's strategic interests. For example, in an October 10, 2005, speech at the American Enterprise Institute, McCain stated, "We must get Iraq right because America's stake in that conflict is enormous." McCain's unwavering support for the war may damage his presidential bid in 2008. His saving grace could be that his rationale for the war provides him with greater flexibility than President Bush's moralistic orations. If withdrawal from Iraq becomes unavoidable, McCain's rhetoric allows him to pivot by arguing that America's national security dictates a new course of action. In contrast, moral justifications offer no such wiggle room.

The other Republicans in the 2008 race will confront rhetorical challenges, as well. Newt Gingrich, a favorite candidate among the conservative base, will face allegations of hypocrisy if he uses moral language too often. As a Mormon, Mitt Romney may find it difficult to talk about religion effectively to the nationwide electorate. Sam Brownback's conversion to Catholicism and his connection to Opus Dei put his religious beliefs in a potentially controversial spotlight. The Republican candidate with the greatest potential to speak the rhetoric of morality and religion with natural ease is former Arkansas governor Mike Huckabee, who was trained as a Baptist minister, served as a pastor, and ran a religiously based television station. Huckabee is a dark horse candidate, and may not raise enough money to guarantee that his rhetorical message reaches a broad segment of Republican primary voters.

All candidates struggle to find their voice on the campaign trail. Unlike gubernatorial and congressional office-seekers, presidential candidates have the added pressure of trying to sound like they belong in the White House. As this book has shown, presidents use the language of morality and religion with varying frequency and in different contexts. Presidential candidates know they must try to speak moralistically, but finding the right script is an onerous task for most. According to the National Election Pool exit poll, 22 percent of 2004 voters responded that "moral values" mattered more to them than any other issue. Almost four years later, pundits and scholars are still debating the impact of these ubiquitous "moral values" voters. Despite the fuzziness, it seems risky for 2008 candidates to ignore such a large chunk of the electorate. While the meaning of the term "moral values" is not always crystal clear, it is a safe bet that the winning candidate in 2008 will have figured out how to maximize the strategic utility of moral and religious rhetoric.

METHODOLOGICAL APPENDIX

Coding Rules: Annual Addresses

1. Description of American policies and the policies of foreign nations: Policies or policy proposals are "just, moral, wicked, humane, evil, good, magnanimous, right (versus wrong), demoralizing, immoral, compassionate, merciful, humane, upright, inhumane, immoral, unjust, righteous." Policies or policy proposals exhibit or encourage "justice, liberality, immorality, moral force, spirituality, spiritual progress, integrity, honesty, faith, values."

2. Description of citizenry/nation (foreign or United States): Citizens or the nation are "virtuous, just, moral, immoral, wicked, atheistic, irreverent, humane, disinterested, honest, evil, pious, merciful, upright, temperate, compassionate, spiritual, righteous, moderate." Citizens or the nation possess or exhibit "integrity, fortitude, ideals, good character, moral force, faith, principles of humanity, spiritual power, moderation, immorality, spiritual progress, values." Citizens or the nation lack "virtue, morality, humanity, honesty, faith, ideals, piety, mercifulness, uprightness, spirituality, righteousness, values."

3. General appeals: References to "national honor, national character, national conscience, values, ideals, morals, justice, national ideals, laws of morality, moral guardianship, American spirit, national spirit."

4. Defense or criticism of political actions, both domestic and foreign: Actions were "virtuous, just, moral, humane, honest, disinterested, unjust, immoral, wicked, inhumane, evil, merciful, upright, temperate, compassionate, righteous, right." Actions exhibited and exemplified "integrity, good character, ideals, faith, morality, morals, honesty, mercifulness, piety, compassion, justice, uprightness, virtue, humanity, spirituality, righteousness, values."

5. Religious language: All references to spiritual beings or religious ideals, such as "Providence, God, Supreme Being, Christianity, Christendom,

the Almighty." Also, all general references to the importance of religion, religious principles, or religious values.

EXAMPLES OF MORAL AND RELIGIOUS RHETORIC: ANNUAL ADDRESSES

"Here and throughout our country may simple manners, pure morals, and true religion flourish forever!"
—JOHN ADAMS, NOVEMBER 22, 1800, FOURTH ANNUAL ADDRESS

"No country has been so much favored, or should acknowledge with deeper reverence the manifestations of the divine protection. An all wise Creator directed and guarded us in our infant struggle for freedom and has constantly watched over our surprising progress until we have become one of the great nations of the earth."
—JAMES K. POLK, DECEMBER 7, 1847, THIRD ANNUAL ADDRESS

"It is impossible, where so many trusts are to be allotted, that the right parties should be chosen in every instance. History shows that no Administration from the time of Washington to the present has been free from these mistakes. But I leave comparisons to history, claiming only that I have acted in every instance from a conscientious desire to do what was right, constitutional, within the law, and for the very best interests of the whole people. Failures have been errors of judgment, not of intent."
—ULYSSES S. GRANT, DECEMBER 5, 1876, EIGHTH ANNUAL ADDRESS

"No man can take part in the torture of a human being without having his own moral nature permanently lowered. Every lynching means just so much moral deterioration in all the children who have any knowledge in it, and therefore just so much additional trouble for the next generation of Americans."
—THEODORE ROOSEVELT, DECEMBER 5, 1905, FIFTH ANNUAL ADDRESS

"As far as the writ of Federal law will run, we must abolish not some, but all racial discrimination. For this is not merely an economic issue, or a social, political, or international issue. It is a moral issue, and it must be met by the passage this session of the bill now pending in the House."
—LYNDON B. JOHNSON, JANUARY 8, 1964, FIRST ANNUAL ADDRESS

"To those imprisoned in regimes held captive, to those beaten for daring to fight for freedom and democracy—for their right to worship, to speak, to live and to prosper in the family of free nations—we say to you tonight: You are not alone Freedom Fighters. America will support you with moral and material assistance—your right not just to fight and die for freedom, but to fight and with freedom—to win freedom in Afghanistan; in Angola; in Cambodia; and in Nicaragua. This is a great moral challenge for the entire world."

—RONALD REAGAN, FEBRUARY 4, 1986, FIFTH ANNUAL ADDRESS

"Beyond all differences of race or creed, we are one country, mourning together and facing danger together. Deep in the American character, there is honor, and it is stronger than cynicism. Many have discovered again that even in tragedy, God is near."

—GEORGE W. BUSH, JANUARY 29, 2002, FIRST ANNUAL ADDRESS

CODING RULES FOR VISIONARY AND TRADITIONALIST APPEALS: INAUGURALS

Visionary rhetoric was defined as:

1. Appeals that celebrated new, emerging, revised, reconstructed, or changing values, principles, insights, ideals, or morals, including all references to vision, changes in morals or the national spirit, organic law, new promises, new horizons, new insights, new promises, a "seeking" nation, and a new America; any endorsement of "moving forward" instead of "standing still"

2. Criticisms of old values or traditional insights; condemnation of retrospection

3. Appeals to the collective moral or principled nature of America, including the national spirit, national pride, the unity of America, the heart of America, the limits of the individual, and the nation's moral strength

Traditionalist rhetoric was defined as:

1. Appeals that call for a return to earlier, traditional principles, morals, ideals; a restoration or renewal of older ideals, principles, or beginning standards; references to the truths, principles, or ideals of the Founders; laudatory references to America's heritage; preservation of older ideals, traditions, foundations, or basic ideals

2. Appeals that describe ideals or principles as fixed, immutable, steadfast, continuous, permanent, universal, old-fashioned

3. Appeals that stress the importance of individual responsibility, self-reliance, discipline, personal character, private character, courage, duty

4. Appeals that stress an explicit categorical distinction between right and wrong or good and evil

EXAMPLES OF VISIONARY AND TRADITIONALIST RHETORIC: INAUGURALS

Visionary Rhetoric

"We do not retreat. We are not content to stand still. As Americans, we go forward, in the service of our country, by the will of God."

—FRANKLIN ROOSEVELT, 1941

"And if a beach-head of cooperation may push back the jungle of suspicion, let both sides join in creating a new endeavor, not a new balance of power, but a new world of law, where the strong are just and the weak secure and the peace preserved."

—JOHN F. KENNEDY, 1961

Categorical/Retrospective Rhetoric

"The great essential to our happiness and prosperity is that we adhere to the principles upon which the Government was established and insist upon their faithful observance."

—WILLIAM MCKINLEY, 1897

"Each and every one of us in our own way must assume personal responsibility not only for ourselves and our families, but for our neighbors and our nation."

—BILL CLINTON, 1997

NOTES

Chapter 1. Presidential Moral Leadership and Rhetoric

1. "President Delivers State of the Union Address," http://www.whitehouse.gov/news/releases/2002/01/20020129–11.html (accessed Apr. 10, 2004).

2. Bush admitted that he specifically used moralistic rhetoric because it was "very important for the American president at this point in history to speak very clearly about the evils the world faces." See Woodward, *Plan of Attack*, 88.

3. Gallup News Service. http://www.gallup.com/poll/releases (accessed Feb. 12, 2002).

4. Fathi, "A Nation Challenged," A10; Chafets, "Judge Dubya," 37; O' Hanlon, "Choosing the Right Enemies," A21.

5. For an examination of the Puritan origins of the American jeremiad, or political sermon, see Bercovitch, *American Jeremiad.*

6. Gerring, *Party Ideologies in America,* 290. Gerring uses content analysis of party platforms to measure partisan ideology across time. See Hinckley, *Symbolic Presidency,* 73–86 and 115–21 for an attempt to quantify moral and religious rhetoric from Theodore Roosevelt through Reagan.

7. For example, Ellis, *Speaking to the People;* Bimes, *Metamorphosis of Presidential Populism;* Tulis, *Rhetorical Presidency;* Laracey, *Presidents and the People;* Germino, *Inaugural Addresses of American Presidents;* Hinckley, *Symbolic Presidency.*

8. Hart and Pauley, *Political Pulpit Revisited;* Medhurst, "Religious Rhetoric and the *Ethos* of Democracy"; Medhurst, "American Cosmology and the Rhetoric of Inaugural Prayer"; Lee and Barton, "Clinton's Rhetoric of Contrition"; Campbell and Jamieson, "Inaugurating the Presidency." On the influence of the Old Testament on American political rhetoric in general, see Darsey, *Prophetic Tradition and Radical Rhetoric in America.*

9. Barber, *Presidential Character;* George and George, *Presidential Personality and Performance;* Robert Shogan, *Double-Edged Sword;* Pfiffner, *Character Factor;* Singer, *President of Good and Evil;* Novak, *Choosing Our King;* Alley, *So Help Me God;* Bellah, "Civil Religion in America"; Pierard and Linder, *Civil Religion and the Presidency;* Hart and Pauley, *Political Pulpit Revisited;* Fairbanks, "Priestly Functions of the Presidency"; Roelofs, "Prophetic President."

10. Hargrove, *President as Leader.*

11. Stuckey, *Defining Americans.* See chapter 3 on Grover Cleveland for an explanation of why the rhetoric of virtue as criteria for citizenship lessened during this time period.

12. Beasley, *You, the People,* 17. On the strategic versus constitutive study of rhetoric, see Stuckey and Antczak, "Rhetorical Presidency: Deepening Vision, Widening Exchange."

13. Bitzer, "Rhetorical Situation."

14. Earlier research established an empirical fact: in varying degrees, presidents have used moral and religious rhetoric in their public discourse. With the exception of the scholars who studied the evolution of the Inaugural Address, this research has concentrated on the twentieth-century presidents. From a quantitative standpoint, scholars know little about the moral and religious speech of the "pre-modern" presidential era or whether this type of rhetorical argument has changed over time. See McDiarmid, "Presidential Inaugural Addresses"; Sigelman, "Presidential Inaugurals"; Hinckley, *Symbolic Presidency,* 65–88.

15. These variables may be more pertinent to scholarship in political science and presidential studies.

16. Riker, *Art of Political Manipulation,* ix.

17. See Mansfield, *Taming the Prince.*

18. See Skowronek, *Politics Presidents Make.*

19. See Moe, "Politicized Presidency"; Moe, "Presidents, Institutions, and Theory"; Rudalevige, *Managing the President's Program;* Kenneth R. Mayer, *With the Stroke of a Pen.*

20. Self, "Rhetoric and *Phronesis,*" 141; Hariman, "Theory without Modernity," 5.

21. The notable exceptions include Hart and Pauley, *Political Pulpit Revisited* and Hart, *Verbal Style and the Presidency.* Analyses of individual presidents include Stuckey, *Playing the Game;* Dallek, *Ronald Reagan;* Dorsey, *Reconstituting the American Spirit;* Kraig, *Woodrow Wilson and the Lost World;* Motter, "Jimmy Carter in Context"; Goldzwig and Dionisopoulos, *In a Perilous Hour;* Medhurst, *Dwight D. Eisenhower.*

22. Campbell and Jamieson, *Deeds Done in Words;* Beasley, *You, the People.*

23. Rossiter, *American Presidency.*

24. Skowronek, *Politics Presidents Make,* 18.

25. Moe, "Presidents, Institutions, and Theory," 338.

26. Stuckey, *Strategic Failures.*

27. For a discussion of rhetorical limits, see Bruner, "Rhetorical Criticism."

28. For a detailed examination of several presidential failures, see Stuckey, *Strategic Failures.*

29. Skowronek, *Politics Presidents Make,* 34–36.

30. I follow Stuckey's *Strategic Failures* in this regard. Stuckey is concerned primarily with the political ramifications of rhetorical decisions, rather than the ethical or constitutive impact a communication strategy may have on policy.

CHAPTER 2. RHETORICAL PATTERNS OF THE ANNUAL AND INAUGURAL ADDRESSES

1. To complete the data collection, I analyzed approximately five thousand pages of text. A research assistant recoded 25 percent of the addresses; inter-coder reliability was high at .92.

2. For several reasons why the Annual Addresses are a good source of data for studying rhetorical development, see Teten, "Evolution of the Modern Rhetorical Presidency," 335; Campbell and Jamieson, *Deeds Done in Words*, 54; Campbell and Jamieson, "Rhetorical Hybrids."

3. Follett, *Speaker of the House of Representatives*, 325.

4. One example of inspirational rhetoric that was not coded as an example of moral or religious rhetoric is contained in John Kennedy's 1963 Annual Address. At the conclusion of the speech, Kennedy stated, "We are not lulled by the momentary calm of the sea or the somewhat clearer skies above. We know the turbulence that lies below, and the storms that are beyond the horizon this year. But now the winds of change appear to be blowing more strongly than ever, in the world of communism as well as our own." This is certainly an inspirational statement, but it does not contain explicit moral or religious argumentation.

5. Hinckley, *Symbolic Presidency*; Cohen, *Presidential Responsiveness and Public Policy-Making*.

6. From Washington through Taft, the average number of words per sentence was thirty-six. After Wilson, this average dropped to twenty-three. Shorter sentences increase the denominator of the ratio but also provide more opportunities for the president to engage in moral and religious argumentation. To correct any shortcomings of this methodology, I include an alternate analysis that measures the total number of moral and religious appeals per Annual Address without correcting for the length of the speech.

7. Neustadt, *Presidential Power*; Greenstein, "Change and Continuity in the Modern Presidency"; Greenstein, Berman, and Felzenberg, *Evolution of the Modern Presidency*. For a critical examination of bifurcated periodization in presidential studies, see Galvin and Shogan, "Presidential Politicization and Centralization." Tulis, "Reflections on the Rhetorical Presidency in American Political Development," 211. As Tulis notes, other scholars have made similar observations, including Theodore Lowi, James Ceaser, Roderick Hart, George Edwards III, Samuel Kernell, and Bruce Miroff.

8. Ketcham, *Presidents above Party*.

9. Skowronek, *Politics Presidents Make*, 52–54.

10. Tulis, *Rhetorical Presidency*, 136; Ellis, *Speaking to the People*. In varying degrees, many of the essays in this volume challenge Tulis's historical depiction of presidential rhetoric. In particular, see David Nichols, "A Marriage Made in Philadelphia: The Constitution and the Rhetorical Presidency"; Mel Laracey, "The Presidential Newspaper: The Forgotten Way of Going Public"; Gerald Gamm and Renee Smith, "Presidents, Parties, and the Public: Evolving Patterns of Interaction, 1877–1929"; Richard Ellis, "Accepting the Nomination: From Martin Van Buren to Franklin Delano Roosevelt", Terri Bimes and Stephen Skowronek, "Woodrow Wilson's Critique of Popular Leadership: Reassessing the Modern-Traditional Divide in Presidential History"; and Daniel Stid, "Rhetorical Leadership and 'Common Counsel' in the Presidency of Woodrow Wilson." Another volume that offers alternatives to Tulis's approach is Medhurst, *Beyond the Rhetorical Presidency*. For a clarification of the differences between the study of "presidential rhetoric" and the "rhetorical presidency" see Medhurst, "The Tale of Two Constructs"and Hoffman, "'Going Public' in the Nineteenth Century" in *Beyond the Rhetorical Presidency*.

11. Because they never gave an Annual Address, William Henry Harrison and James Garfield are omitted.

12. Novak, *On Two Wings*, 7. Novak argues that scholars have concentrated on how the Enlightenment influenced the Founders but have forgotten the importance of religion. In particular, the stories of the Hebrew Bible served as a "political doctrine" for early Americans.

13. Colleen Shogan, "Rhetorical Moralism in the Plebiscitary Presidency." Zachary Taylor and Warren Harding have been omitted from this graph because their total number of coded moral and religious sentences was less than ten, making the denominator of the ratio too small for reliable analysis.

14. My analysis questions Gronbeck's conclusion that the changes described by Tulis in *The Rhetorical Presidency* are in fact products of the "electronic revolution." Gronbeck is unable to explain why abrupt changes in presidential rhetoric occurred before the advent of the electronic presidency, which he dates at 1924. See Gronbeck, "Presidency in the Age of Secondary Orality."

15. Tulis, *Rhetorical Presidency*, 135.

16. Thurow, "Dimensions of Presidential Character," 22–23.

17. In *Rhetoric*, Aristotle labeled ceremonial speech that either "praises or blames" as epideictic. The Greek term *epideictic* means "fit for display." See Aristotle, *Rhetoric and the Poetics of Aristotle*, 1385b. Condit, "Functions of Epideictic," 290; Campbell and Jamieson, *Deeds Done in Words*, 15.

18. The category of "visionary" rhetoric comes directly from Tulis, who uses the term to describe Wilson's speech. See Tulis, *Rhetorical Presidency*, 135. Tulis contends that Wilson captured public sentiment and articulated its wishes rather than appealing to established principles. The category of "retrospective" rhetoric is my own invention, which I created after realizing that there was a whole other ideological orientation of twentieth-century presidential rhetoric missing in *The Rhetorical Presidency*.

19. For example, the entire first half of George Washington's First Inaugural Address described his feeling of moral responsibility in accepting the presidency. Washington stated, "In this conflict of emotions all I dare aver is that it has been my faithful study to collect my duty from a just appreciation of every circumstance by which it might be affected."

20. See Kraig, *Woodrow Wilson and the Lost World* for an extension of Tulis's interpretation of Wilson's importance. Other political scientists have also emphasized Wilson's innovative contributions. See Bessette, *Mild Voice of Reason*; Thurow, "Dimensions of Presidential Character"; Kesler, "Woodrow Wilson and the Statesmanship of Progress."

21. Gerring, *Party Ideologies in America*, 107. I follow Gerring in treating the Whigs and Republicans as possessing a cohesive party ideology. Kelley, *Cultural Pattern in American Politics*, 167.

22. Bostdorff, *Presidency and the Rhetoric of Foreign Crisis*; Holloway, "Keeping the Faith," 48; Wander, "Rhetoric of American Foreign Policy," 342; Campbell and Jamieson, *Deeds Done in Words*, 107.

23. Mayhew, *Divided We Govern*; Edwards, Barrett, and Peake, "Legislative Impact of Divided Government"; Weatherford, "Responsiveness and Deliberation in Divided Government."

24. Dahl, "Myth of the Presidential Mandate," 356; Conley, *Presidential Mandates*, 6.

25. Hager and Sullivan, "President-centered and Presidency-centered Explanations,"1083; Lawrence, "Collapse of the Democratic Majority," 799.

26. Skowronek, *Politics Presidents Make*, 34–44.

27. Table 2 begins in 1801 with the presidency of Thomas Jefferson and the beginning of a party system in the United States. Both George Washington and John Adams might be considered as Federalists but cannot be coded as either a "Whig/Republican" or "Democratic/Democratic Republican" in the dichotomous party variable used in the regressions. For this reason, they are omitted from the analysis.

28. For additional qualitative evidence of the ideological nature of modern presidential moralizing, see Colleen Shogan, "Rhetorical Moralism in the Plebiscitary Presidency."

29. The Annual Addresses included in the first regression were: 1812–14, 1846, 1847, 1898, 1917, 1918, and 1941–45. In addition to these addresses, the years added to the second regression model were: 1861–64, 1951–53, 1966, 1967, 1991, 2002, and 2003. An address was included if 25 percent of its paragraphs concerned the foreign conflict at hand. For example, Johnson's 1968 speech did not meet the 25 percent criteria. Minor foreign conflicts, such as the undeclared war with France, the war with Tripoli, the Second Barbary War, the Boxer Rebellion, Nicaragua (1926–33), the invasion of Panama, Lebanon, and Grenada were not included because such incidents were mentioned, but not highlighted, in the Annual Addresses.

30. The data come from the website "Economic History Services." See http://www .eh.net/hmit/gdp/ (accessed Mar. 10, 2004). Although not the best indicator of economic prosperity, yearly real GDP estimates are available from 1789 through 2003.

31. Conley, *Presidential Mandates*, 62. Conley has shown that the Electoral College vote percentage is a better indicator of presidential mandate-claiming than popular vote share.

32. Washington was excluded because he does not fit into one of Skowronek's four categories. George W. Bush was classified as an "orthodox innovator" in a lecture presented by Skowronek. See Skowronek, "Leadership by Definition."

33. Skowronek, *Politics Presidents Make*, 39.

34. Hutcheson, *God in the White House*, 50.

CHAPTER 3. THE POLITICS OF REINFORCING MORAL RHETORIC

1. Ketcham, *Presidents above Party*; Phelps, *George Washington and American Constitutionalism*; Brookhiser, *Founding Father*; Lipset, "Setting the Standard"; Colleen Shogan, "George Washington."

2. Notable exceptions that discuss Washington's rhetoric other than the Farewell Address are Lucas, "Genre Criticism and Historical Context" and Lucas, "George Washington and the Rhetoric of Presidential Leadership."

3. Phelps, *George Washington and American Constitutionalism*. Ketcham acknowledged Washington's "tone-setting moral ways" but did not explicitly describe his establishment of the moral spokesman role. See Ketcham, *Presidents above Party*, 91.

4. Howe, "Republican Thought and the Political Violence of the 1790s," 158.

5. Phelps, "George Washington and the Paradox of Party."

6. Lucas, "George Washington and the Rhetoric of Presidential Leadership," 47; Lucas, "Genre Criticism and Historical Context," 363.

7. Washington, *George Washington*, 460.

8. Lucas, "Genre Criticism and Historical Context," 359.

9. Smolin, "Consecrating the President."

10. Washington, *George Washington*, 461; Flexner, *George Washington and the New Nation*, 184.

11. Washington, *George Washington*, 463.

12. Ibid., 461–62.

13. Howe, "Republican Thought and the Political Violence of the 1790s," 147–65.

14. Elkins and McKitrick, *Age of Federalism*, 462; Hamilton, *Papers of Alexander Hamilton*, 24–27.

15. McDonald, *Presidency of George Washington*, 146; Washington, *Writings*, 476.

16. Phelps, *George Washington and American Constitutionalism*, 134; Kohn, "Washington Administration's Decision to Crush the Whiskey Rebellion," 572.

17. Washington, *Writings*, 509.

18. Ibid., 508.

19. McDonald, *Presidency of George Washington*, 145.

20. Israel, *State of the Union Messages*, 21.

21. Ibid.

22. Ibid., 27.

23. McDonald, *Presidency of George Washington*, 147; Lucas, "George Washington and the Rhetoric of Presidential Leadership," 55–57; Elkins and McKitrick, *Age of Federalism*, 461.

24. For the most comprehensive account of the formulation of the Farewell Address, see Binney, *An Inquiry into the Formation of Washington's Farewell Address*. In scrupulous detail, Binney analyzed the various drafts of the address and the principles contained in them. Flexner, *George Washington and the New Nation*, 307; Bemis, "Washington's Farewell Address," 99.

25. Flexner, *George Washington and the New Nation*, 304; Washington, *George Washington*, 514.

26. Ryan, "Rhetoric of George Washington's Farewell Address." For a listing of all the senators who have read Washington's Farewell Address on the Senate floor, see: http://www.senate.gov/artandhistory/history/minute/Washingtons_Farewell_Address .htm. Felix Gilbert, *To the Farewell Address*; Kaufman, *Washington's Farewell Address*; Campbell and Jamieson, *Deeds Done in Words*, 191, 197; Spalding, "Command of Its Own Fortunes."

27. Lucas, "George Washington and the Rhetoric of Presidential Leadership," 53; Hostetler, "Washington's Farewell Address."

28. Washington, *George Washington*, 515.

29. Ibid., 520, 521; Campbell and Jamieson, *Deeds Done in Words*, 202; Spaulding and Garrity, *Sacred Union of Citizens*.

30. Washington, *George Washington*, 523.

31. Blum, *Republican*, 13.

32. Roosevelt, *Strenuous Life*, 20–21.

33. Blum, *Republican Roosevelt*, 107.

34. Dorsey, *Reconstituting the American Spirit*.

35. Dorsey, *Reconstituting the American Spirit*; Blum, *Republican Roosevelt*; Friedenberg, *Theodore Roosevelt and the Rhetoric of Militant Decency*.

36. Gould, *Presidency of Theodore Roosevelt*, 133–34.

37. Blum, *Republican Roosevelt*, 75–81.

38. Ibid., 80.

39. Ibid., 82.

40. Ibid., 55; Gould, *Presidency of Theodore Roosevelt*, 141–45; Cooper, *Warrior and the Priest*, 79; Blum, *Republican Roosevelt*, 3.

41. Cooper, *Warrior and the Priest*, 85; Harbaugh, *Power and Responsibility*; Kolko, *Railroads and Regulation*.

42. Blum, *Republican Roosevelt*, 85. According to Blum, Roosevelt did not view tariff reform in moral terms.

43. Ibid., 29.

44. Dorsey, *Reconstituting the American Spirit*, 16.

45. Roosevelt, *Roosevelt Policy*, 249.

46. Blum, *Republican Roosevelt*, 72.

47. Roosevelt, *Roosevelt Policy*, 54, 244.

48. Ibid., 308.

49. Ibid., 299, 304.

50. Harbaugh, *Power and Responsibility*, 242.

51. Roosevelt, *Roosevelt Policy*, 71–372.

52. Gould, *Presidency of Theodore Roosevelt*, 162.

53. Blum, *Republican Roosevelt*, 101–103; Skowronek, *Politics Presidents Make*, 249; Gould, *Presidency of Theodore Roosevelt*, 164.

54. La Follette, *La Follette's Autobiography*, 166.

55. Roosevelt, *Autobiography of Theodore Roosevelt*, 195–96. Roosevelt stated that his swings around the circle allowed him to present his arguments to the American people, who then influenced GOP senators to side with him. According to Roosevelt's autobiography, this success enabled the Republican Party to become "once more the progressive and indeed the fairly radical progressive party of the nation."

56. Cooper, *Warrior and the Priest*, 115.

57. Gould, *Presidency of Theodore Roosevelt*, 276.

58. Roosevelt, *Roosevelt Policy*, 722.

59. Ibid., 724, 737.

60. Several motives for the Special Message have been offered. Besides trying to use public opinion to persuade Congress, it is possible that Roosevelt issued the address to mute Gov. Charles Evans Hughes's (New York) message about presidential leadership, which was released the same day. Hughes was thought to be a serious Republican contender for the presidency in the 1908 election, but at this point, TR had already thrown his support behind Taft. Others believed Roosevelt issued the message because he was incensed by the Supreme Court's recent invalidation of the Employers' Liability Act of 1906. See Hatch, *Big Stick*, 34, 62; Roosevelt, *Theodore Roosevelt: An Autobiography*, 367; Gould, *Presidency of Theodore Roosevelt*, 276.

61. Hatch, *Big Stick*, 37; Gould, *Presidency of Theodore Roosevelt*, 279–81; Johnson, "Antitrust Policy in Transition," 433.

62. Hatch, *Big Stick*, 43.

63. Israel, *State of the Union Messages*, 2323; Hatch, *Big Stick*, 56.

64. Skowronek, *Politics Presidents Make*, 254; Cooper, *Warrior and the Priest*, 117.

65. Skowronek, *Politics Presidents Make*, 234.

66. Carter, *Government as Good*, 102.

67. Hargrove, *Jimmy Carter as President;* Morris, *Jimmy Carter*, 4; Patton, "Jimmy Carter," 187.

68. Carter, *Government as Good*, 130.

69. Hochman, et al. "Interview with Jimmy Carter," 226.

70. Ibid., 252.

71. The fact that the address is known as the "malaise" speech is quite telling. The word "malaise" does not appear anywhere in the text, yet within weeks of July 15, the speech became well known as the "malaise" speech. Only a president who was desperately reaching to find a source of authority or legitimacy would fall victim to such a label.

72. Barrow, "Age of Limits," 173.

73. Carter, *Keeping Faith*, 93.

74. Carter, *Public Papers of the Presidents: 1977*, 656.

75. Rozell, *Press and the Carter Presidency*, 37.

76. Carter, *Keeping Faith*, 127.

77. Rozell, *Press and the Carter Presidency*, 50.

78. Stuckey, *Strategic Failures*, 126.

79. Ibid., 122; Morris, *Jimmy Carter*, 2.

80. Kaufman, *Washington's Farewell Address*, 144; Morris, *Jimmy Carter*, 4.

81. Jones, *Trusteeship Presidency*, 177; Hahn, "Flailing the Profligate," 298.

82. Carter, *Public Papers of the Presidents: 1979*, 1237, 1238.

83. Ibid., 1240. Robert Bellah, a Berkeley sociologist, was extremely critical of the July speech. Bellah had been one of Carter's chosen guests at the Camp David retreat days earlier and had expected a more coherent speech. The main problem, Bellah charged, was the inconsistencies contained in the speech. Carter told the American people "how wonderful they are" but then stated that they didn't have "any confidence or faith." Bellah wondered, "How can these moral people have such bad characteristics?" According to Bellah, Carter exemplified moral leadership in only the most "superficial sense." For an interview with Bellah after the July 1979 speech, see Raeside, "Night at Camp David."

84. Morris, *Jimmy Carter*, 6.

85. Rozell, *Press and the Carter Presidency*, 137; Hochman, et al., "Interview with Jimmy Carter," 251.

86. Referring to the political situation of the Carter presidency in 1979, Hamilton Jordan lamented, "We had no unifying Democratic consensus, no program, no set of principles on which a majority of Democrats agreed." See Morris, *Jimmy Carter*, 244.

87. In roll call votes in the House, more than a third of Republicans supported Carter, much more than expected. But securing this support was very costly for Carter: for every Republican that over-supported Carter by ten or more points, there

were three Democrats that under-supported Carter by ten or more points. See Fleisher and Bond, "Assessing Presidential Support in the House."

88. Hochman, et al., "Interview with Jimmy Carter," 252.

89. Self, "Rhetoric and *Phronesis*," 133; Aristotle, *Nicomachean Ethics*, 157; Lucas, "George Washington and the Rhetoric of Presidential Leadership," 53; Spaulding and Garrity, *Sacred Union*, 11.

CHAPTER 4. THE POLITICS OF MORAL RESTRAINT

1. The more commonly known title is *Jefferson's Bible*. Jefferson actually cut apart text from the Gospel and arranged it in a way he thought stressed the moral teachings of Jesus. The book was not published until 1903, when Congress printed 9,000 copies. New members of Congress received a copy of *Jefferson's Bible* every year until 1957. An economist, Judd Patton, has taken it upon himself to reestablish the practice. Since 1997, he has sent 753 copies of the republished *Jefferson's Bible* to members of Congress, with Jesus' words featured in red. See Holly Lebowitz Rossi, "People's Bible Goes to Washington," http://www.beliefnet.com/story/161/story_16121_1.html (accessed May 11, 2005).

2. Jefferson, "Query XIX: Manufactures," 165.

3. Sheldon, *The Political Philosophy of Thomas Jefferson*, 15–16; Yarbrough, *American Virtues*, 145.

4. Jefferson, *Memoirs*, 507.

5. Jefferson, "Query XIX: Manufactures," 163.

6. Banning, *Jeffersonian Persuasion*, 266; Johnstone, *Jefferson and the Presidency*, 45.

7. Skowronek, *Politics Presidents Make*, 70.

8. DeConde, *This Affair of Louisiana*, 98–103.

9. Ibid., 119–22.

10. Ibid., 127.

11. Jefferson, *Messages*, 343.

12. Ibid., 358; Balleck, "When the Ends Justify the Means."

13. Johnstone, *Jefferson and the Presidency*, 71.

14. Aristotle, *Nicomachean Ethics*, 163.

15. Johnstone, *Jefferson and the Presidency*, 256–69.

16. Ibid., 263.

17. Ibid., 265.

18. Sears, *Jefferson and the Embargo*, 59–60.

19. Johnstone, *Jefferson and the Presidency*, 267–68.

20. Sears, *Jefferson and the Embargo*, 58, 61.

21. Johnstone, *Jefferson and the Presidency*, 270.

22. Jefferson, *Essential Jefferson*, 477–78; Johnstone, *Jefferson and the Presidency*, 238–39.

23. Sears, *Jefferson and the Embargo*, 106–107.

24. Johnstone, *Jefferson and the Presidency*, 275; Levy, *Jefferson and Civil Liberties*, 124; Johnstone, *Jefferson and the Presidency*, 299; McDonald, *Presidency of Thomas Jefferson*, 152; Gallatin, *Writings*, 398.

25. Johnstone, *Jefferson and the Presidency*, 269.

26. Ibid., 263.

27. Sears, *Jefferson and the Embargo*, 88, 103, 112.

28. Levy, *Jefferson and Civil Liberties*, 130.

29. Skowronek, *Politics Presidents Make*, 84.

30. Holzer, *Lincoln Seen and Heard*, 163.

31. Greenstone, *Lincoln Persuasion*, 220.

32. For example, Neuhaus, *Naked Public Square*; Diggins, *Lost Soul of American Politics*; Thurow, *Abraham Lincoln and American Political Religion*; Jaffa, *Crisis of the House Divided*.

33. Lincoln, *Lincoln: Selected Speeches*, 147, 152, 210.

34. Zarefsky, *Lincoln Douglas and Slavery*, 166.

35. Jaffa, *Crisis of the House Divided*, 243–44; White, *Eloquent President*, 92, 120; Wilson, "Paradox of Lincoln's Rhetorical Leadership," 27; Lincoln, *Lincoln: Selected Speeches*, 36.

36. Jaffa, *Crisis of the House Divided*, 272; Donald, *Lincoln*, 332; Williams, *Lincoln and the Radicals*, 4.

37. Williams, *Lincoln and the Radicals*, 6; Donald, *Lincoln Reconsidered*, 105; Greenstone, *Lincoln Persuasion*, 273; Williams, "Shall We Keep the Radicals?" 102.

38. Lincoln, *Lincoln: Selected Speeches*, 421.

39. Williams, *Lincoln and the Radicals*, 173; McPherson, *Abraham Lincoln and the Second American Revolution*, 31; Donald, *Lincoln*, 314, 345; Lincoln, *Lincoln: Selected Speeches*, 421.

40. Donald, *Lincoln*, 260; Jaffa, *New Birth of Freedom*, 240–41.

41. Lincoln, *Lincoln: Selected Speeches*, 344.

42. Ibid., 329.

43. Klingaman, *Abraham Lincoln and the Road to Emancipation*, 187.

44. Hofstadter, *American Political Tradition*; Holzer, *Lincoln Seen and Heard*, 182; Boritt, "Did He Dream of a Lily-White America?" 16.

45. Lincoln, *Lincoln: Selected Speeches*, 369.

46. Donald, *Lincoln*, 405–406.

47. Lincoln, *Lincoln: Selected Speeches*, 349.

48. Holzer, *Lincoln Seen and Heard*, 187.

49. Franklin, *Emancipation Proclamation*, 85; Holzer, *Lincoln Seen and Heard*, 187.

50. Boritt, "Did He Dream of a Lily-White America?" 12.

51. Donald, *Lincoln*, 397.

52. Lincoln, *Lincoln: Selected Speeches*, 364.

53. Zarefsky, "Lincoln's 1862 Annual Message."

54. Donald, *Lincoln*, 441–44; Lincoln, *Lincoln: Selected Speeches*, 376, 391.

55. Wills, *Lincoln at Gettysburg*, 25; White, *Eloquent President*, 227; Donald, *Lincoln*, 458.

56. Eulogies are often rhetorical hybrids that remember the deceased and propose new policies. It is an acceptable practice to discuss policy in a eulogy, as long as the proposals are subordinate to the memorial of the deceased. See Mister, "Reagan's Challenger Tribute"; Carpenter and Seltzer, "Situational Style and the Rotunda Eulogies."

57. Black, "Gettysburg and Silence."

58. White, *Eloquent President*, 243–53.

59. Selzer, "Historicizing Lincoln."

60. Wills, *Lincoln at Gettysburg*, 134.

61. Mister, "Reagan's Challenger Tribute," 164; Reid, "Newspaper Response to the Gettysburg Address."

62. Donald, *Lincoln*, 473.

63. Ibid., 552–53.

64. White, *Lincoln's Greatest Speech*, 47.

65. Ibid., 87.

66. Wills, "Lincoln's Greatest Speech?" 68.

67. Black, "Ultimate Voice of Lincoln," 51. Black argues that the most striking aspect of Lincoln's presidential rhetoric is his "disappearance." White, *Lincoln's Greatest Speech*, 101.

68. Lincoln, *Lincoln: Selected Speeches*, 450.

69. White, *Lincoln's Greatest Speech*, 59.

70. Ibid., 114.

71. Wills, "Lincoln's Greatest Speech?" 62–63.

72. Donald, *Lincoln*, 568.

73. White, *Lincoln's Greatest Speech*, 191–92.

74. Lincoln, *Lincoln: Selected Speeches*, 451

75. Pauley, *Modern Presidency*, 4.

76. Schlesinger, *Thousand Days*, 3539–40.

77. Miroff, *Pragmatic Illusions*, 229–30.

78. Mayer, *Running on Race*, 28, 39.

79. Schlesinger, *Thousand Days*, 939.

80. Goldzwig and Dionisopoulos, "John F. Kennedy's Civil Rights Discourse," 182; Bernstein, *Promises Kept*, 295; Schlesinger, *Thousand Days*, 931.

81. On the disappointment of civil rights leaders with Kennedy, see Pauley, *The Modern Presidency*, 109–10, 114, and 117.

82. Shull, *American Civil Rights Policy*, 23.

83. Parmet, *Democrats*, 184.

84. Kennedy, *Public Papers of the President: 1962*, 517.

85. Miroff, *Pragmatic Illusions*, 235.

86. Dudziak, *Cold War Civil Rights*, 159; Goldzwig and Dionisopoulos, "John F. Kennedy's Civil Rights Discourse," 183.

87. Israel, *State of the Union Messages*, 3135.

88. Brauer, *John F. Kennedy and the Second Reconstruction*, 131.

89. Kennedy, *Public Papers of the President: 1962*, 727, 728; Pauley, *Modern Presidency*, 105–106.

90. Ashmore, *Hearts and Minds*, 346; Pauley, *Modern Presidency*, 122; Reeves, *Question of Character*, 347.

91. Shull, *American Civil Rights Policy*, 49.

92. Pauley, *Modern Presidency*, 122.

93. Weisbrot, *Freedom Bound*, 68.

94. Brauer, *John F. Kennedy and the Second Reconstruction*, 213.

95. Ibid., 222.

96. Kennedy, *Public Papers of the President: 1962*, 221–30; Brauer, *John F. Kennedy and the Second Reconstruction*, 222; King, "Bold Design for a New South," 260.

97. Miroff, *Pragmatic Illusions*, 251; Pauley, *Modern Presidency*, 124; Kennedy, *Public Papers of the President: 1963*, 397.

98. Pauley, *Modern Presidency*, 124–25; Goldzwig and Dionisopoulos, "John F. Kennedy's Civil Rights Discourse," 190.

99. Stern, *Calculating Visions*, 92–93; Dudziak, *Cold War Civil Rights*, 179.

100. Pauley, *Modern Presidency*, 134; Brauer, *John F. Kennedy and the Second Reconstruction*, 263.

101. Kennedy, *Public Papers of the President: 1963*, 468–69; Pauley, *Modern Presidency*, 141; Miroff, *Pragmatic Illusions*, 7.

102. Pauley, *Modern Presidency*, 146–47; Brauer, *John F. Kennedy and the Second Reconstruction*, 263; Dudziak, *Cold War Civil Rights*, 181; Schlesinger, *Thousand Days*, 965.

103. Brauer, *John F. Kennedy and the Second Reconstruction*, 263–64; Gilbert, "Moral Leadership in Civil Rights," 13.

104. Miroff, *Pragmatic Illusions*, 267; Gilbert, "Moral Leadership in Civil Rights," 14, 16; Brauer, *John F. Kennedy and the Second Reconstruction*, 302–303.

105. Brauer, *John F. Kennedy and the Second Reconstruction*, 273.

106. Gilbert, "Moral Leadership in Civil Rights," 14.

107. Schlesinger, *Thousand Days*, 1019.

108. For a discussion of Lincoln's presidential leadership and *phronesis* unrelated to rhetoric, see Fishman, *Prudential Presidency*, 35–39; Ruderman, "Aristotle and the Recovery of Political Judgment." Ruderman distinguishes *phronesis* from mere shrewdness, in that *phronesis* aims at the moral good, or "living well"; Zarefsky, *Lincoln, Douglas and Slavery*, 196.

109. Fishman, *Prudential Presidency*, 18.

CHAPTER 5. THE POLITICS OF STRATEGIC MORAL RHETORIC

1. McCoy, *Last of the Fathers*, 26.

2. Sheldon, *Political Philosophy of James Madison*, 24–28; McLean, "Before and after Publius," 17.

3. Ketcham, "James Madison and the Nature of Man," 67–68; Lindsay, "James Madison on Religion and Politics,"1321; Sheldon, *Political Philosophy of Thomas Jefferson*, 15.

4. Stagg, "James Madison and the 'Malcontents,'" 560; Sheldon, *Political Philosophy of James Madison*, 106; Rutland, *Presidency of James Madison*, 85, 100; Bostdorff, *Presidency and the Rhetoric of Foreign Crisis*, 5; Buel, *Securing the Revolution*, 280; Campbell and Jamieson, *Deeds Done in Words*, 107.

5. Stagg, "James Madison and the 'Malcontents,'" 575, 584; Hatzenbuehler and Ivie, *Congress Declares War*, 26–33.

6. Sheldon, *Political Philosophy of James Madison*, 106.

7. Stagg, "Preface," xxvii; Rutland, *Presidency of James Madison*, 96.

8. Rutland, *Presidency of James Madison*, 85.

9. Madison and Rutland, *Papers of James Madison*, 3.

10. Ketcham, *James Madison*, 510; Madison and Rutland, *Papers of James Madison*, 7; Laracey, "Presidential Newspaper," 70.

11. Madison and Rutland, *Papers of James Madison*, 10. Stuart Leibiger argued in *Founding Friendship* it was no coincidence that George Washington and James Madison exhibited many similar characteristics of personality. According to Leibiger, it is likely that Madison consciously modeled his behavior after Washington. See Leibiger, *Founding Friendship*, 225.

12. McCoy, *Last of the Fathers*, 62.

13. Madison and Rutland, *Papers of James Madison*, 287.

14. Ibid., 437.

15. Stagg, "James Madison and the 'Malcontents,'" 585; Ketcham, "James Madison and the Presidency," 356.

16. Ketcham, *James Madison*, 537; Rutland, *Presidency of James Madison*, 116.

17. *Annals of Congress 1811–1812*, 2199–2201.

18. Lowell, *Mr. Madison's War*, 23, 29.

19. Ketcham, *James Madison*, 547.

20. Israel, *State of the Union Messages*, 122.

21. *Annals of Congress 1812–1813*, 660; Madison, *Messages*, 524; Ketcham, *James Madison*, 556.

22. Madison, *Messages*, 525.

23. Bostdorff, *Presidency and the Rhetoric of Foreign Crisis*, 9.

24. Ketcham, *James Madison*, 556–57; Israel, *State of the Union Messages*, 122–29.

25. Ketcham, *James Madison*, 587.

26. Rutland, *Presidency of James Madison*, 211.

27. See table 7 for an empirical comparison of Buchanan's and Lincoln's use of moral and religious rhetoric in their Annual Addresses.

28. Pendleton, "James Buchanan's Attitude toward Slavery," 7, 18, and 26.

29. Buchanan, *Mr. Buchanan's Administration*, 11; Smith, *Presidency of James Buchanan*, 17.

30. Stampp, Fehrenbacher, Johannsen, and Smith, "Presidency of James Buchanan," 201.

31. Gienapp, "No Bed of Roses"; Smith, *Presidency of James Buchanan*, 81.

32. Pendleton, *Slavery*, 317; Smith, *Presidency of James Buchanan*, 16.

33. Pendleton, *Slavery*, 239.

34. Ibid., 238.

35. Unlike most nineteenth-century presidents, Buchanan wrote his addresses and speeches with little or no assistance from cabinet members or advisors. It is thought that Buchanan did not think through the political implications of his rhetoric very clearly. If Buchanan had circulated his addresses prior to issuing them, it is possible that his rhetoric might have been more strategically beneficial and politically sensitive. See Stampp et al., "Presidency of James Buchanan," 172.

36. Johannsen, *Stephen A. Douglas*, 576; Wells, *Stephen Douglas*, 22.

37. Pendleton, *Slavery*, 307; Buchanan, *Works of James Buchanan*, vol. 10, 122; Klein, *President James Buchanan*, 297.

38. Klein, *President James Buchanan*, 336.

39. Buchanan, *Works of James Buchanan,* vol. 10, 341.

40. Ibid., 345.

41. Smith, *Presidency of James Buchanan,* 108–109.

42. Buchanan, *Works of James Buchanan,* vol. 10, 346.

43. Davis, "James Buchanan and the Suppression of the Slave Trade," 458.

44. Smith, *Presidency of James Buchanan,* 94.

45. Buchanan, *Works of James Buchanan,* vol. 10, 339; Klein, *President James Buchanan,* 337.

46. Smith, *Presidency of James Buchanan,* 151.

47. Klein, *President James Buchanan,* 339; Smith, *Presidency of James Buchanan,* 98.

48. Buchanan, *Works of James Buchanan,* vol. 11, 8.

49. Israel, *State of the Union Messages,* 1027.

50. Zarefsky, "Lyndon Johnson," 223; Pauley, *Modern Presidency,* 159.

51. Stern, *Calculating Visions,* 105.

52. Campbell and Jamieson, *Deeds Done in Words,* 38; Johnson, *Public Papers of the President: 1963–64,* 12.

53. Campbell and Jamieson, *Deeds Done in Words,* 39.

54. Israel, *State of the Union Messages,* 3156, 3159.

55. Zarefsky, "Lyndon Johnson," 224.

56. Mann, *Jericho,* 390–91.

57. Ibid., 398.

58. Stern, *Calculating Visions,* 162; "Strong Rights Bill," 1205–1206.

59. Mann, *Walls of Jericho,* 389.

60. Ibid., 412.

61. Ibid., 413.

62. "Cloture on Civil Rights," 1169.

63. Mann, *Walls of Jericho,* 400.

64. Johnson, *Public Papers of the President: 1965,* 74.

65. Mann, *Walls of Jericho,* 444.

66. Pauley, *Modern Presidency,* 182.

67. Ibid., 177–78.

68. Mann, *Walls of Jericho,* 460.

69. Stern, *Calculating Visions,* 218; Johnson, *Vantage Point,* 164.

70. Johnson, *Public Papers of the President: 1965,* 281; Black, *Rhetorical Questions,* 40.

71. Johnson, *Public Papers of the President: 1965,* 283.

72. Ibid., 285; Pauley, *Modern Presidency,* 181.

73. Pauley, *Modern Presidency,* 187, 197.

74. Stern, *Calculating Visions,* 217; Miroff, "Presidential Leverage over Social Movements," 2–23.

75. "Sweeping Voting Rights Bill Introduced in Congress," 435; Mann, *Walls of Jericho,* 465.

76. Brady and Sinclair, "Building Majorities for Policy Changes," 1054; Mann, *Walls of Jericho,* 474.

77. Pauley, *Modern Presidency,* 194; Stern, *Calculating Visions,* 229; Miroff, "Presidential Leverage over Social Movements," 20; for poll numbers, see LexisNexis Aca-

demic Universe Polls and Surveys, http://web.lexis-nexis.com/universe (accessed Nov. 16, 2001).

78. Goldzwig, "LBJ, the Rhetoric of Transcendence," 36. Goldzwig outlines the political restrictions that influenced Johnson's civil rights rhetoric concerning the Fair Housing Act.

79. Zarefsky, "Lyndon Johnson," 225.

80. Dorsey, "Introduction," 10.

CHAPTER 6. THE FUTURE OF RHETORICAL MORALISM IN THE PRESIDENCY

1. Rudalevige, *Managing the President's Program*; Heclo, "Changing Presidential Office."

2. Ruderman, "Aristotle and the Recovery of Political Judgment," 409, 413.

3. Skowronek and Orren, *Search for American Political Development*, 13–19.

4. Shogan, "Rhetorical Moralism in the Plebiscitary Presidency."

5. Miroff, "Presidency and the Public."

6. Edwards, *On Deaf Ears*, 251.

7. Ibid., 244–46.

8. There is also a report that Bush claimed publicly that "God speaks through me." The alleged declaration occurred during a private meeting with an Amish community in Pennsylvania, but since the White House has not included the speech in Bush's official Public Papers, it is impossible to confirm. See Jack Brubaker, "Bush Quietly Meets with Amish Here," July 16, 2004, http://lancasteronline.com/pages/news/local/4/7565 (accessed Sept. 14, 2004). Murphy, "Our Mission and Our Moment."

9. "Remarks by the President on Stem Cell Research," http://www.whitehouse.gov/news/releases/2001/08/20010809–2.html (accessed Apr. 2, 2004).

10. David Kusnet, Clinton's chief speechwriter, remarked, "He certainly found his voice as a national and world leader." Reagan speechwriter Lyn Nofziger called it "the toughest speech I've ever heard." John Murphy, a professor of speech communication, classified the speech as "excellent" and reminiscent of the "echoes of Abe Lincoln and Winston Churchill." There were some criticisms of the speech. Theodore Sorensen, Kennedy's speechwriter, dismissed it as a "pep talk" that failed to provide specific evidence that bin Laden was responsible for the attacks. However, the majority of commentators gave the address high marks. See Chen, "Helping Bush Sound Presidential," A5; Smith, George, and McNamara, "Bush Drew on Strengths in His Address to the Nation," A4; "Mr. Bush's Most Important Speech," A34.

11. "President Bush Outlines Iraqi Threat," http://www.whitehouse.gov/news/releases/2002/10 (accessed Apr. 4, 2004).

12. Woodward, *Plan of Attack*, 131; "President Bush Delivers West Point Speech," http://www.whitehouse.gov/news/releases/2002/06/20020601–3.html (accessed Apr. 10, 2004); Gelernter, "Bush's Rhetoric Deficit."

13. "President Addresses the Nation in Prime Time Press Conference," http://www.whitehouse.gov/news/releases/2004/04/20040413–20.html (accessed Apr. 15, 2004); Gould, "Leadership," B1; Hiatt, "A Foreign Policy to Match Bush's Rhetoric?" A25.

14. Fineman and Lipper, "The Gospel According to George," 18; Lemann, "Without a Doubt."

15. Skowronek, "Leadership by Definition"; Brooks, "Strength in Disunity."

16. Zarefsky, "George W. Bush Discovers Rhetoric," 153.

17. "Views of a Changing World," 22, 115, http://people-press.org/reports/display.php3?ReportID=185 (accessed Apr. 6, 2004). The nine countries surveyed were the United States, France, Great Britain, Russia, Germany, Turkey, Morocco, Jordan, and Pakistan. "A Year after the Iraq War," The Pew Research Center for the People and the Press, http://people-press.org/reports/display.php3?ReportID=206 (accessed Apr. 4, 2005), 21; Kagan, *Of Paradise and Power*, 3, 29.

18. Woodward, *Plan of Attack*, 88; BBC World News, "Iran and the Axis of Evil," http://news.bbc.co.uk/1/hi/world/middle_east/1814659.stm (accessed Apr. 4, 2004); PBS Frontline, "Iran and the Axis of Evil," http://www.pbs.org/wgbh/pages/frontline/shows/tehran/axis/ (accessed Apr. 4 2004); National Review Online, "Iran and the Axis of Evil," http://www.nationalreview.com/contributors/ledeen030402.shtml (accessed Apr. 10, 2004).

19. Fletcher, "Bush Honors President Lincoln," A4.

20. At the conclusion of his 2003 State of the Union Address, President Bush did pronounce that Americans cannot fully understand God's will. He stated, "We do not know—we do not claim to know all the ways of Providence, yet we can trust in them, placing our confidence in the loving God behind all of life, and all of history." This statement was unusual for Bush, who usually premises his moral and religious rhetoric upon firm stances that leave little room for wavering.

BIBLIOGRAPHY

Alley, Robert. *So Help Me God: Religion and the Presidency, Wilson to Nixon.* Richmond, Va.: John Knox Press, 1972.

Annals of Congress 1811–1812. Washington, D.C.: Gales and Seaton, 1853.

Annals of Congress 1812–1813. Washington, D.C.: Gales and Seaton, 1853.

Aristotle. *Nicomachean Ethics.* Translated by Martin Ostwald. Indianapolis: Bobbs Merrill, 1962.

———. *Rhetoric.* Translated by W. Rhys Roberts. *Poetics.* Translated by Ingram Bywater. New York: Modern Library, 1984.

Ashmore, Harry S. *Hearts and Minds: A Personal Chronicle of Race in America.* Washington, D.C.: Seven Locks Press, 1988.

Balleck, Barry J. "When the Ends Justify the Means: Thomas Jefferson and the Louisiana Purchase." *Presidential Studies Quarterly* 22 (1992): 679–97.

Banning, Lance. *The Jeffersonian Persuasion: Evolution of a Party Ideology.* Ithaca, N.Y.: Cornell University Press, 1978.

Barber, James David. *The Presidential Character.* 4th ed. Englewood Cliffs, N.J.: Prentice Hall, 1992.

Barrow, John C. "An Age of Limits: Jimmy Carter and the Quest for a National Energy Policy." In *The Carter Presidency: Policy Choices in the Post–New Deal Era,* edited by Gary Fink and Hugh Davis Graham, 158–78. Lawrence: University Press of Kansas, 1998.

Beasley, Vanessa B. *You, the People.* College Station: Texas A&M University Press, 2004.

Bellah, Robert N. "Civil Religion in America." *Daedalus* 96 (1967): 1–21.

Bemis, Samuel. "Washington's Farewell Address: A Foreign Policy of Independence." *American Historical Review* 39 (1934): 250–68.

Bercovitch, Sacvan. *The American Jeremiad.* Madison: University of Wisconsin Press, 1978.

Bernstein, Irving. *Promises Kept: John F. Kennedy's New Frontier.* New York: Oxford University Press, 1991.

Bessette, Joseph M. *The Mild Voice of Reason: Deliberative Democracy and American National Government.* Chicago: University of Chicago Press, 1994.

Bimes, Terri. "The Metamorphosis of Presidential Populism." PhD diss., Yale University, 1999.

Binney, Horace. *An Inquiry into the Formation of Washington's Farewell Address.* New York: DeCapo Press, 1859.

Bitzer, Lloyd F. "The Rhetorical Situation." *Philosophy and Rhetoric* 1 (1969): 1–15.

Black, Edwin. "Gettysburg and Silence." *Quarterly Journal of Speech* 80 (1994): 21–36.

———. *Rhetorical Questions: Studies of Public Discourse.* Chicago: University of Chicago Press, 1992.

———. "The Ultimate Voice of Lincoln." *Rhetoric and Public Affairs* 3 (2000): 49–57.

Blum, John Morton. *The Republican Roosevelt.* 2d ed. Cambridge, Mass.: Harvard University Press, 1977.

Boritt, Gabor. "Did He Dream of a Lily-White America? The Voyage to Linconia." In *The Lincoln Enigma: The Changing Faces of an American Icon,* edited by Gabor Boritt, 1–19. Oxford, England: Oxford University Press, 2001.

Bostdorff, Denise. *The Presidency and the Rhetoric of Foreign Crisis.* Columbia: University of South Carolina Press, 1994.

Brady, David, and Barbara Sinclair. "Building Majorities for Policy Changes in the House of Representatives." *Journal of Politics* 46 (1984): 1033–60.

Brauer, Carl M. *John F. Kennedy and the Second Reconstruction.* New York: Columbia University Press, 1977.

Brookhiser, Richard. *Founding Father: Rediscovering George Washington.* New York: Free Press, 1996.

Brooks, David. "Strength in Disunity." *New York Times,* November 23, 2004.

Bruner, M. Lane. "Rhetorical Criticism: A Limit Work." *Western Journal of Communication* 66 (2002): 281–99.

Buchanan, James. *Mr. Buchanan's Administration on the Eve of the Rebellion.* New York: D. Appleton and Company, 1866.

———. *The Works of James Buchanan.* Vol. 10, edited by John Bassett Moore. Philadelphia, Pa.: J. B. Lippincott Company, 1910.

———. *The Works of James Buchanan.* Vol. 11, edited by John Bassett Moore. Philadelphia, Pa.: J. B. Lippincott Company, 1910.

Buel, Richard, Jr. *Securing the Revolution: Ideology in American Politics, 1789–1815.* Ithaca, N.Y.: Cornell University Press, 1972.

Campbell, Karlyn Kohrs, and Kathleen Hall Jamieson. *Deeds Done in Words: Presidential Rhetoric and the Genres of Governance.* Chicago: University of Chicago Press, 1990.

———. "Inaugurating the Presidency." *Presidential Studies Quarterly* 15 (1985): 394–411.

———. "Rhetorical Hybrids: Fusions of Generic Elements." *Quarterly Journal of Speech* 68 (1982): 146–57.

Carpenter, Ronald H., and Robert V. Seltzer. "Situational Style and the Rotunda Eulogies." *Central States Speech Journal* 22 (1971): 11–15.

Carter, Jimmy. *A Government as Good as Its People.* New York: Simon and Schuster, 1975.

———. *Keeping Faith: Memoirs of a President.* New York: Bantam Books, 1982.

———. *Public Papers of the Presidents: 1977.* Washington, D.C.: Government Printing Office, 1977.

———. *Public Papers of the Presidents: 1979.* Washington, D.C.: Government Printing Office, 1980.

Chafets, Zev. "Judge Dubya: New Bush Doctrine Casts U.S. as World's Moral Arbiter." *New York Daily News,* February 3, 2002.

Chen, Edwin. "Helping Bush Sound Presidential." *Los Angeles Times,* September 22, 2001.

"Cloture on Civil Rights Breaks 26-Year Precedent." *Congressional Quarterly Weekly Report.* June 12, 1964: 1169.

Cohen, Jeffrey. *Presidential Responsiveness and Public Policy-Making.* Ann Arbor: University of Michigan Press, 1997.

Condit, Celeste Michelle. "The Functions of Epideictic: The Boston Massacre Orations as Exemplar." *Communication Quarterly* 33 (1985): 284–99.

Conley, Patricia Heidotting. *Presidential Mandates: How Elections Shape the National Agenda.* Chicago: University of Chicago Press, 2001.

Cooper, John Milton. *The Warrior and the Priest: Woodrow Wilson and Theodore Roosevelt.* Cambridge, Mass.: Harvard University Press, 1983.

Dahl, Robert. "Myth of the Presidential Mandate." *Political Science Quarterly* 105 (1990): 355–72.

Dallek, Robert. *Ronald Reagan: The Politics of Symbolism.* Cambridge, Mass.: Harvard University Press, 1984.

Darsey, James. *The Prophetic Tradition and Radical Rhetoric in America.* New York: New York University Press, 1997.

Davis, Robert Ralph. "James Buchanan and the Suppression of the Slave Trade, 1858–1861." *Pennsylvania History* 33 (1966): 446–59.

DeConde, Alexander. *This Affair of Louisiana.* New York: Charles Scribner's Sons, 1976.

Diggins, John P. *The Lost Soul of American Politics: Virtue, Self-Interest and the Foundations of Liberalism.* Chicago: University of Chicago Press, 1986.

Donald, David. *Lincoln.* New York: Simon and Schuster, 1995.

———. *Lincoln Reconsidered.* New York: Alfred A. Knopf, 1956.

Dorsey, Leroy G. "Introduction: The President as a Rhetorical Leader." In *The Presidency and Rhetorical Leadership,* edited by Leroy G. Dorsey, 3–19. College Station: Texas A&M University Press, 2002.

———. "Reconstituting the American Spirit: Theodore Roosevelt's Rhetorical Presidency." PhD diss., Indiana University, 1993.

Dudziak, Mary L. *Cold War Civil Rights: Race and the Image of American Democracy.* Princeton, N.J.: Princeton University Press, 2000.

Edwards, George C., III. *On Deaf Ears: The Limits of the Bully Pulpit.* New Haven, Conn.: Yale University Press, 2003.

Edwards, George C., III, Andrew Barrett, and Jeffrey Peake. "The Legislative Impact of Divided Government." *American Journal of Political Science* 41 (1997): 545–63.

Elkins, Stanley, and Eric McKitrick. *The Age of Federalism.* New York: Oxford University Press, 1993.

Ellis, Richard, ed. *Speaking to the People: The Rhetorical Presidency in Historical Perspective.* Amherst: University of Massachusetts Press, 1998.

Fairbanks, James David. "The Priestly Functions of the Presidency: A Discussion of the Literature on Civil Religion and Its Implications for the Study of Presidential Leadership." *Presidential Studies Quarterly* 11 (1981): 214–32.

Fathi, Nazila. "A Nation Challenged: The Rogue List." *New York Times*, February 1, 2002.

Fineman, Howard, and Tamara Lipper. "The Gospel According to George." *Newsweek*, April 26, 2004.

Fishman, Ethan M. *The Prudential Presidency.* Westport, Conn.: Praeger, 2001.

Fleisher, Richard, and Jon Bond. "Assessing Presidential Support in the House: Lessons from Reagan and Carter." *Journal of Politics* 45 (1983): 745–58.

Fletcher, Michael A. "Bush Honors President Lincoln." *Washington Post*, April 20, 2005.

Flexner, James. *George Washington and the New Nation.* Boston: Little, Brown and Company, 1969.

Follett, Mary Parker. *The Speaker of the House of Representatives.* New York: Longman, Green, and Co., 1896.

Franklin, John Hope. *The Emancipation Proclamation.* Garden City, N.Y.: Doubleday, 1963.

Friedenberg, Robert V. *Theodore Roosevelt and the Rhetoric of Militant Decency.* New York: Greenwood Press, 1990.

Gallatin, Albert. *The Writings of Albert Gallatin.* Vol. 1, edited by Henry Adams. Philadelphia, Pa.: J. B. Lippincott and Co., 1879.

Galvin, Daniel, and Colleen Shogan, "Presidential Politicization and Centralization across the Modern-Traditional Divide." *Polity* 36 (2004): 477–504.

Gelernter, David. "Bush's Rhetoric Deficit." *Weekly Standard,* October 6, 2003.

George, Alexander L., and Juliette L. George. *Presidential Personality and Performance.* Boulder, Colo.: Westview Press, 1998.

Germino, Dante. *The Inaugural Addresses of American Presidents: The Public Philosophy and Rhetoric.* Lanham, Md.: University Press of America, 1984.

Gerring, John. *Party Ideologies in America, 1828–1996.* Cambridge: Cambridge University Press, 1998.

Gienapp, William. "No Bed of Roses: James Buchanan, Abraham Lincoln, and Presidential Leadership in the Civil War Era." In *James Buchanan and the Political Crisis of the 1850s,* edited by Michael J. Birkner, 93–122. London: Associated University Presses, 1996.

Gilbert, Felix. *To the Farewell Address.* Princeton, N.J.: Princeton University Press, 1961.

Gilbert, Robert E. "Moral Leadership in Civil Rights: An Evaluation of John F. Kennedy." *Political Communication and Persuasion* 6 (1989): 1–19.

Goldzwig, Steven. "LBJ, the Rhetoric of Transcendence, and the Civil Rights Act of 1968." *Rhetoric and Public Affairs* 6 (2003): 25–54.

Goldzwig, Steven, and G. N. Dionisopoulos. *In a Perilous Hour: The Public Addresses of John F. Kennedy.* Westport, Conn.: Greenwood Press, 1995.

———. "John F. Kennedy's Civil Rights Discourse: The Evolution from 'Principled Bystander' to Public Advocate." *Communication Monographs* 56 (1989): 179–98.

Gould, Lewis L. "Leadership: Now, the Nation Needs Answers More than Exhortations." *Washington Post,* April 18, 2004.

———. *The Presidency of Theodore Roosevelt.* Lawrence: University Press of Kansas, 1991.

Greenstein, Fred. "Change and Continuity in the Modern Presidency." In *The New American Political System,* edited by Anthony King, 45–86. Washington, D.C.: American Enterprise Institute, 1978.

Greenstein, Fred, Larry Berman, and Alvin Felzenberg. *Evolution of the Modern Presidency: A Bibliographic Survey.* Washington, D.C.: American Enterprise Institute, 1977.

Greenstone, J. David. *The Lincoln Persuasion.* Princeton, N.J.: Princeton University Press, 1993.

Gronbeck, Bruce E. "The Presidency in the Age of Secondary Orality." In *Beyond the Rhetorical Presidency,* edited by Martin Medhurst, 30–49. College Station: Texas A&M University Press, 1996.

Hager, Gregory, and Terry Sullivan. "President-centered and Presidency-centered Explanations of Presidential Public Activity." *American Journal of Political Science* 38 (1994): 675–92.

Hahn, Dan F. "Flailing the Profligate: Carter's Energy Sermon of 1979." In *Essays in Presidential Rhetoric,* edited by Theodore Windt, 294–300. Dubuque, Iowa: Kendall/Hunt Publishing, 1983.

Hamilton, Alexander. *The Papers of Alexander Hamilton.* Vol. 17, edited by Harold Syrett. New York: Columbia University Press, 1961.

Harbaugh, William Henry. *Power and Responsibility: The Life and Times of Theodore Roosevelt.* New York: Farrar, Straus and Cudahy, 1961.

Hargrove, Erwin C. *Jimmy Carter as President: Leadership and the Politics of the Public Good.* Baton Rouge: Louisiana State University Press, 1988.

———. *The President as Leader: Appealing to the Better Angels of Our Nature.* Lawrence: University Press of Kansas, 1998.

Hariman, Robert. "Theory without Modernity." In *Prudence,* edited by Robert Hariman, 1–32. University Park: Pennsylvania State University Press, 2003.

Hart, Roderick P. *Verbal Style and the Presidency.* Orlando, Fla.: Academic Press, 1984.

Hart, Roderick P., and John L. Pauley II. *The Political Pulpit Revisited.* West Lafayette, Ind.: Purdue University Press, 2005.

Hatch, Carl E. *The Big Stick and the Congressional Gavel.* New York: Pageant Press, 1967.

Hatzenbuehler, Ronald L., and Robert L. Ivie. *Congress Declares War: Rhetoric, Leadership, and Partisanship in the Early Republic.* Kent, Ohio: Kent State University Press, 1983.

Heclo, Hugh. "The Changing Presidential Office." In *The Managerial Presidency,* edited by James Pfiffner, 23–36. College Station: Texas A&M University Press, 1999.

Hiatt, Fred. "A Foreign Policy to Match Bush's Rhetoric?" *Washington Post,* November 15, 2004.

Hinckley, Barbara. *The Symbolic Presidency: How Presidents Portray Themselves.* New York: Routledge, 1990.

Hochman, Steven H., et al. "Interview with Jimmy Carter, Nov. 29, 1982, Miller Center Interviews, Carter Presidency Project." In *Conversations with Carter,* edited by Don Richardson, 221–57. Boulder, Colo.: Lynne Rienner Publishers, 1998.

Hoffman, Karen S. "'Going Public' in the Nineteenth Century: Grover Cleveland's Repeal of the Sherman Silver Purchase Act." *Rhetoric and Public Affairs* 5 (2002): 57–77.

Hofstadter, Richard. *The American Political Tradition and the Men Who Made It.* New York: Vintage, 1974.

Holloway, Rachel. "Keeping the Faith: Eisenhower Introduces the Hydrogen Age." In *Eisenhower's War of Words,* edited by Martin Medhurst, 47–72. East Lansing: Michigan State University Press, 1994.

Holzer, Harold. *Lincoln Seen and Heard.* Lawrence: University Press of Kansas, 2000.

Hostetler, Michael J. "Washington's Farewell Address: Distance as Bane and Blessing." *Rhetoric and Public Affairs* 5 (2002): 393–407.

Howe, John R. "Republican Thought and the Political Violence of the 1790s." *American Quarterly* 19 (1967): 147–65.

Hutcheson, Richard G. *God in the White House.* New York: Collier Books, 1988.

Israel, Fred, ed. *The State of the Union Messages of the Presidents of the United States.* New York: Chelsea House, 1966.

Jaffa, Harry V. *Crisis of the House Divided.* Chicago: University of Chicago Press, 1982.

———. *A New Birth of Freedom: Abraham Lincoln and the Coming of the Civil War.* Lanham, Md.: Rowman and Littlefield Publishers, 2000.

Jefferson, Thomas. *The Essential Jefferson,* edited by Albert Fried. New York: Collier Books, 1963.

———. *Memoirs, Correspondences, and Miscellanies from the Papers of Thomas Jefferson.* Vol. 3, edited by Thomas Jefferson Randolph. Boston, Mass.: Gray and Bowen, 1830.

———. *Messages and Papers of the Presidents.* Vol. I, edited by James Richardson. Washington, D.C.: Government Printing Office, 1896.

———. "Query XIX: Manufactures." In *Notes on the State of Virginia,* edited by William Peden. Chapel Hill: University of North Carolina Press, 1955.

Johannsen, Robert W. *Stephen A. Douglas.* New York: Oxford University Press, 1973.

Johnson, Arthur M. "Antitrust Policy in Transition, 1908: Ideal and Reality." *Mississippi Valley Historical Review* 48 (1961): 415–34.

Johnson, Lyndon. *Public Papers of the President: 1963–64.* Washington, D.C.: Government Printing Office, 1965.

———. *Public Papers of the President: 1965.* Washington, D.C.: Government Printing Office, 1966.

———. *The Vantage Point.* New York: Holt, Rinehard, and Winston, 1971.

Johnstone, Robert M. *Jefferson and the Presidency.* Ithaca, N.Y.: Cornell University Press, 1978.

Jones, Charles O. *The Trusteeship Presidency.* Baton Rouge: Louisiana State University Press, 1988.

Kagan, Robert. *Of Paradise and Power: America and Europe in the New World Order.* New York: Alfred A. Knopf, 2003.

Kaufman, Burton Ira., ed. *Washington's Farewell Address: The View from the Twentieth Century.* Chicago: Quadrangle Books, 1969.

Kelley, Robert. *The Cultural Pattern in American Politics: The First Century.* New York: Alfred A. Knopf, 1979.

Kennedy, John F. *Public Papers of the President: 1962.* Washington, D.C.: Government Printing Office, 1963.

———. *Public Papers of the President: 1963.* Washington, DC: Government Printing Office, 1964.

Kesler, Charles. "Woodrow Wilson and the Statesmanship of Progress." In *Natural Right and Political Right: Essays in Honor of Harry V. Jaffa,* edited by Thomas Silver and Peter Schramm, 103–27. Durham, N.C.: Carolina Academic Press, 1984.

Ketcham, Ralph. *James Madison: A Biography.* Charlottesville: University of Virginia Press, 1990.

———. "James Madison and the Nature of Man." *Journal of the History of Ideas* 19 (1958): 62–76.

———. "James Madison and the Presidency." In *Inventing the American Presidency,* edited by Thomas Cronin, 347–62. Lawrence: University Press of Kansas, 1989.

———. *Presidents above Party.* Chapel Hill: University of North Carolina Press, 1984.

King, Martin Luther, Jr. "Bold Design for a New South." *Nation* (1963): 260.

Klein, Philip. *President James Buchanan: A Biography.* Falls Creek, Pa.: Gray Printing Company, 1962.

Klingaman, William K. *Abraham Lincoln and the Road to Emancipation, 1861–1865.* New York: Viking, 2001.

Kohn, Richard H. "The Washington Administration's Decision to Crush the Whiskey Rebellion." *Journal of American History* 59 (1972): 567–84.

Kolko, Gabriel. *Railroads and Regulation.* Princeton, N.J.: Princeton University Press, 1965.

Kraig, Robert. *Woodrow Wilson and the Lost World of the Oratorical Statesman.* College Station: Texas A&M University Press, 2004.

La Follette, Robert M. *La Follette's Autobiography.* Madison: University of Wisconsin Press, 1968.

Laracey, Mel. "The Presidential Newspaper: The Forgotten Way of Going Public." In *Speaking to the People,* edited by Richard Ellis, 66–86. Amherst: University of Massachusetts Press, 1998.

———. *Presidents and the People: The Partisan Story of Going Public.* College Station: Texas A&M University Press, 2002.

Lawrence, David G. "The Collapse of the Democratic Majority: Economics and Vote Choice since 1952." *Western Political Quarterly* 44 (1991): 797–820.

Lee, Ronald, and Matthew H. Barton. "Clinton's Rhetoric of Contrition." In *Images, Scandal, and Communication Strategies of the Clinton Presidency,* edited by Robert E. Denton Jr. and Rachel L. Holloway, 219–46. Westport, Conn.: Praeger, 2003.

Leibiger, Stuart. *Founding Friendship: George Washington, James Madison, and the Creation of the American Republic.* Charlottesville: University Press of Virginia, 1999.

Lemann, Nicolas. "Without a Doubt." *New Yorker,* October 14, 2002.

Levy, Leonard. *Jefferson and Civil Liberties: The Darker Side.* Cambridge, Mass.: Belknap Press of Harvard University Press, 1963.

Lincoln, Abraham. *Lincoln: Selected Speeches and Writings.* New York: Library of America, 1992.

Lindsay, Thomas. "James Madison on Religion and Politics: Rhetoric and Reality." *American Political Science Review* 85 (1991): 1321–37.

Lipset, Seymour Martin. "Setting the Standard: George Washington's Leadership." *Current* 411 (1999): 10–16.

Lowell, John. *Mr. Madison's War.* New York: Beach, 1812.

Lucas, Stephen E. "Genre Criticism and Historical Context: The Case of George Washington's First Inaugural Address." *Southern Speech Communication Journal* 51 (1986): 354–71.

———. "George Washington and the Rhetoric of Presidential Leadership." In *The Presidency and Rhetorical Leadership,* edited by Leroy Dorsey, 42–72. College Station: Texas A&M University Press, 2002.

McCoy, Drew R. *The Last of the Fathers: James Madison and the Republican Legacy.* Cambridge: Cambridge University Press, 1989.

McDiarmid, John. "Presidential Inaugural Addresses—A Study in Verbal Symbols." *Public Opinion Quarterly* 1 (1937): 79–82.

McDonald, Forrest. *The Presidency of George Washington.* Lawrence: University Press of Kansas, 1974.

———. *The Presidency of Thomas Jefferson.* Lawrence: The University Press of Kansas, 1976.

McLean, Iain. "Before and after Publius: The Sources and Influence of Madison's Political Thought." In *James Madison: The Theory and Practice of Republican Government,* edited by Samuel Kernell, 14–40. Stanford, Calif.: Stanford University Press, 2003.

McPherson, James M. *Abraham Lincoln and the Second American Revolution.* New York: Oxford University Press, 1990.

Madison, James. *Messages and Papers of the Presidents,* edited by James Richardson. Washington, D.C.: Government Printing Office, 1896.

Madison, James, and Robert Allen Rutland. *The Papers of James Madison.* Charlottesville: University Press of Virginia, 1999.

Mann, Robert. *The Walls of Jericho.* New York: Harcourt Brace and Company, 1996.

Mansfield, Harvey C., Jr. *Taming the Prince.* Baltimore, Md.: John Hopkins University Press, 1993.

Mayer, Jeremy D. *Running on Race: Racial Politics in Presidential Campaigns, 1960–2000*. New York: Random House, 2002.

Mayer, Kenneth R. *With the Stroke of a Pen*. Princeton, N.J.: Princeton University Press, 2001.

Mayhew, David. *Divided We Govern*. New Haven, Conn.: Yale University Press, 1991.

Medhurst, Martin J. "American Cosmology and the Rhetoric of Inaugural Prayer." *Central States Speech Journal* 28 (1977): 277–82.

———. *Dwight D. Eisenhower: Strategic Communicator*. Westport, Conn.: Greenwood Press, 1993.

———. "Religious Rhetoric and the *Ethos* of Democracy." In *The Ethos of Rhetoric*, edited by Michael J. Hyde, 114–35. Columbia: University of South Carolina, 2004.

———, ed. *Beyond the Rhetorical Presidency*. College Station: Texas A&M University Press, 1996.

Miroff, Bruce. *Pragmatic Illusions: The Presidential Politics of John F. Kennedy*. New York: David McKay Company, 1976.

———. "The Presidency and the Public: Leadership as Spectacle." In *The Presidency and the Political System*, edited by Michael Nelson, 278–304. 7th ed. Washington, D.C.: CQ Press, 2003.

———. "Presidential Leverage over Social Movements: The Johnson White House and Civil Rights." *Journal of Politics* 43 (1981): 2–23.

Mister, Stephen. "Reagan's Challenger Tribute: Combing Generic Constraints and Situational Demands." *Central States Speech Journal* 37 (1986): 158–65.

Moe, Terry. "The Politicized Presidency." In *New Directions in American Politics*, edited by John Chubb and Paul Peterson, 235–72. Washington, D.C.: Brookings, 1985.

———. "Presidents, Institutions, and Theory." In *Researching the Presidency*, edited by George Edwards III, John Kessel, and Bert Rockman, 337–85. Pittsburgh, Pa: University of Pittsburgh Press, 1993.

Morris, Kenneth E. *Jimmy Carter: American Moralist*. Athens: University of Georgia Press, 1996.

Motter, Russell. "Jimmy Carter in Context." *Mississippi Quarterly* 45 (1992): 467–82.

"Mr. Bush's Most Important Speech," *New York Times*, September 21, 2001.

Murphy, John M. "Our Mission and Our Moment: George W. Bush and September 11th." *Rhetoric and Public Affairs* 6 (2003): 607–32.

Neuhaus, Richard John. *The Naked Public Square*. Grand Rapids, Mich.: Eerdmans, 1991.

Neustadt, Richard. *Presidential Power*. New York: Wiley, 1960.

Novak, Michael. *Choosing Our King*. New York: MacMillan Publishing Co., 1974.

———. *On Two Wings: Humble Faith and Common Sense at the American Founding*. San Francisco: Encounter Books, 2002.

O' Hanlon, Michael. "Choosing the Right Enemies." *New York Times*, February 6, 2002.

Parmet, Herbert S. *The Democrats: The Years after FDR*. Oxford: Oxford University Press, 1976.

Patton, John H. "Jimmy Carter: The Language of Politics and the Practice of Integrity." In *Presidential Speechwriting*, edited by Kurt Ritter and Martin Medhurst, 165–93. College Station: Texas A&M University Press, 2003.

Pauley, Garth. *The Modern Presidency and Civil Rights: Rhetoric on Race from Roosevelt to Nixon*. College Station: Texas A&M University Press, 2001.

Pendleton, Lawson Alan. "James Buchanan's Attitude toward Slavery." PhD diss., University of North Carolina, 1964.

Pfiffner, James. *The Character Factor*. College Station: Texas A&M University Press, 2004.

Phelps, Glenn. *George Washington and American Constitutionalism*. Lawrence: University Press of Kansas, 1993.

———. "George Washington and the Paradox of Party." *Presidential Studies Quarterly* (1989): 733–46.

Pierard, Richard V., and Robert D. Linder. *Civil Religion and the Presidency*. Grand Rapids, Mich.: Academie Books, 1988.

Raeside, John. "A Night at Camp David." *East Bay Express*, July 27, 1979.

Reeves, Thomas C. *A Question of Character: A Life of John F. Kennedy*. New York: Free Press, 1991.

Reid, Ronald F. "Newspaper Response to the Gettysburg Address." *Quarterly Journal of Speech* 53 (1967): 50–60.

Riker, William H. *The Art of Political Manipulation*. New Haven, Conn.: Yale University Press, 1986.

Roelofs, H. Mark. "The Prophetic President: Charisma in the American Political Tradition." *Polity* 25 (1992): 1–20.

Roosevelt, Theodore. *The Autobiography of Theodore Roosevelt*. Edited by Wayne Andrews. New York: Charles Scribner's Sons, 1958.

———. *The Roosevelt Policy*. New York: Current Literature Publishing Company, 1908.

———. *The Strenuous Life*. New York: Century Co., 1902.

———. *Theodore Roosevelt: An Autobiography*. New York: Da Capo Press, 1985.

Rossiter, Clinton. *The American Presidency*. New York: Harcourt, Brace and World, 1960.

Rozell, Mark. *The Press and the Carter Presidency*. Boulder, Colo.: Westview Press, 1989.

Rudalevige, Andrew. *Managing the President's Program*. Princeton, N.J.: Princeton University Press, 2002.

Ruderman, Richard S. "Aristotle and the Recovery of Political Judgment." *American Political Science Review* 91 (1997): 409–20.

Rutland, Robert Allen. *The Presidency of James Madison*. Lawrence: University Press of Kansas, 1990.

Ryan, Halford. "The Rhetoric of George Washington's Farewell Address." *Speaker and Gavel* 38 (2001): 1–15.

Schlesinger, Arthur M., Jr. *A Thousand Days: John F. Kennedy in the White House*. Boston: Houghton Mifflin Company, 1965.

Sears, Louis. *Jefferson and the Embargo*. Durham, N.C.: Duke University Press, 1927.

Self, Lois S. "Rhetoric and *Phronesis:* The Aristotelian Ideal." *Philosophy and Rhetoric* 12 (1979): 130–45.

Selzer, Linda. "Historicizing Lincoln: Garry Wills and the Canonization of the Gettysburg Address." *Rhetoric Review* 16 (1997): 120–37.

Sheldon, Garrett Ward. *The Political Philosophy of James Madison*. Baltimore, Md.: John Hopkins University Press, 2001.

———. *The Political Philosophy of Thomas Jefferson*. Baltimore, Md.: John Hopkins University Press, 1991.

Shogan, Colleen J. "George Washington: Can Aristotle Recapture What His Countrymen Have Forgotten?" In *George Washington: Foundation of Presidential Leadership and Character,* edited by Ethan Fishman, William D. Pederson, and Mark J. Rozell, 53–69. Westport, Conn.: Praeger Press, 2001.

———. "Rhetorical Moralism in the Plebiscitary Presidency: New Speech Forms and Their Ideological Entailments." *Studies in American Political Development* 17 (2003): 149–67.

Shogan, Robert. *The Double-Edged Sword*. Boulder, Colo.: Westview Press, 1999.

Shull, Steven A. *American Civil Rights Policy from Truman to Clinton*. Armonk, N.Y.: M. E. Sharpe, 1999.

Sigelman, Lee. "Presidential Inaugurals: The Modernization of a Genre." *Political Communication* 13 (1996): 81–92.

Singer, Peter. *The President of Good and Evil: The Ethics of George W. Bush*. New York: Dutton, 2004.

Skowronek, Stephen. "Leadership by Definition: George W. Bush and the Politics of Orthodox Innovation." Paper presented at the Sondermann Symposium, Colorado College, Colorado Springs, Colorado, December 6, 2004.

———. *The Politics Presidents Make*. Cambridge, Mass.: Belknap Press, 1997.

Skowronek, Stephen, and Karen Orren. *The Search for American Political Development*. Cambridge: Cambridge University Press, 2004.

Smith, Elbert. *The Presidency of James Buchanan*. Lawrence: University Press of Kansas, 1975.

Smith, Lynn, Lynell George, and Mary McNamara. "Bush Drew on Strengths in His Address to the Nation." *Los Angeles Times,* September 22, 2001.

Smolin, David. "Consecrating the President." *First Things* 69 (1997): 14–18.

Spalding, Matthew. "The Command of Its Own Fortunes: Reconsidering Washington's Farewell Address," In *George Washington: Foundation of Presidential Leadership and Character,* edited by Ethan Fishman, William D. Pederson, and Mark Rozell, 19–31. Westport, Conn.: Praeger Press, 2001.

Spalding, Matthew, and Patrick J. Garrity. *A Sacred Union of Citizens: George Washington's Farewell Address and the American Character*. New York: Rowman and Littlefield Publishers, 1996.

Stagg, J. C. A. "James Madison and the 'Malcontents': The Political Origins of the War of 1812." *William and Mary Quarterly* 33 (1976): 557–85.

———. "Preface." In *The Papers of James Madison: Presidential Series*. Vol. 4. Charlottesville: University Press of Virginia, 1996.

Stampp, Kenneth, Don E. Fehrenbacher, Robert Johannsen, and Elbert Smith. "The Presidency of James Buchanan: A Reassessment." In *James Buchanan 1791–1868,* edited by Irving Sloan. Dobbs Ferry, N.Y.: Oceana Publications, 1968.

Stern, Mark. *Calculating Visions: Kennedy, Johnson, and Civil Rights.* New Brunswick, N.J.: Rutgers University Press, 1992.

"Strong Rights Bill Due to Leaders' Tactics, Southern Errors." *Congressional Quarterly Weekly Report,* June 19, 1964: 1205–1206.

Stuckey, Mary E. *Defining Americans: The Presidency and National Identity.* Lawrence: University Press of Kansas, 2004.

———. *Playing the Game: The Presidential Rhetoric of Ronald Reagan.* Westport, Conn.: Praeger, 1990.

———. *Strategic Failures in the Modern Presidency.* Cresskill, N.J.: Hampton Press, 1997.

Stuckey, Mary E., and Frederick J. Antczak. "The Rhetorical Presidency: Deepening Vision, Widening Exchange." In *Communication Yearbook,* edited by Michael E. Roloff, 405–42. Thousand Oaks, Calif.: Sage Publications, 1998.

"Sweeping Voting Rights Bill Introduced in Congress." *Congressional Quarterly Weekly Report,* March 19, 1965: 435.

Teten, Ryan. "Evolution of the Modern Rhetorical Presidency: Presidential Presentation and Development of the State of the Union Address." *Presidential Studies Quarterly* 33 (2003): 333–46.

Thurow, Glen E. *Abraham Lincoln and American Political Religion.* Albany: State University of New York Press, 1976.

———. "Dimensions of Presidential Character." In *Beyond the Rhetorical Presidency,* edited by Martin Medhurst, 15–29. College Station: Texas A&M University Press, 1996.

Tulis, Jeffrey K. "Reflections on the Rhetorical Presidency in American Political Development." In *Speaking to the People,* edited by Richard Ellis, 211–22. Amherst: University of Massachusetts Press, 1998.

———. *The Rhetorical Presidency.* Princeton, N.J.: Princeton University Press, 1987.

Wander, Philip. "The Rhetoric of American Foreign Policy." *Quarterly Journal of Speech* 70 (1984): 347–50.

Washington, George. *George Washington: A Collection,* edited by W. B. Allen. Indianapolis, Ind.: Liberty Fund, 1988.

———. *Writings of Washington.* Vol. 33, edited by John C. Fitzpatrick. Washington, D.C.: Government Printing Office, 1938.

Weatherford, M. Stephen. "Responsiveness and Deliberation in Divided Government: Presidential Leadership in Tax Policy Making." *British Journal of Political Science* 24 (1994): 1–31.

Weisbrot, Robert. *Freedom Bound: A History of America's Civil Rights Movement.* New York: W. W. Norton and Company, 1990.

Wells, Damon. *Stephen Douglas: The Last Years, 1857–1861.* Austin: University of Texas Press, 1971.

White, Ronald C., Jr. *The Eloquent President: A Portrait of Lincoln through His Words*. New York: Random House, 2005.

———. *Lincoln's Greatest Speech: The Second Inaugural*. New York: Simon and Schuster, 2002.

Williams, T. Harry. *Lincoln and the Radicals*. Madison: University of Wisconsin Press, 1941.

———. "Shall We Keep the Radicals?" In *The Leadership of Abraham Lincoln*, edited by Don E. Fehrenbacher, 99–110. New York: John Wiley and Sons, 1970.

Wills, Garry. *Lincoln at Gettysburg: The Words That Remade America*. New York: Simon and Schuster, 1992.

———. "Lincoln's Greatest Speech?" *Atlantic Monthly* 284 (September 1999): 60–70.

Wilson, Kirt H. "Paradox of Lincoln's Rhetorical Leadership." *Rhetoric and Public Affairs* 3 (2000): 15–32.

Woodward, Bob. *Plan of Attack*. New York: Simon and Schuster, 2004.

Yarbrough, Jean M. *American Virtues: Thomas Jefferson on the Character of a Free People*. Lawrence: University Press of Kansas, 1998.

Zarefsky, David. "George W. Bush Discovers Rhetoric." In *The Ethos of Rhetoric*, edited by Michael J. Hyde, 136–55. Columbia: University of South Carolina Press, 2004.

———. *Lincoln Douglas and Slavery: In the Crucible of Public Debate*. Chicago: University of Chicago Press, 1990.

———. "Lincoln's 1862 Annual Message: A Paradigm of Rhetorical Leadership." *Rhetoric and Public Affairs* 3 (2000): 5–14.

———. "Lyndon Johnson." In *American Orators of the Twentieth Century*, edited by Bernard Duffy and Halford Ryan, 223–31. New York: Greenwood Press, 1987.

INDEX

civil rights themes. *See* Johnson, Lyndon; Kennedy, John F.

Clay, Henry, 96, 139

Clinton, Bill, 4, 24–27, 173, 186

Cobb, Howell, 148

coding methodology, 21–23, 183–84, 185–86, 189*n*4

Coles, Edward, 133

Condit, Celeste, 29

Conkling, James, 106

Connecticut citizens, Buchanan's reply, 147–48

Conservatives, Republican Party, Lincoln presidency, 98–101, 102–104, 106, 108–10

content analysis approach, methodology of, 7–9, 20–23, 39–41, 183–86, 189*n*4, *n*6

Coolidge, Calvin, 28, 83

Cooper, John Milton, 66, 69

Corning, Erastus, 105–106

Covode Committee report, 153

"crisis of spirit" theme, 77–79

Cronkite, Walter, 126

Dean, Howard, 5

Defining Americans (Stuckey), 6–7

Democratic Party: Buchanan presidency, 145–46, 148, 150–51, 153; Carter presidency, 71, 73, 80, 194–95*nn*86–87; Kennedy presidency, 113, 116–18, 120, 121–22, 126–27; L. Johnson presidency, 158–59, 160–61, 165–67; Lincoln presidency, 104, 105–106; as political variable, 31–32, 34–37; T. Roosevelt presidency, 64–65

Democratic Societies, Washington's era, 50–53, 52

disjunctive presidents, 35, 38–39, 40

divided government variable, rhetoric patterns, 32, 35, 38

domestic policy statements, graphed data, 27–28

Donald, David, 104

Dorsey, Leroy, 58, 168

Douglas, Stephen, 148

Eastland, James, 117

economic conditions, as political variable, 33

Edwards, George, 174–75

Eisenhower, Dwight D., 41, 114

Eizenstat, Stuart, 77–78

electoral mandate variable, rhetoric patterns, 33, 35, 38

electronic presidency, 190*n*14

Emancipation Proclamation, 102–104

embargo conflicts, Jefferson years, 89–94

Employers' Liability Act, 193*n*60

energy themes, Carter's, 73–79

Enforcement Act, 92

England, U.S. shipping embargo, 89–94

eulogies, 106–108, 196*n*56

Evans, Roland, 75

factionalism theme, Washington's rhetoric: consistency of, 45–46; Farewell Address, 53–56; Inaugural Address, 46–48; Whiskey Rebellion, 49–53. *See also* Roosevelt, Theodore; unity theme

Fallows, James, 71, 77

Farewell Address, Washington's, 53–56

Federalist Papers, 131, 175

Federalists: Jefferson presidency, 85–86; Madison presidency, 134–38, 139–40, 142

Flexner, James, 47

Follett, Mary Parker, 21

foreign policy themes: graphed data, 27–28; Washington, 54, 55, 56. *See also* war-oriented rhetoric

Forney, John, 146

France, 86–87

Kennedy, John F (*cont.*)
rhetoric, 122, 124–25, 129; on
moral leadership, 170; moral
rhetoric and political authority
summarized, 127–29; political
circumstances, 116–18, 119–20,
121–24, 125–27, 157
Kennedy, Robert F., 123–24, 159–60
Ketcham, Ralph, 23, 131, 191*n*3
King, Martin Luther, Jr., 115–16,
117, 120, 122, 125
Kolko, Gabriel, 60
Kusnet, David, 201*n*10

LaFollette, Robert, 64–65
Lance affair, Carter administration,
72, 74–75
LeCompton Constitution, 147–48, 153
Lee, Henry, 134
The Life and Morals of Jesus
(Jefferson), 83, 195*n*1
Lincoln, Abraham: civil war themes,
106–108, 110–12, 140–41,
154; in graphed/charted data,
24–27, 95; moral rhetoric and
political authority summarized,
112–13, 127–29, 182; as
phronesis exemplar, 127–28, 182;
political circumstances, 97–101,
102–104, 105–106, 108–10;
religious beliefs, 41, 101; slavery
statements, 96–97, 99, 101–102,
104–105, 110–12
Livingston, Robert, 87
Louisiana Purchase rhetoric, 86–89
Lowell, John, 137–38
Lucas, Stephen, 47

Macon, Nathaniel, 89
Madison, James: moral rhetoric and
political authority summarized,
142–43, 168–69; political
circumstances, 131–32, 134–38,
139, 142–43, 152; religious views,
130–31; war-oriented rhetoric,

133–34, 135, 138–42; Whiskey
Rebellion, 53
"malaise" speech, Carter's, 72, 77–
80, 194*n*71, *n*83
mandate variable, rhetoric patterns,
33, 35, 38
Marston, David, 75
Martin, Louis, 122
Mayhew, David, 32
McKinley, William, 186
Medill, Joseph, 101
"Meditation on the Divine Will"
(Lincoln), 101, 111
M.E.O.W. jibes, 75, 77
Meredith, James, 119–20
methodology, 7–9, 20–23, 39–41,
183–86, 189*n*4, *n*6
Mifflin, Governor, 50
military preparedness theme, 133–
34. *See also* war-oriented rhetoric
Miroff, Bruce, 125
Mississippi, civil rights conflicts,
119–20
Mondale, Walter, 77–78
Monroe, James, 134–35
Morales, Juan, 87
moral leadership role, generally:
and rhetorical choices, 9–11,
15–17, 41–43, 170–71; scholarly
approaches, 5–7; Washington's
impact, 46–48, 56
moral restraint. *See* restraint-
oriented rhetoric *entries*
moral rhetoric patterns, generally:
content analysis approach, 7–9,
20–23, 39–41, 183–86, 189*n*4, *n*6,
191*n*29; historical development,
23–31; and political
circumstances, 13–16, 31–39;
strategic choice hypothesis, 11–
12, 41–43
Murphy, John, 201*n*10

Napoleon, 86–87
National Intelligencer, 136

Neville, John, 50
Newsweek, 75
The New Yorker, 125
New York Herald, 112
New York Times, 69, 104, 112, 165
New York Tribune, 105
Nixon, Richard, 4, 28
Nofziger, Lyn, 201n10
Non-Importation Act, 90
non-policy moralizing: graphed
    data, 27–28; modern trend,
    171–74
Notes on the State of Virginia
    (Jefferson), 83, 85
Novak, Michael, 190n12
Novak, Robert, 75

On Deaf Ears (Edwards), 174–75
orthodox innovator presidents,
    rhetoric patterns, 35, 38–39

Parker, Alton Brooks, 60
party affiliation variable, rhetoric
    patterns, 31–32, 34–37
"party" presidents, generally, 23–27
patrician presidents, generally, 23–
    27, 190n12. *See also* Washington,
    George
patrician statesman theme:
    Roosevelt, 62–63; Washington,
    46–48
Pauley, Garth, 156
Pennsylvania, Whiskey Rebellion,
    49–53
Philadelphia Inquirer, 112
Philadelphia Press, 148
phronesis: absence in Bush rhetoric,
    179, 182; Lincoln as exemplar,
    127–28, 182; and political circum-
    stances, 81, 128–29, 168–69; as
    political strategy, 88, 170–71;
    as rhetorical tradition, 11;
    Washington as exemplar, 81, 171
Plumer, William, 134
policy detachment trend, 171–74

political authority, generally:
    defined, 13; and moral
    argumentation timing, 81–82;
    and rhetorical decisionmaking,
    10–17; with strategic moral
    rhetoric, 10–11
political authority variable, rhetoric
    patterns, 33, 38–39, 40
political circumstances, generally,
    13–16, 31–39
Polk, James K., 184
The President as Leader (Hargrove), 6
presidential rhetoric, generally:
    limits of, 174–76; policy
    detachment trend, 171–74; and
    political circumstances, 13–16;
    scholarly approaches, 5–7, 11–13,
    188n14; as strategic choice, 9–12,
    16–17, 170–71
prudence. *See phronesis*
public opinion: British shipping
    embargo, 91, 92, 94; Bush
    polls, 3, 4, 180, 202n17; Carter
    poll, 77; Kennedy polls, 125; L.
    Johnson polls, 166–67; Louisiana
    Purchase, 88; Roosevelt's strategy,
    59, 63, 67, 193n55; voting rights,
    163; Whiskey Rebellion, 49
public *vs.* private effort, generally,
    174–76

race discrimination themes. *See*
    Johnson, Lyndon; Kennedy,
    John F.
Radicals, Republican Party, Lincoln
    presidency, 98–101, 102–104,
    106, 108–10
railroad legislation: political
    circumstances, 58–60, 63–66;
    Roosevelt's rhetoric, 60–63, 64
Randolph, John, 135
Reagan, Ronald, 4, 24–27, 28, 80,
    173, 185
reconstructive presidents, rhetoric
    patterns, 35, 38–39, 40

130–43, 168–69; selection criteria, 17–19
strategic moral rhetoric, generally, 11–12, 41–43. *See also phronesis*
Strong, Caleb, 136
Stuckey, Mary, 6–7
Sullivan, James, 91
Sumner, Charles, 100, 103, 106

Taft, William Howard, 24–27, 69–70
tariff policy, T. Roosevelt's approach, 58, 59
terrorism speeches, 3–4, 177–78, 180–81, 201n10
Thurow, Glen E., 29
traditionalist rhetoric, defined, 185–86
Tulis, Jeffrey, 24, 29, 97, 174, 190n18

unity theme: Buchanan, 154; Bush, 185; L. Johnson, 161; Lincoln, 106–108, 111–12; Madison, 133–36; T. Roosevelt, 62–63, 66
unity theme, Washington's rhetoric: consistency of, 45–46; Farewell Address, 53–56; Inaugural Address, 46–48; Whiskey Rebellion, 49–53

Van Buren, Martin, 25–27
Vantage Point (Johnson), 161
Varnum, Joseph B., 89
visionary rhetoric, generally: defined, 185, 186, 190n18; in Inaugural Addresses, 29–31; political variables, 34, 36–39
Voting Rights Act, 161–67

Wallace, George, 123
War of *1812*. *See* Madison, James

war-oriented rhetoric: Buchanan, 152–55; Bush, 3–4, 177–79, 180–81, 201n10; Lincoln, 106–108, 110–12; Madison and the opposition, 133–34, 135, 136–42
war variable, rhetoric patterns, 32, 35, 37–38, 191n29
Washington, George: Farewell Address, 53–56; Inaugural Address, 46–48, 190n19; moral rhetoric and political authority summarized, 44, 81–82; as patriot king, 45–46; as *phronesis* exemplar, 81, 171; political circumstances, 47, 49–51; Whiskey Rebellion rhetoric, 49–53, 66, 93, 140
Washington Daily National Intelligencer, 112
Washington Post, 74, 75, 79
Weed, Thurlow, 110, 112
Whig Party, as political variable, 31–32, 34–37
Whiskey Rebellion rhetoric, 49–53, 66, 93, 140
White, Ronald, 107, 109
Why Not the Best? (Carter), 71
Wilkins, Roy, 125
Williams, T. Harry, 98
Wills, Garry, 107
Wilson, Woodrow, 26–31, 175, 190n18
Wofford, Harris, 115, 116, 118

Yancey, William Lowndes, 150
You, the People (Beasley), 6, 7

Zarefsky, David, 105, 167